The State of the Environment of England and Wales: Fresh Waters

May 1998

LONDON: THE STATIONERY OFFICE

Commissioning Organisation:
Environment Agency
Rio House
Waterside Drive
Almondsbury
Bristol
BS32 4UD
Tel: 01454 624400
Fax: 01454 624409

Foreword

The state of the environment at any one time is always difficult to assess. The Agency has therefore developed a framework whereby it recognises that the environment is often looked at from different points of view, and that the many pressures placed upon it create a number of stresses and strains which need to be resolved over different time scales. Using this framework, the Agency has embarked upon a programme of analysing the state of the environment in England and Wales, sector by sector, in order to provide a basis for its more sustainable management into the new millennium. This first report covers the freshwater environment and the second will examine the coastal environment.

An assessment of the state of the freshwater environment is timely for many reasons. Following recent droughts, and with mounting concern about climate change, much fundamental thinking has been taking place on the future management of water resources. This has resulted in a variety of reviews and reports being produced by a range of bodies, such as the one by the House of Commons Environment Committee on *Water Conservation and Supply* in 1996, the former Department of the Environment's *Agenda for Action* on water resources, published in the same year, the UK Round Table on Sustainable Development's report on *Freshwater* in February 1997, and English Nature's report on *Wildlife and FreshWater* in March 1997.

The new government called a Water Summit early in its term of office, resulting in a set of actions to address the current situation on water resources. Reviews of abstraction licensing and fisheries legislation have also been announced. A major review of water policy has been taking place in Europe leading to the proposed Framework Directive on Water which provides for a common approach based on integrated river basin management. The European Environment Agency has also reviewed the current situation on water resources in its report on *Water Stress in Europe*. In view of this general interest in water issues, it was therefore felt important that the Environment Agency should have its own considered opinion on the state of the freshwater environment in England and Wales, based on an analysis of all the information available.

It is now more than eight years since the privatisation of the water industry. Significant changes have taken place over this period. A Periodic Review of water prices has already been carried out by the Director General of Water Services and, in preparing for the next review, it is necessary to take stock of the impact that privatisation and the significant accompanying capital investment have actually had on the water environment. In short, what has been achieved, what benefits to the environment have resulted, what remains to be done and, in consequence, what should the future priorities be? This report attempts to provide answers to these questions.

Dr R J Pentreath
Chief Scientist and Director of Environmental Strategy

Contents

List of Figures

SECTION 4

SECTION 5

List of Tables

Symbols

Bq/kg	becquerels per kilogramme (radiation activity per unit mass)
Bq/l	becquerels per litre (radiation activity per unit volume)
cm	centimetres (unit distance)
°C	degrees Celsius (standard temperature scale)
d	day
ha	hectare (unit area)
ha/yr	hectares per year (unit area in relation to time)
kg	kilogrammes (unit mass)
kgN/ha	kilogrammes of nitrogen per hectare
km	kilometres (unit distance)
l	litres (unit volume)
m^2	square metres (unit area)
m^3	cubic metres (unit volume)
m^3/d	cubic metres per day
m^3/s	cubic metres per second
Mm^3	megacubic metres, one million cubic metres (unit volume)
Mm^3/yr	megacubic metres per year (unit volume in relation to time)
Ml/d	megalitres per day, that is one million litres per day (unit volume in relation to time)
mSv	milli-Sieverts (measure of radioactivity)
µg/kg	microgrammes per kilogramme weight
µg/l	microgrammes per litre, one millionth of a gramme per litre (level of concentration)
mgN/l	milligrammes of nitrogen per litre (level of nitrogen concentration)
mg/l as N	milligrammes of nitrogen per litre (level of nitrogen concentration)
mg NO_3/l	milligrammes of nitrate per litre
mg/l	milligrammes per litre (level of concentration)
mm	millimetres
mm/yr	millimetres per year (distance in relation to time)
ng/ml	nanogrammes per millilitre
pH	measure of acidity/alkalinity (e.g. pH7 = neutral)
yr	year

Abbreviations

BMWP	Biological Monitoring Working Party
BOD	Biochemical oxygen demand
CSO	Combined sewer overflow
DDT	Dichlorodiphenyltrichloroethane
DO	Dissolved oxygen
DoE	Department of Environment
DETR	Department of the Environment, Transport and the Regions
EC	European Commission
EQI	Environmental Quality Index
EQS	Environmental quality standard
GQA	General Quality Assessment
HCH	Hexachlorocyclohexane
HMIP	Her Majesty's Inspectorate of Pollution
HMS	Harmonised Monitoring Scheme
HSE	Health and Safety Executive
LEAP	Local Environment Agency Plan
MAFF	Ministry of Agriculture, Fisheries and Food
NRA	National Rivers Authority
OECD	Organisation for Economic Cooperation and Development
OFWAT	Office of Water Services
OSPARCOM	Oslo and Paris Commissions
PCB	Polychlorinated biphenyls
RIVPACS	River Invertebrate Prediction and Classification System
SEPA	Scottish Environmental Protection Agency
SSSI	Site of Special Scientific Interest
STW	Sewage-treatment works
TBT	Tributyltins
UPM	Urban Pollution Management
UWWTD	Urban Waste Water Treatment Directive (91/271/EEC)
WSA	Water Services Association
WHO	World Health Organisation

Executive Summary

Introduction

This report provides a detailed assessment of the state of the freshwater environment in England and Wales. It brings together and examines information on the various stresses placed upon it and the consequent state of it as looked at from different points of view. In the light of this information the report considers how well the freshwater environment is being managed to meet the needs of today's society, and how well it is being protected to meet the needs of future generations. The report concludes with an overall opinion on the state of the freshwater environment and identifies a set of priority issues that require further management action to bring about improvements.

Stresses on the Freshwater Environment

Since 1988 the UK has experienced exceptional climatic extremes, including the wettest winter period (December 1994 to February 1995) followed by the driest summer (June to August 1995) on record. The average temperatures over the period have been the highest since 1845. These extremes have already exerted significant pressures on the freshwater environment and presented real management challenges. Predicted long-term climate changes also have potentially serious implications for the state of the environment as a whole. They could exacerbate pressures on water resources, particularly in the south and east of England where they are already under pressure, affect other water uses and natural ecosystems, and increase the frequency of storms and flooding.

There has been a continuing increase in the number of households. The distribution of the human population has also been changing, resulting in increased pressures on fresh waters in certain parts of the country by creating new demands for water abstraction and sewage disposal. Between 1991 and 2016 the number of households is projected to increase by more than 4 million, with the greatest demands likely in those parts of the country where pressures on fresh waters are already acute. Development of urban areas and roads in floodplains continues to impact upon freshwater habitats, changing natural flow regimes and reducing the amount of infiltration of rainfall into groundwaters. Runoff from urban surfaces can have a significant impact on the quality of rivers. Changing lifestyles are also placing new demands on fresh waters; the increase in recreational use, for example, has to be carefully managed to avoid conflicts with other water uses and the protection of the environment.

The total amount of water abstracted from fresh waters in England and Wales has actually fallen since 1971, mainly because of reduced demands by industry, particularly for power generation. Over the same period, abstraction for potable supply has increased by more than a quarter. The increase in water supplied to domestic properties currently exceeds the rate of population increase and, in part, relates to the increasing number of households and changing lifestyles. The loss of water through leakage from distribution systems is a waste of valuable water resources and concerted effort to meet leakage reduction targets is needed before further resource development schemes will be considered. Demands for irrigation are also predicted to increase significantly by 2020, particularly in the east and south east of England.

There have been significant reductions in the amounts of contaminants discharged to fresh waters from sewage-treatment works and direct industrial discharges since 1989. The quantities of organic matter, certain metals and pesticides discharged have decreased as a result of increased investment, effective regulation, and changing patterns of use. But although pollution from point sources is improving, that from diffuse sources continues to be of concern. Localised water quality problems associated with pesticides (including synthetic pyrethroid sheep dips), nutrients, industrial solvents, urban and road runoff, waste disposal sites, and abandoned mines persist and require further action. The extent of groundwater pollution is difficult and expensive to quantify, but seems to be widespread. This is of particular concern because of its long-term nature, and the difficulties and large costs of any remedy, yet in some parts of the country groundwaters provide up to 70 per cent of potable water supply.

The number of substantiated pollution incidents caused by accidents or illegal practices has fallen since 1990, and those that are classified as serious have also declined. This is an encouraging sign. The efforts that have been put into pollution prevention and into the raising of awareness through education, and into targeted campaigns is therefore paying dividends, but continued action is needed to further reduce pollution incidents to manageable levels.

The State of the Freshwater Environment

Although England and Wales have substantial water resources, their distribution, both regionally and seasonally, is not well matched with patterns of demand. Over 30 rivers and other sites have been recognised nationally as suffering from low-flows because of over-use and others are being considered. Many Sites of Special Scientific Interest (SSSIs) are reported to be at risk from low water levels. Contrary to the current status of depleted water resources, groundwater levels in some urban areas are rising because of reducing demands for abstraction by industry. This could create potentially serious problems and the Agency is monitoring water levels in affected areas very closely.

There has been a significant decline in the extent of wetlands, streamside habitats, and ponds, and about 40 per cent of river habitat sites across England and Wales have been subject to modification. Seven freshwater habitat types (chalk rivers, mesotrophic lakes, eutrophic standing waters, aquifer fed waterbodies, reedbeds, fens and grazing marsh) are of particular concern because of their vulnerability to change.

General improvements in water quality and habitat are allowing freshwater species, such as otters, to recover in parts of the country. Salmon are returning to rivers for the first time in decades, but other rivers show declining numbers due to land use changes causing siltation, low flows, acidification, and the impact of activities at sea. Populations of some bird species, including swans, are increasing. Other species remain at risk because of factors such as habitat loss, nutrient enrichment and competition with non-native species. Forty-seven freshwater species have been identified as rare, threatened, or vulnerable.

In 1990, a nationally-consistent chemical and biological monitoring programme for water quality in rivers across England and Wales was introduced by the then National Rivers Authority. Results show that net improvements in both chemical and biological quality have since taken place in more than a quarter of the total length of rivers. Compliance with statutory water quality standards arising from European legislation is high but still needs to be improved. Against this general pattern of improving water quality, a small proportion of river stretches has recently deteriorated. About 10 per cent of the monitored river network is still of Poor or Bad quality, mainly in urban areas, and requires investment to bring about improvements.

More direct measurements of the health of the environment are urgently needed. There is increasing concern over the possible ecological and human health effects of exposure to chemicals present in the environment at low concentrations, such as those which can cause hormonal disruption in wildlife. Further investigation into the effects of nutrient enrichment of fresh waters is also needed because, although the available evidence suggests that nutrient concentrations in rivers are generally falling, they are still high in parts of the country particularly in the southern and eastern areas. About three-quarters of the lakes with SSSI status are affected by nutrient enrichment and many lakes, reservoirs and ponds suffer from blue-green algae blooms. With the increasing use of fresh waters for recreation, further attention also needs to be given to assessing health risks associated with microbiological quality.

A few long-term monitoring programmes provide a valuable perspective on overall trends in the state of fresh waters. These have shown that there has been a general reduction in the levels of degradable, organic pollution in rivers since the 1970s. Concentrations of certain organochlorine pesticides have fallen significantly over the same period. The pattern for nutrients in surface and groundwaters is more complex, with increased concentrations in parts of the country and decreases in others. Catchment-based modelling suggests that a significant proportion of lakes have become enriched with nutrients since the 1930s. Monitoring of selected lakes confirms this and demonstrates the difficulties in reversing the effects of nutrient enrichment.

The aesthetic quality of the freshwater environment is also important. Rivers show a wide range in aesthetic quality. Many river stretches in urban areas are still of poor quality because of littering, pollution, sewage-derived debris, and poor habitats. Further effort needs to be put into determining what the priorities are from a public perception viewpoint and how they can be assessed.

The Agency's Response

This analysis of available information on the stresses on the freshwater environment and its consequent state shows the varied nature of the many issues that require active management. Based upon this analysis, 10 priority areas for further concerted action have been identified, along with the specific responses that are necessary. These are:

- current climatic variability and potential long-term climate change;

- pressures on water resources;

- habitat loss and modification;

- changes in flora and fauna;

- groundwater contamination;

- pollution from hazardous substances;

- nutrient enrichment in some lakes and rivers, and groundwaters;

- poor and deteriorating water quality in some rivers, mainly in urban areas;

- aesthetic quality of fresh waters and the increasing demand for recreational uses;

- the pressures caused by changing lifestyles, demands for new housing, and increasing urbanisation.

The Agency has recently published its *Environmental Strategy for the Millennium and Beyond* which addresses a range of specific issues to be progressively addressed across its environmental management functions. Further action in the freshwater environment will be tackled as part of this overall strategy by:

- addressing the causes of, and ameliorating the effects of, climate change;

- improving air quality and thus the specific causes of acidification of fresh waters;

- improving the biodiversity of our freshwater habitats;

- managing our freshwater fisheries in a sustainable way;

- ensuring long-term and integrated approaches to our management of water resources;

- delivering an integrated approach to the management of river basins generally, with respect to their multiple use by both industry and the public;

- reducing the impact of land use on diffuse sources of pollutants and soil erosion on surface waters and the long-term impact of pollution on groundwaters;

- managing wastes so that they do not add to the polluting pressures on fresh waters, particularly groundwaters;

- ensuring that industrial impact on the freshwater environment is progressively reduced, both for the benefit of industry itself and for the enjoyment of fresh waters by everyone.

The Agency cannot bring about all the necessary changes on its own. An important element of our environmental strategy is developing proper working relationships with others to ensure that their actions contribute to the achievement of environmental goals. Of particular importance in this respect is ensuring that the investment by other sectors is properly targeted to maximise environmental benefits. The water industry in particular has a very important part to play in bringing about necessary improvements to the state of the freshwater environment. The Agency wishes to see that an appropriate level of investment is committed in order to tackle leakage from distribution systems and to find environmentally sensitive solutions for managing water resources. There is a need for further improvement to water quality by upgrading sewer systems and sewage treatment facilities. The extent to which the goals of sustainable development can be achieved ultimately depends upon the willingness of all sectors, including the general public to take responsibility. This is certainly true in the case of the freshwater environment, which continues to be subject of significant pressures to meet society's needs. The Agency therefore attaches great importance to the role of education in improving general awareness and in changing behaviours where necessary.

1 Introduction

This report forms an opinion on the State of the Freshwater Environment by addressing the following questions.

- What is the state of fresh waters (rivers, canals, lakes and groundwaters) in England and Wales and have they improved or deteriorated over time?

- Why are fresh waters in this state and how much are human activities influencing them?

- How much money has been invested in tackling the impact of human activities on fresh waters and has this money been well spent?

- Are there any causes for concern in the state of fresh waters and any further problems predicted in the near future?

- What are the priorities for action and investment in the future?

Section 2 of the report provides a general background to the freshwater environment including a historical perspective on the dependence that society has placed on water, the regulation of water, and conflicts of interest. It also gives an overview of the hydrological cycle, how fresh waters vary naturally across England and Wales and describes, in broad terms, how man's activities are influencing them.

Section 3 then looks at 'pressures' on the environment in more depth and shows how these have changed over the last 10 to 20 years and how they are expected to change over the next 20 to 30 years. Recognising these pressures before problems are created is important in environmental management because investment planning can lead to an effective balance between human and environmental needs.

Section 4 provides information on the state of fresh waters. It is organised into the following six viewpoints which the Agency has devised in order to examine the state of the environment generally and which recognise the role of many organisations in providing information on the state of the environment:

- land use and environmental resources;

- the status of key biological populations and communities, and of biodiversity;

- the quality of the environment as determined by assessing compliance with standards and targets;

- the 'health' of environmental resources;

- environmental changes at long-term reference sites;

- the aesthetic quality of the environment.

Section 5 builds on Sections 3 and 4 by attempting to explain why fresh waters are in their current state and what accounts for trends over time. Human activities in one form or another can explain many of the changes and the present state. To identify how much effort has been placed in trying to minimise the effects of human activities on the freshwater environment, the amount of investment by industry, farming and others is presented, together with planned investment where known. It also considers how much people are willing to pay for investment in the freshwater environment.

Having looked at the information in the pressures, states, response framework, Section 6 pulls this together to present the Agency's opinion on the State of Fresh Waters. This identifies the key successes and key areas where further effort is needed.

The information contained in this report has been acquired from as many sources as possible and unless otherwise stated, refers to England and Wales. Regional data presented from Agency sources relates to the river catchments managed by each Agency Region (shown inside the back cover). All the raw data owned by the Agency are available on the Public Registers held in the Agency's Regional Offices, and summary data are available on the World Wide Web which can be found at http://www.environment-agency.gov.uk.

2 Background to the Freshwater Environment

2.1 Hydrological Cycle

To evaluate the impact of human activities on fresh waters, it is necessary to have a broad understanding of the water cycle (Figure 2.1). The water cycle is essentially a closed system with water neither lost nor gained. Water is evaporated from the oceans and land, and then moves by air circulation over the land where it condenses and falls as precipitation. The water runs off the land into channels (rivers) or soaks into the ground and may become stored in the rocks (aquifers). Where the water table (saturated surface) in these rocks meets the surface, springs and seepages connect the groundwater system to rivers. Rivers return the water to the oceans and the cycle continues. Water is therefore a renewable resource.

Our knowledge of the quantities of fresh water in the environment depends on measurements at different points in the hydrological cycle. Precipitation is measured at more than 3000 sites and flows at 1000 river gauging stations in England and Wales, many recording continuously. This network is amongst the highest density of all European countries. Many gauges are linked to offices by telephones or radio to give data quickly, typically at 15 minute intervals which are essential for flood forecasting. Over half the gauging stations use weirs or engineered structures for flow measurements, and most of the others use estimation techniques. The UK is the main user of ultrasonic flow gauging in Europe and the only European country to use modern electromagnetic

techniques, although these methods are only used at a small proportion of the total number of stations. Groundwater levels are monitored at 50,000 observation boreholes in England and Wales. Hydrological models have been developed to link components of the water cycle together from these critical measurements. With improvements in electronics, measurements have increased in precision in the last 10 years. Knowledge about the components of the physical water cycle far outweighs knowledge of the chemical and biological components of the system.

There are significant natural variations in the water cycle across England and Wales due to climatic, geographical and geological differences. Greater precipitation occurs in the higher areas of Wales (average annual rainfall 2400mm), the Lake District and south west England, and lower rainfalls occur in the east and south east (500mm per yr). The amount of rainfall affects the amount of runoff to rivers and the amount that infiltrates (recharges) aquifers and hence the amount of flow in rivers and the quantity of water stored as groundwater. Not all rainfall reaches rivers or aquifers because of evaporation and transpiration losses. These losses are temperature dependent resulting in greater losses to the atmosphere during the summer than winter. Evaporation losses account for about 75 per cent of the rainfall in the English lowlands, but there are further local differences depending on the vegetation or type of land use.

Figure 2.1
The water cycle

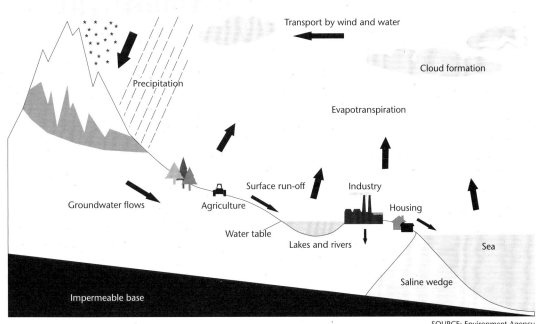

SOURCE: Environment Agency

Climate records show that extreme weather conditions are not common in England and Wales when considering the extremes suffered by other countries. However, the 1980s and 1990s have recorded extremes in winter and summer temperatures, and winter and summer rainfall. There has been a trend towards warmer, drier summers, along with a marked accentuation of the north west to south east rainfall gradient across England and Wales. However, the extremes in winter temperature do not seem to have reached those recorded in earlier times, when 'Frost Fairs' were held on the River Thames. Records show that these took place in 1683, 1740, 1895 with the most elaborate on record being in 1814. Whilst the river froze in 1996, it is doubtful as to whether a fair could have been held! Droughts and floods occur naturally and can cause serious local deterioration and there is some evidence to show that the severity of floods is increasing. Human activities can affect the severity of flooding, for example, canalisation can help to speed up runoff but building in floodplains reduces the natural area over which high flood flows can be accommodated.

Average annual air temperatures across England and Wales range from about 9.0°C in the north to 11.5°C in the south. Temperatures affect rates of evapotranspiration, with the consequence that 75 per cent of evaporation occurs during April to September, with minimum surface runoff during these times. Temperatures also influence the growth of algae in rivers, the demand for water abstractions, and the rate at which rivers self-purify naturally; for example, the breakdown of organic pollution doubles with a 10°C rise in temperature. Sunshine hours also naturally affect the state of fresh waters because algae need sunshine to grow. The south and east have the most sunshine hours, averaging four to five hours daily.

The physical and chemical characteristics of fresh waters are influenced by their underlying geology. This determines stream gradients, densities, sediment types, runoff characteristics and aquifer types, as well as the natural chemistry of fresh waters. Slightly acid waters occur, for example, over granite and sandstone areas and alkaline waters occur in limestone and chalk areas. Some groundwaters are naturally rich in dissolved salts whilst others are extremely poor. The variability in geology across England and Wales accounts for much of the natural physical, chemical and consequent ecological variability of rivers. In general terms, the relatively impermeable rocks in the higher regions of the north and west have led to slightly acid, nutrient poor streams, a predominance of surface waters and a lack of important aquifers. The limestones and chalk of south and east England have led to well buffered, nutrient rich waters and the occurrence of major aquifers.

Soils and vegetation can also affect runoff characteristics, infiltration rates, evapotranspiration

rates and chemical quality. The colour of rivers can be determined by soil type. For example, runoff from peat in the Pennines gives rise to naturally brown coloured rivers. Soils tend to correspond with underlying geology and work together in their effects on fresh waters. Vegetation is more variable and has changed significantly over the 10,000 years since the last ice-age and since humans have progressively farmed and developed the natural landscape.

The natural ecosystems of fresh waters reflect the physical and chemical characteristics and range from wetlands to ponds to river ecosystems. In terms of biodiversity, wetlands support about one-third of all British vascular plants (660 species). Many invertebrates and all amphibians are dependent on fresh waters and there are 38 species of freshwater fish native to Great Britain. A large number of bird species and three rare or threatened mammals (water shrew, water vole and otter) are dependent on aquatic habitats. Biological colonisation of England and Wales has taken place in the 10,000 years since the last ice-age. This is relatively short on geological time scales, but ever since humans arrived in England and Wales, their activities have been affecting the ecosystem. During the 20th century, there has been an increase in the pace and scale of human intervention which has led to concerns about the loss of biodiversity. Whilst some of society's activities have reduced certain types of habitats, others have created new freshwater habitats, for example the construction of reservoirs and garden ponds.

2.2 Historical Perspective

Fresh waters meet essential needs of humans, including health, and they also support much of our economic well-being. The 'uses' to which we put fresh waters have grown through time reflecting industrial, agricultural and economic history. Humans require water to live; early settlements were therefore based around sources of fresh water, but the amount of water that humans use in day-to-day activities has increased significantly through time. In the 19th century there was a need to provide basic services via an infrastructure to keep pace with the expansion of urban communities. Figure 2.2 shows the growth in abstractions from the River Thames over the past century. The increase reflects the growing population during this time (Figure 2.3) as well as the increased number of uses for which society requires water. This also implies that less flow is being left in rivers to support other non-abstractive uses. Internal bathrooms, washing machines and car washing are uses which have become prevalent in the last 50 years. Potable abstraction in England and Wales in the 1960s was estimated to be 12,000Ml/d but now runs at 17,000Ml/d. Based on a population of 51.4 million, this averages out at 331 litres/person/day.

The demand for abstracted water has increased steadily over the last century reflecting an increasing

SOURCE: Environment Agency

Figure 2.2
Annual mean abstraction from the River Thames, 1890 to 1996

population in the first half of the century (at a rate of about 0.5 per cent per year although this has now fallen to 0.37 per cent per year), increased uses of water in the home, increased consumption of power (the production of which uses water for cooling), and increased number of households in the second half of the 20th century. Over the last 20 years, there has been a 15 per cent increase in quantities put into public supply, though only a 3 per cent increase in the last 10 years. Some of this slowing down of the trend is due to less use and greater efficiency by industry as well as a decline in the number of industries that use water. However, with an anticipated increase in the number of households and an increase in population predicted at about 0.29 per cent per year in the next 20 years, the Environment Agency expects demand to continue to rise by 12 to 38 per cent by 2021 unless it can be reduced. The volume abstracted for irrigation purposes has tripled since 1969. This causes concern because this use is consumptive, that is, the next stage in the cycle after irrigation is evapotranspiration,

whereas other uses are less consumptive due to reuse in the cycle. Water returned from the sewerage system to rivers can be re-abstracted and reused further down the catchment. In the south east, for example, water from the River Thames is abstracted and returned many times through discharges from sewage-treatment works before finally entering the sea.

Demands for water vary from season to season with peak demands in the summer months typically 20 per cent higher than average, when river flows are at their lowest. Storage reservoirs have been constructed since the mid-19th century in order to safeguard supplies in the summer though the capacity of many of these is being stretched by current demands. Figure 2.4 shows the increase in total reservoir capacity in England and Wales since 1850, reflecting the similar growth in population and water demand. The large increases in the late 1970s and early 1980s reflect the commissioning of the Queen Mother Reservoir near London in 1974 and Kielder Reservoir in

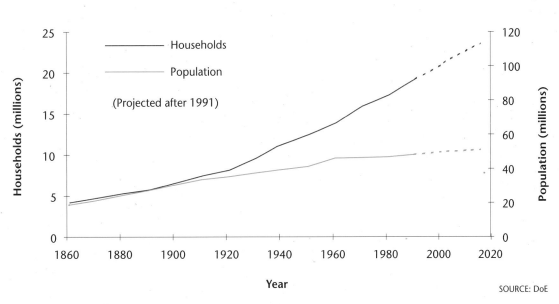

SOURCE: DoE

Figure 2.3
Demographic trends in England, 1861 to 2016

Figure 2.4
Increase in total reservoir capacity since 1857

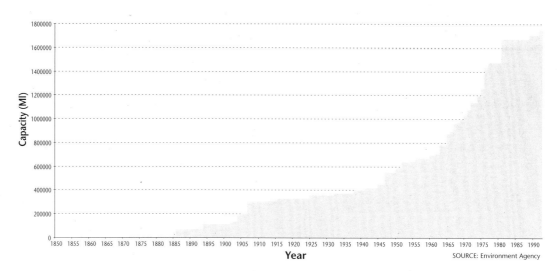

SOURCE: Environment Agency

Northumberland in 1981. Reservoirs have generally been planned to meet a 25-year time horizon in demand growth. The area covered by reservoirs is about 24,000 hectares or 0.16 per cent of the land surface of England and Wales and whilst this may appear small, the figure has increased substantially since the 1960s. Although this represents a loss of land for other purposes, it also represents an increase in the number of freshwater sites available for wildlife and recreation. Any new proposals for reservoirs need careful evaluation to assess their environmental impact and their impact on sustainable development.

Before the water supply network was built, water was freely available to everyone but for the last century or so, households have had to pay for the service of provision to the tap. Domestic, commercial and industrial users require water supplies at a reasonable price and of sufficient quality, together with facilities for carrying away, treating and disposing of effluents, both reliably and efficiently. Businesses do not expect processes to be shut down because of interrupted water supplies or inadequate pressure. Both economic considerations and environmental aspects govern the management of the abstraction, treatment and supply of water and the treatment and disposal of effluents.

Water bills have risen significantly in real terms in England and Wales, from £1.29 per week in 1982 to £4.19 per week in 1996. In 1996/97, the average household water supply bill for households without meters was £102; the highest was £161 and the lowest £72. The average sewage bill was £117 in 1996/97; the highest £206 and the lowest £93 (Water Services Association, 1996). There are wide variations nationally.

Historically, rivers have been used to carry away domestic effluent, ever since the water closet was introduced in about 1810. This, together with a period of rapid industrialisation, resulted in many rivers becoming severely polluted in the 19th century, with the consequences of loss of all fish life and severe outbreaks of cholera. In 1831, London's first cholera epidemic occurred resulting in more than 6,000 deaths and in the following 30 years many more died, including 5,000 in 1866 alone. This intolerable situation was rectified by the construction of vast sewer networks and sewage-treatment works, as well as water treatment works, many of which survive today.

The public health problems caused by effluent in the 19th and early 20th centuries led to the development of pollution control legislation in England and Wales. This recognised that whilst effluent can be returned to fresh waters, the quality needs to be controlled to avoid pollution. The increase in life expectancy over the last two centuries has been very closely linked to improvements in water supply and sanitation, and water-borne diseases in England and Wales are now rare. Some 98 per cent of the population are now connected to sewers and about 79 per cent of sewage receives secondary (biological) or tertiary (advanced) treatment in sewage-treatment works. Of the remaining, 8 per cent receives primary treatment (settlement) and 11 per cent preliminary (screens) or no treatment, but these tend to discharge to areas of high dilution (the sea) rather than to fresh waters (Water Services Association, 1996). Discharges from the sewerage system comprise the largest proportion of planned discharges to the freshwater environment, others being made by industry, fish farms, and mineral workings. Whilst organic pollution was the main concern in the 1800s, other issues have come to light since, ranging from the impact of radioactive waste to acidification, although organic pollution is still a major motivation for investment today (Figure 2.5). With rivers being used as effluent carriers, many rivers became devoid of fish life in the 19th and early 20th centuries. The River Trent downstream of Birmingham was essentially 'dead' before the 1960s; it has now improved so much that it is being considered as a potential drinking water source (after treatment), and its biological status has been restored, although only after 'clean-up' costs of about £750 million.

These two main human uses of fresh waters – to meet demands for water and to carry away effluent – can, in

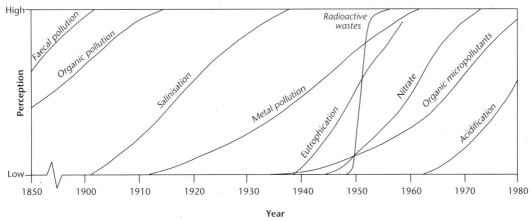

SOURCE: Meybeck & Helmer

Figure 2.5
Growth in the perception of freshwater pollution problems in industrialised countries

some circumstances benefit each other, but at other times conflict. They can also conflict with maintaining aquatic life. The return of effluent to rivers increases the flow in the river and the water can be abstracted again further downstream. At times of average flow, 30 per cent of the River Thames at Teddington (West London) is estimated to be treated effluent. This figure rises to 70 per cent at times of low flow so the effluent returned is providing an essential resource. Most standards for effluent treatment assume a certain minimum flow is available in the receiving watercourse. If over-use or drought causes this to fall, then water quality in the watercourse could decline too, with further consequences for aquatic life.

Rivers are natural drainage channels, but over the centuries human activities have resulted in changed river courses, land drains, culverts, weirs and impoundments, channels, reservoirs and the dredging of rivers. These activities have been carried out for various purposes but include dams for mill-ponds in the middle ages, and locks for the needs of navigation when water was used much more for the transport of goods than today. The first three locks on the River Thames were completed in 1630 and much of the canal network was built during the 18th Century, although the Romans also built canals in

England at a much earlier date. The estimated total length of canal monitored by the Agency is 2,500km compared with a total monitored river and canal length of 40,000km. Canals provide a valuable extra length of available freshwater environment to support various uses, both recreational and for biodiversity.

In the last 100 years the greatest changes to the physical structure of rivers and the drainage system have been for two main purposes: to meet the needs of flood defence in protecting land and people from risk of flooding, and to drain low-lying areas so that land can be brought into agricultural production. The former was driven by the great floods of 1894, 1915, 1928, 1929, 1947, 1953 and 1963 in which many people drowned. There is evidence from historical records of a progressive increase in significant flooding, erosion and deposition events affecting people and property (Figure 2.6). Although such data are selective and subject to changes in reporting, they indicate a large increase in the frequency of events over the last 200 years, but with a decline in events over the last 30 years due to flood defence schemes. The demand for drainage to create more agricultural land for food production was driven by the needs of both World Wars and an increasing population in the 20th century. The desires of the longer living

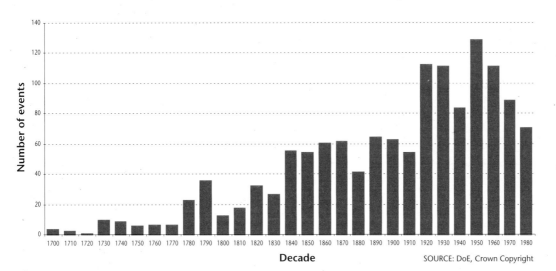

SOURCE: DoE, Crown Copyright

Figure 2.6
The frequency of significant erosion, deposition and flooding events in England, Wales and Scotland, per decade, 1700 to 1980

population for an ever more varied and changing diet puts different demands on agriculture, which has to compete economically and change to meet these needs. Many of these changes impact on fresh waters.

In the last 150 years, other physical changes of rivers have been due to the growth of towns. In many cases, these have led to the culverting or diversion of rivers to allow construction of urban areas or roads. The building of towns, extending the amount of paved areas which increase the intensity of runoff during storms, can lead to flooding. As the Black Country developed during the industrial revolution, urban development in the headwaters of the River Tame led to increased flooding of Birmingham further downstream. Schemes to store water and regulate flows have largely alleviated these effects, but further urbanisation requires adequate planning to minimise flood risk. In rural areas, changing economic patterns are affecting land use, including afforestation and overgrazing by stock, which have affected patterns of runoff and sediment load. Other economic changes leading to the closing of metal and coal mines have led to significant local pollution problems with approximately 170 discharges currently from these abandoned mines, affecting 620km of rivers, mainly in Wales, the north and the south west.

These changes to fresh waters that have occurred due to human activities, create conflicts with the need to maintain the biodiversity of aquatic ecosystems because much of the physical structure of rivers can be damaged temporarily, and water levels in wetlands affected permanently. This latter change can have knock-on effects for water resource availability because it can lead to a lower storage of water than wetlands provided in the past. Pollution from agriculture, industry and sewage effluents can threaten the quality of water needed to support these economic activities and potable supply. There is a need for effective management.

The human activities dependent on fresh waters identified so far relate to basic needs, including economic needs. There are two distinct further needs. Firstly, fresh waters are essential for maintaining biodiversity, and secondly, fresh waters are becoming increasingly important as a recreational resource with the increased leisure time that affluence and technology have provided, compared with 50 years ago. Fishing has always taken place on fresh waters but whereas previously it was to meet consumptive needs, it is now largely a leisure activity. The Agency sells over one million fishing licences every year and surveys suggest that angling is one of the most popular sports in the UK with over three million participants. There is concern that the genetic integrity of fish stocks, particularly trout may have been adversely affected, primarily by extensive stocking programmes and escapees from fish farms.

Fresh waters also support other leisure activities such as boating, canoeing and riverside walks. Some of these activities conflict with each other, for example canoeing can conflict with angling, or with other river uses. The use of rivers as effluent carriers conflicts with new demands for water contact sports, and all recreational activities require certain minimum water levels to be maintained. The introduction of exotic flora and fauna species in gardens and managed water areas since Victorian times has led to some of these becoming naturalised which in turn has led to competitive pressures on the natural species and to the introduction of diseases.

2.3 Regulation of Fresh Waters

Even though fresh waters have long been used for human activities, abstractions have only been regulated since the Water Resources Act, 1963 which followed a severe drought in 1959. The Act lead to the setting up of 29 River Authorities to provide regional catchment-based integrated management of water resources, and to the introduction of abstraction licensing. It allowed for 'licences of right' to be granted to anyone abstracting water at that time, regardless of the effect on catchment water resources, but any new applications for abstractions could be licensed based on resource availability in the catchment. A major weakness of this Act was the inadequate provision for the coordination of water resources development and water quality control, because Rivers Boards had been responsible for the pollution control of entire catchments since 1948. The 1973 Water Act addressed this weakness by setting up 10 Regional Water Authorities, responsible for sewerage and sewage treatment as well as water resources management.

The regulation of discharges to fresh waters has a longer history than abstraction licensing. Early concerns dealt mainly with the obvious effects of sewage. Water pollution was first legally prohibited in 1388 by the Act for Punishing Nuisances which Cause Corruption of the Air near Cities and Great Towns. This was intended to control foul smells, but the problem reached a peak with the infamous Great Stink of the Thames in London in 1858. The Rivers Pollution Prevention Act 1876 required sewage discharges to be rendered inoffensive prior to discharge to an inland watercourse. This led to a series of developments in sewage treatment technology which stemmed from some of the worst organic pollution. The Act was poorly enforced, however, and did nothing to control industrial pollution. A significant step came with the Royal Commission on Sewage Disposal report of 1912. This advocated emission standards for biochemical oxygen demand (BOD) and suspended solids which were related to the river dilution available for an effluent. Although non-statutory, this approach was generally applied.

Industrial effluents were addressed by The Rivers (Prevention of Pollution) Act, 1951 which required new dischargers of trade or sewage effluent to inland waters to have a consent from the river boards specifying limits on the quality and quantity of the discharge. It also became an offence to cause or knowingly permit any poisonous, noxious or polluting matter to enter a river. The Rivers (Prevention of Pollution) Act, 1961 extended these controls to industrial discharges existing before 1951, and for the first time brought in controls over direct discharges to groundwater. Attempts to control discharges from septic tanks had been made by local authorities in the mid-1920s to avoid pollution of wells, e.g. in Brighton and Margate. This enabled a two-mile exclusion zone in the vicinity of these wells to be enforced by legislation, but the Rivers Act made control much easier.

The Control of Pollution Act, 1974 introduced public participation in decisions, established public registers of information and allowed for private prosecutions; although it was nearly 10 years before parts of the Act were fully implemented. This was an important change in the legislation because it made public the details of discharges for the first time and helped to raise public awareness of pollution. The important division between sewage undertaking by public limited companies and the regulation of pollution by the National Rivers Authority (NRA) was made in the Water Act, 1989. This Act set up the NRA and led to the privatisation of the water and sewerage undertakers to give rise to the water utility companies. The 1991 Water Resources Act consolidated the NRA's duties and superseded all previous water legislation. It maintained the offences of discharging trade or sewage effluent to controlled waters unless in compliance with a discharge consent, and the need for abstraction licences. The NRA had the key duty to conserve, redistribute or otherwise augment water resources in England and Wales and to secure the proper use of those resources, but the water companies were left with the duty to supply wholesome drinking water.

The Water Industry Act, 1991 set out various duties to be undertaken by the Director General of Water Services, many of which are shared with the Secretary of State. The primary duty of the Director General is to ensure that the functions of water and sewerage undertakers are properly carried out and that appointed companies are able to finance the proper carrying out of their functions. The price of water is regulated by the Director General, whose office is known as the Office of Water Services (OFWAT) and who is also responsible for standards of service delivered by the water companies and for operating customer service committees. Price increases in the water industry are limited to the Retail Prices Index plus a variable factor, K. The K factors reflect what a company needs to charge in order to finance services

to customers. These are set for a 10-year period with the provision for a five-year review if necessary. A review took place in 1994 and another has been announced for 1999.

The duties and powers of the water and sewerage undertakers are also specified in the Water Industry Act, which include the provision of a supply of water sufficient for domestic purposes which is wholesome, and to provide a sewer system with suitable treatment. Discharges to the sewer system require consent from the undertaker and conditions may be specified on the volume, nature and composition of the effluent. However, there is no requirement for the monitoring results for trade discharges to sewer to be made public, contrary to the legislation on discharges to rivers

Integrated Pollution Control was introduced by the Environmental Protection Act, 1990. It applies to the most complex and polluting industrial processes and substances and is enforced by the Agency (previously by Her Majesty's Inspectorate of Pollution) for Part A processes (e.g. large chemical works, power stations). Smaller scale processes, Part B, are subject to air pollution control by local authorities. Integrated Pollution Control aims to prevent or minimise the release of prescribed substances (dangerous substances) and to render harmless any such substances which are released by means of the Best Available Techniques Not Entailing Excessive Cost. Its major conceptual advance in pollution control is that it considers discharges and environmental effects to all media: water, air and land, and selects the Best Practicable Environmental Option for disposal. Prescribed substances released to the sewer must be referred by sewerage undertakers to the Secretary of State so that notices imposing conditions of Best Available Techniques Not Entailing Excessive Cost can be applied. The Radioactive Substances Act, 1993 provides for controls to be exercised over the use and keeping of radioactive materials, and the accumulation and disposal of radioactive wastes. It applies to all users of radioactive substances including hospitals, universities, industrial research, manufacturing centres, and the nuclear industry. The Agency's powers on licensed nuclear sites are limited to the regulation of disposal of radioactive waste, including discharges to the environment. In the process of determining applications for nuclear site authorisations, the Agency consults MAFF and the Health and Safety Executive.

The Environment Act, 1995 created the Environment Agency for England and Wales which took over all the functions of the NRA, together with those of Her Majesty's Inspectorate of Pollution and Waste Regulation Authorities. The duties with respect to fresh waters encompass all those of its predecessors, together with some new duties which are of particular relevance to this report. The Agency has written this report in recognition of its principal aim, *"to protect or enhance the environment taken as a whole, as to make the contribution towards attaining the objective of achieving sustainable development"* (Environment Act, Section 4). The Act specifies that the Agency's pollution control powers shall be exercisable for the purpose of preventing or minimising, or remedying or mitigating the effects of pollution of the environment. The Agency is also required to compile information so as *"to form an opinion on the general state of pollution of the environment"* (Environment Act, Section 5). In regulating fresh waters, the Agency is required to take account of any International and European commitments that have been translated in UK law, although the Department of the Environment, Transport and the Regions (DETR) is responsible for reporting compliance to Europe. At present, there are 26 pieces of European legislation which require specific actions to be taken by the Agency as well as International Commitments to the Paris Commission and North Sea Conferences on reductions of substances input to the marine environment. Appendix 1 gives more details.

The Agency is the licensing authority for water abstraction and this is the only power it has to fulfill its water resources duties. New licences to abstract will only be granted if the Agency is satisfied with the need for new resources through a thorough analysis of demand, the scope for demand management, and an appropriate environmental assessment. However, there are many 'licences of right' given to abstractors who were taking water before the Water Resources Act of 1963, and 'licences of entitlement' given to other specific users by the Water Resources Act, 1991. The Agency does not have the power to revoke these licences without compensation, even if they are in conflict with the overall duty and environmental needs. The Environment Act also amended Section 93 of the Water Industry Act, 1991 to impose a duty on water undertakers to promote the efficient use of water by its customers.

As well as its water resources and pollution control functions, the Agency has inherited a duty to promote the conservation and enhancement of fresh waters and to promote the recreational use of fresh water. It is the navigation authority for some watercourses. The Agency has a duty to maintain, improve and develop the salmon, trout, freshwater and eel fisheries under its jurisdiction and has a duty to regulate these fisheries and prevent their illegal exploitation. The Agency also has powers to: help ensure the unobstructed migration of salmon and sea trout from the sea to their spawning grounds; monitor catches, fish stocks and the occurrence of disease; and to raise income through duties on rod and net licences as well as contributions from fishery owners. Other bodies have powers and duties relating to fisheries as well. MAFF and the Secretary of State for Wales are required to consider all new fishery byelaws and Net Limitation Orders made by the Agency, and approve changes to licence duties. Fisheries legislation in England and Wales is currently being reviewed to take account of the need to maintain, and where appropriate enhance, biodiversity, and the need to maximise the economic, social and recreational benefits derived from salmon and freshwater fisheries on a fully sustainable basis. The review is also considering the institutional arrangements for regulation and management.

The Agency also has an important flood defence function, including flood warning and provision of defences to reduce the risk of sea and fluvial flooding, and to issue land drainage consents. Legislation dealing with land drainage has existed in England and Wales for at least five and a half centuries, although it was fragmented until the Land Drainage Act 1930 with further consolidations in 1976 and 1991. The Land Drainage Act 1991 re-enacts most of the previous land drainage provisions but those relating to main rivers appear in the Water Resources Act 1991. These Acts distinguish between 'main rivers' and 'ordinary watercourses'. The Agency has responsibility for the former and local authorities and Internal Drainage Boards have responsibilities for all other watercourses. The Land Drainage Act 1994 added new environmental duties. Many of the duties of the Agency impinge on each other but by taking an integrated approach to regulation and planning, an effective balance should be achieved.

The quality of drinking water is regulated by the Drinking Water Inspectorate of the Department of the Environment, Transport and the Regions. This inspectorate was created in January 1990, and the supply of wholesome water is the responsibility of the privatised water companies. Whilst the Agency is responsible for aspects of pollution control, public health responsibilities lie with the environmental health departments of local authorities, who also have specific pollution control powers.

3 Pressures on the Freshwater Environment

This section looks in more detail at pressures on fresh waters caused by human activities, their trends over the last decade or so, and projected future pressures. Climate change is considered as the first pressure that needs to be addressed. Climate change may be due to natural causes – there have been large shifts in climate in the past – but it also may be accelerating due to human activities. It is included in this section for completeness and because it is perceived to be a large threat.

The section continues by describing how society and lifestyles cause pressure on fresh waters. The demands of humans are the ultimate reason for the economic activities that lead to pressures on the environment described later in the chapter – abstractions and discharges. Various economic activities, for example industry and agriculture, are the 'driving forces' for many of these pressures and are described within the subsections. The pressure from illegal discharges (pollution incidents) is also considered. Data are presented on how these pressures have changed over past years, so that an appreciation of which pressures cause greatest concern for future management can be drawn out. A summary table at the end attempts to draw all the pressures together.

3.1 Climate Change

There is good evidence of global warming with average air temperatures increasing by 0.3°C to 0.6°C during the 20th century (Figure 3.1). This is consistent with the expected effect of increased greenhouse gases on air temperatures, but it is also within the bounds of normal climate variability. The increase in air temperature could lead to higher rates of evapotranspiration which in turn could lead to changes in the amount of river and groundwater flow, although predictions of future climate are uncertain (DoE, 1996a). An increase of about 1.5°C by 2050

could reduce annual river flows in southern England substantially but lead to increases in northern England (Figure 3.2). Winter flows may show an increase in some regions, but marked decreases may also occur in the summer months (Figure 3.3) when demands for water are high. A higher frequency of storms is also possible. These predictions are based on models which have large uncertainties and so the direction of climate change is also uncertain.

An analysis of the recent trends in rainfall, temperature, and effective rainfall (i.e. rainfall minus evapotranspiration) provides several interesting facts about climate change in England and Wales.

- The 1988 to 1992 drought was the driest 28-month sequence since the 1850s. When this ended in the summer of 1992, it was followed by the wettest 32-month sequence this century. December 1994 to February 1995 was the wettest December to February on record but this was followed by the driest summer (June to August 1995) in 229 years, with rainfall less than 15 per cent of the average in July and August.

- Average air temperatures over the seven years ending in 1995 were the highest on record since 1845, and for the last 20 years taken together, mean temperatures have been 0.5°C greater than the preceding average. This has affected evaporation losses which have been notably higher in the 1990s than in the 1960s (Figure 3.4), and in the summer of 1995 were more than 20 per cent above average.

- The combination of 20 per cent rainfall deficiency and higher evaporative losses in 1988 to 1992 translated into a 50 per cent reduction in recharge to some aquifers, although the long residence times of aquifers have buffered

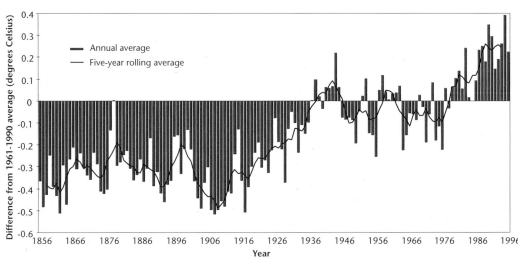

Figure 3.1
Annual average global temperature anomalies (relative to 1961-1990) from 1856 to 1996

SOURCE: University of East Anglia, Norwich and the Hadley Centre

29

Figure 3.2
Projected percentage change in average annual runoff by the 2050s under the 1996 Climate Change Impacts Review Group scenario

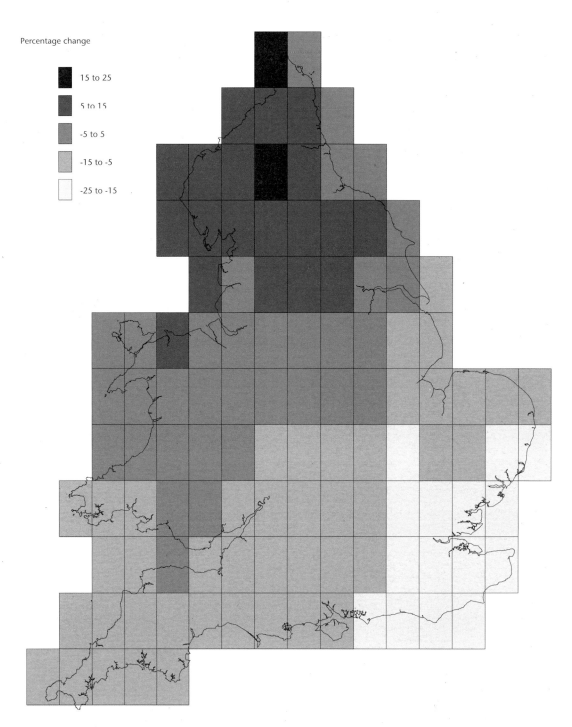

Percentage change

15 to 25

5 to 15

-5 to 5

-15 to -5

-25 to -15

SOURCE: Department of the Environment, Transport and the Regions
Crown copyright is reproduced with the permission of the Controller of
Her Majesty's Stationery Office

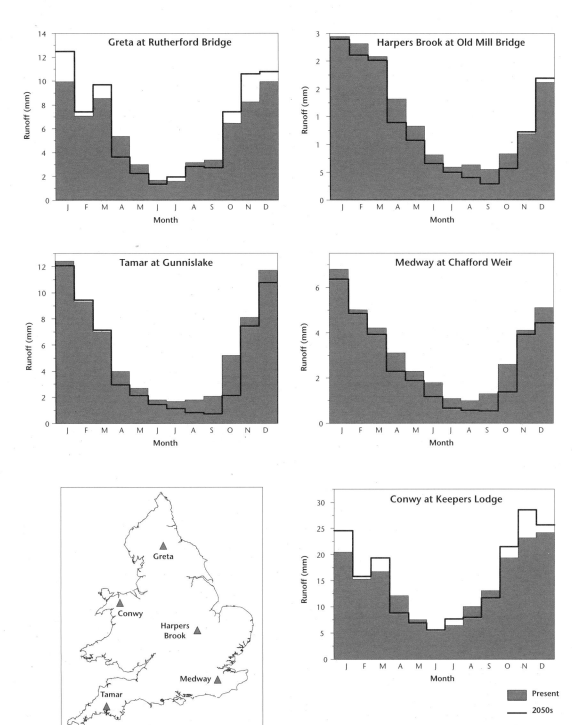

SOURCE: Department of the Environment, Transport and the Regions
Crown copyright is reproduced with the permission of the Controller of
Her Majesty's Stationery Office

Figure 3.3
Monthly average runoff at present and in the 2050s under the 1996 Climate Change Impacts Review Group scenario

Figure 3.4
*Potential
evaporation, 1960
to 1995 (three-year
running mean)*

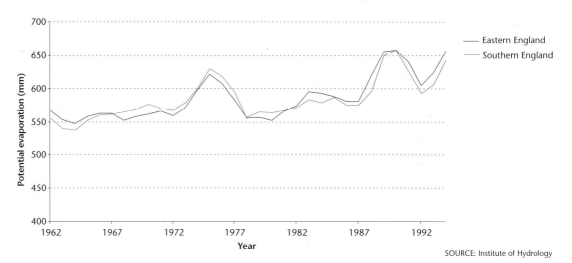

SOURCE: Institute of Hydrology

variability to some extent. Groundwater levels over the period 1988 to 1995, demonstrate a wide range of levels. In the winter of 1994/95 they were at their historical maxima in many locations and in 1992, they were at their historical minima.

Overall, there has been a tendency since 1970 for more distinct rainfall differences between summer and winter with less in the summer. This continues the trend over a much greater time period, from 1760 (Figure 3.5). Figure 3.6 shows the ratio of winter to summer rainfall since 1860 and the recent change to less summer rainfall (below 10 per cent of average) is clear. However, there have been periods in the past (late 1910s, early 1940s) when there were similar ratios to the 1990s (Marsh, 1996).

The air temperatures and rainfall for each of the last 21 years are compared with the years from 1845 to 1975 in Figure 3.7, showing a tendency of warmer, wetter winters and hotter, drier summers in the last two to three decades. These observations are broadly similar to the predictions of climate change induced by burning fossil fuels, but the inherent variability of the climate suggests that caution is needed in accrediting recent climate patterns to climate change produced by humans.

The extent to which these changes are due to the effects of society's activities is unclear but the information on rainfall, temperature, and hence evaporation losses in the recent past suggest that freshwater stocks are now much more variable over time than previously. This has clear implications for the management of these stocks if the day to day needs of abstractors, the environment and other users are to be met.

The pressure from climate change goes beyond droughts. The potential consequences include:

- changed availability of water stocks, particularly in summer, and groundwater recharge, already discussed;

- increased demand for water for crops due to the need for irrigation in any drier, warmer areas, although if the types of crops change then the amount of irrigation required will change too;

- drying out of wetland habitats but there may be other habitats created over a long period, perhaps more like 'Mediterranean' types; we need to determine how to achieve adequate biodiversity;

- loss or northward movement of species – the extent to which this is a threat depends on the rate of climate change and the adaptability of species, and we need to be satisfied that biodiversity will be maintained; biodiversity of freshwater species may well increase in a warmer climate although there may be an initial reduction in diversity as species accommodate to the changes;

- increased flooding and erosion caused by storms, which could increase the frequency of sewer overflows;

- changes in soils and vegetation with an expected increase in growing periods affecting rates of evapotranspiration;

- reduced dilution of pollutants at lower flows, although higher temperatures should make sewage treatment processes more effective;

- increased frequency of algal blooms promoted by warmer temperatures and an extended time of occurrence from earlier in the year to later in the year than currently; if windiness increases, this may mitigate this change to some extent;

- a rise in sea level of 20cm by 2030 without appropriate sea defences would cause losses of freshwater habitats in the Somerset levels, Fens and Broads, and may lead to saline intrusion into coastal aquifers reducing groundwater abstraction yield.

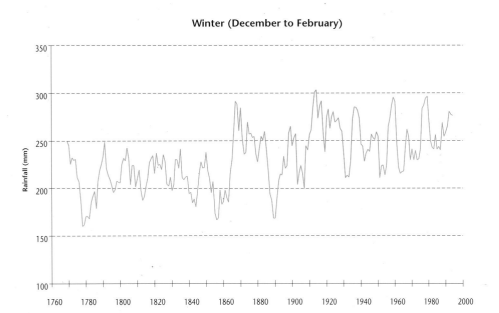

Winter (December to February)

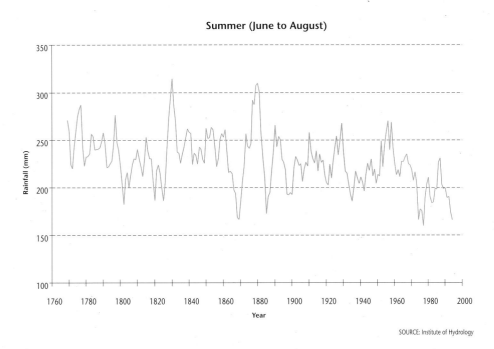

Summer (June to August)

SOURCE: Institute of Hydrology

Figure 3.5
Summer and winter rainfall (five-year running mean) in England and Wales, 1767 to 1996

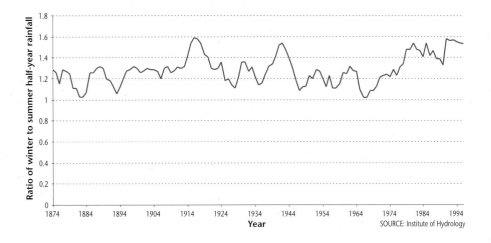

SOURCE: Institute of Hydrology

Figure 3.6
The ratio of winter to summer half-year rainfall for Great Britain, 1874 to 1996 (five-year running mean)

Figure 3.7
The difference in average rainfall and air temperature in England and Wales, 1845 to 1997 compared with the long-term mean

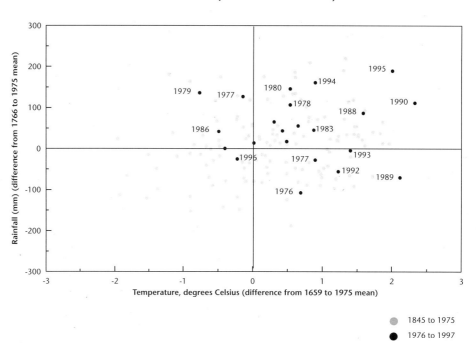

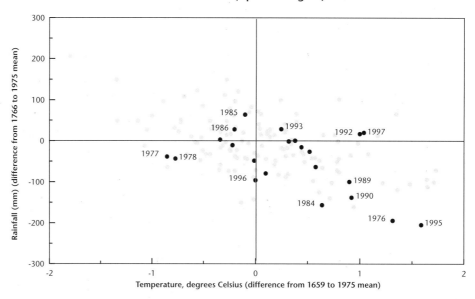

SOURCE: Institute of Hydrology

There is a need to investigate these potential consequences in more depth by appropriate modelling work, so that a strategy based on priorities can be determined. This should then lead to cost-effective planning to minimise the risks to sustainable development.

3.2 Society and Lifestyles

Households

Households put pressure on the freshwater environment in both direct and indirect ways. They represent the 'end of the line' for economic activities which abstract from and discharge to fresh waters,

being the ultimate consumers of most of the products – food, manufactured goods, and electricity. But households also exert direct pressure on the water environment by using much of the water abstracted themselves and they account for most of the waste water draining into sewage-treatment works. It is therefore necessary to consider the current pressures exerted by households, how these have changed with time and how they are projected to change in future.

There has been a steady increase in the number of households in England and Wales since the 1970s reflecting the increase in population and a move to more people living alone (Figure 2.3). The number of households is projected to grow at a faster rate than the population in the next 20 years. This is due to an expected decrease in the average size of household, brought about by the projected rise in households containing only one person. Over the 25 years from 1991 to 2016, there is a projected increase in the number of households by about 4.4 million (23 per cent) in England and 223,000 in Wales. Forty-six per cent of this increase is accounted for by population growth of which 0.5 million is due to net migration, 33 per cent by behavioural changes (e.g. divorce), and 21 per cent by greater life expectancy (DoE, 1995b). Eighty per cent (some 3.5 million households) of the total projected growth are likely to be in one-person households (DoE, 1996c).

These housing needs will mainly be accommodated in the south west (29 per cent increase in households above their present level), south east, Cheshire, East Midlands and eastern regions, with the lowest percentage increase of 13 per cent in Merseyside and 16 per cent in the north east. The projected increase in numbers of households for each county are shown in Figure 3.8. The greatest pressures will occur in those parts of the country where the greatest pressures from abstractions and discharges already exist, where climate change is predicted to have the largest impact and where urbanisation is already extensive. The increase in the number of households will contribute to the expected increase in the area of land in urban use (Figure 3.9) and hence lost to the rural environment. Some 169,000ha (1.3 per cent of England's area) is projected to change from rural use to urban use between 1991 and 2016, that is a rate of 6,800ha/yr. By the year 2016, 11.9 per cent of England's land will be in urban use compared with 10.6 per cent in 1991. This has important implications in terms of loss of habitat, and change to the nature of drainage systems. Runoff from urban areas and development in floodplains are a particular concern because this water will not soak into the ground and recharge aquifers, causing a reduction in available groundwater resources. Furthermore, the timing of runoff can be changed giving rise to 'flashy' rivers with intense peak flows and with low flows at times of no rainfall, unless storage is built into urban drainage systems. The ornamental lake at the National Exhibition Centre in Birmingham balances the impact of the large paved area there to protect the Hollywell Brook from flooding parts of Solihull!

The UK Round Table on Sustainable Development has considered this issue in its report on Housing and Urban Capacity (1997b) and recommends that 75 per cent of new housing should be provided on previously developed land to provide real benefit economically, environmentally and socially. The report highlighted the fact that the present system of land development is failing to make proper use of our land and other resources.

These projections suggest that there have been some important changes in the way people live now, and are likely to live in future, compared with the past, and the kind of housing and other facilities they need. Aspirations and lifestyles have changed in recent decades and these can all cause changing pressures on the environment. At the turn of the century, the extended family was a common feature, with three or more generations living together and an average household size of five. By 1991 the average household size was 2.5, with the main reasons being increased prosperity (people can afford to live separately), improved standards of living and health care so that people are living longer, often on their own, and changes in social behaviour.

The average domestic consumption of water for England and Wales is 140 litres/person/day (Water Services Association, 1996). Household use will depend on the total number of people living there and economies of scale, and households with large gardens may use more for watering during dry times than other types of households. Broken down into elements, rough demands are shown in Table 3.1.

Domestic consumption has increased significantly over time, reflecting changes in the number of household appliances available, lifestyles and expectations. In 1972, 66 per cent of households had washing machines, whereas this figure had risen to 90 per cent by 1996; dishwashers were used in only 4 per cent of households in 1981 but 20 per cent in 1996. Many new households are one person only, and their use of appliances may be less frequent than large households but more frequent in terms of use per person; there is not a straightforward link between the number of households and water use. The variability of water demand according to the type of household is shown in Table 3.2 from data collected in Yorkshire. These suggest that smaller households use more water

Bath	80 litre per bath	Washing machines	80 litre per cycle
Showers	5 litre/min	Dishwashers	35 litre per cycle
Toilets	9.5 litre per flush	Drinking and cooking	10 litre/d
Sprinklers	1,020 litre/hr		

Source: Water Services Association, 1996

Table 3.1
Average household water use

Figure 3.8
Projected growth in the number of households in counties of England, 1991 to 2016

Projected increase - absolute numbers

Over 160,000
120,000 to 160,000
80,000 to 120,000
40,000 to 80,000
Up to 40,000

SOURCE: DoE

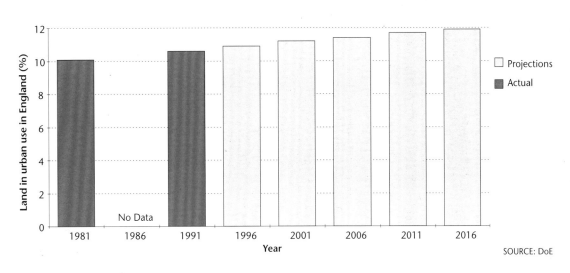

SOURCE: DoE

Figure 3.9
Area of land in urban use in England, 1981 to 2016

per person per day, unless the household is a single resident.

The use of water in the garden has also increased in recent years. This can lead to a greater average demand for water and higher peak demands in the summer months, especially during hot, dry summers. In the United States and Australia, garden watering can account for up to 50 per cent of annual demand, rising to 70 per cent in the summer (Herrington, 1996). Very little research has been done on the demand and trends in England and Wales but Severn Trent Water considered diurnal demands during different summer conditions to estimate the amount of water used in the garden. They monitored the hourly input in a rural suburb of Stourbridge in which all the properties have large gardens (Figure

3.10). The figure clearly shows the effect of a hosepipe ban in reducing demand and also evidence of all-night sprinkler use.

Whilst this study clearly shows the effect of garden watering in hot, dry summers, there is also a need to assess the trend. The unit sales of hosepipes and sprinklers doubled between 1992 and 1995. It is estimated that up to 60 per cent of these are new uses, rather than replacements. Ownership of hosepipes in the UK is about 70 per cent of households whereas the figure exceeds 90 per cent in France and Germany, so there may still be more growth in the UK (OFWAT, 1996c).

Reducing domestic demand for water, or at least minimising the increasing trend for more water, will

Table 3.2
Average household water demand by four attributes: type of household, tenure, number of residents and number of bedrooms (litres/day)

Property type	Litres/day	No. of residents	Litres/day	Use/person
Bungalow	240	1	137	137
Detached	369	2	287	144
Flat	167	3	373	124
Semi-detached	287	4	473	118
Through terrace	280	5	512	102
		6+	1,141	-
Tenure type	**Litres/day**	**No. of bedrooms**	**Litres/day**	
Council rented	224	1	136	
Owner occupied	305	2	199	
Private rented	264	3	291	
Other	256	4	406	
		5	459	
		6+	690	

Source: Clarke *et al.*, 1997

Figure 3.10
The effect of a hosepipe ban (and the use of all-night sprinklers) on the hourly input of water supply in a rural suburb of Stourbridge, 16-27 August, 1995

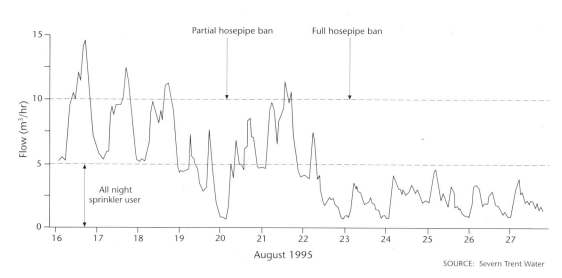

SOURCE: Severn Trent Water

alleviate pressures on the freshwater environment by affecting the quantities that need to be abstracted or stored. Water companies have a duty to promote the efficient use of water and in 1997, a number provided heavy duty plastic bags, 'Hippos', free of charge to customers to reduce water used in toilet cisterns, which account for 10 per cent of household use. There is a need for more water saving devices in the home, an issue that has been tackled elsewhere, and for a greater awareness by individuals of the value of water.

Most of the water used by households, estimated at 80 per cent, is returned to rivers or estuaries via sewers and treatment works which discharge treated effluent. Water returned to fresh waters is then available for further use if discharge points are upstream of intakes, although in many cases, discharges are downstream of intakes and short circuit rivers. However, some water is lost through evaporation in garden use, and lost through leakage in supply pipes and so is not available for further uses.

Households also contribute to the pollution load of fresh waters. Human metabolic processes contribute a large amount of phosphorus to sewage and the use of detergents also contribute phosphorus, although changing formulations have led to a decline in the 1990s (Technical Committee on Detergents and the Environment, 1993). Metal and chemical products are widely used in the home and these contribute to the loads discharged to the environment from sewage-treatment works (STWs) including nickel, copper, lead, zinc and various pesticides. Some of these metals are dissolved from water pipes and solder but others are contained in cosmetics, toiletries, medicines and domestic cleaners. Dilution in STWs normally reduces these to harmless levels but it is not always known what these are. Recent work has suggested that natural oestrogens and those associated with the birth control pill may not be removed in STW processes and these substances have been linked to observations of

intersex in male fish downstream of STW discharges (Environment Agency, 1997f). The use of pesticides and herbicides in gardens also contributes diffuse pollution to fresh waters, misconnections from 'do it yourself' plumbing contaminate surface water sewers, and misuse of road drains for oily residues also create problems in fresh waters. More than 1,000 pollution incidents in 1995 were attributed to domestic or residential premises.

Recreational Activity

Household expenditure on recreation, entertainment and education has increased substantially since 1971, reflecting the rise in real household disposable income over the same period (Figure 3.11). Part of this increase in recreational expenditure relates to time spent in the freshwater environment; 180 million day visits were attributed to freshwater recreation in 1996, consisting mostly of walking, angling and watersports. Boating is a popular leisure time activity in many areas; selected rivers and canals that have navigations under the Agency, the British Waterways Authority and the Broads Authority are shown in Figure 3.12. On average, visitors travelled 21 miles to reach canals or rivers for recreation, further than on most other trips, and the average amount spent per trip was £6.30 (Social and Community Planning Research, 1997). Such visits may have positive economic impact on rural areas. Some activities are on the increase, for example, water skiing, whilst other activities have a continuing high level of participation, for example, angling. Table 3.3 gives details.

Whilst enjoyment of the freshwater environment contributes to the quality of life, recreation can itself create pressures on fresh waters. Recreational users have different needs and the needs of some activities may conflict with the needs of others. Table 3.3 also summarises these. Despite these potential pressures, leisure and tourism do not cause significant

Activity	Level of participation	Potential and perceived environmental impacts	Problems of users
Walking	Ten million visits to Agency navigations, 20 million visits to inland waters.	Noise and other disturbances to wildlife. Litter reducing aesthetic quality. Trampling and loss of vegetation. Disturbance by dogs.	
Watersports	About 700,000 canoeists. Since 1970, number of members of rowing clubs doubled. About 400,000 water skiers but this sport is growing rapidly.	Disturbance and damage to spawning salmonids. Disturbance to breeding birds. Bank erosion at access points. Water skiing may cause physical damage, disturbance to wildlife and other users.	Parking, toilets, access needs, gravel paths and landing stages.
Angling	One million fishing rod licences in 1995. Participation levels about stable. Fifteenth most popular sport in Great Britain.	Disturbance to breeding and non-breeding waterbirds and riparian birds, damage to bankside vegetation. Plant control can cause habitat damage, reduction of species abundance and herbicide pollution. Fish stocking can lead to disease transmission, loss of genetic populations and altered fish communities and ecosystems.	Conflict over access, costs, and increasing demands of all sports on inland waters.
Boating	100,000 boats with access to over 4,000km inland waters; 40,500 craft licensed to use 806km Agency navigations in 1995.	Disturbance to wildlife, notably wildfowl. Aquatic plant damage by direct contact and wash. Bank erosion caused by direct contact and wash. High turbidity limiting ecosystem and aesthetic quality. Discharges of sewage, fuel and oil.	

Sources: NRA, 1995d and House of Commons Environment Committee, 1995

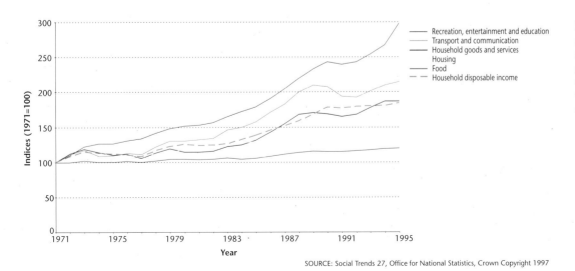

Figure 3.11
Household disposable income per person and household expenditure on selected items, 1971 to 1995

SOURCE: Social Trends 27, Office for National Statistics, Crown Copyright 1997

widespread ecological damage to the countryside although there are local conflicts in specific areas. Cultural conflicts are sometimes more important than the physical problems and are often the cause of various tensions and dissatisfactions that are defined as pressures on the environment (House of Commons Environment Committee, 1995).

With an expected continued growth in recreational activities, there is a need for more positive planning to ensure that the needs of all recreational users are met without increasing pressures on the freshwater environment. This requires providing facilities for all activities, not just for freshwater recreational activities that are aesthetically pleasing. In particular, *"Sites should be sought for watersports, particularly power-boating, water skiing and jet-skiing. These should be developed close to large urban centres so as to reduce leisure travel with its attendant fumes and congestion"* (House of Commons Environment Committee, 1995, page XV).

The Agency has powers to promote Orders under the Transport and Works Act 1992 to help conserve the environment of rivers, to reduce and to eliminate conflicts between those who use the rivers and conflicts between some users and the environment, and to put in place a management framework which will improve the quality of existing recreational use and accommodate increased demand in a sustainable way. The Agency has applied for such an Order on the Rivers Wye and Lugg in the Welsh Region which was the subject of a public enquiry in June 1997.

The Environment Agency considers recreational needs in the development of its Local Environment Agency Plans, which aim to inform and educate visitors on access, facilities and impacts, and to play a full consultative role in strategic plans of the local authorities in the provision of leisure activities.

3.3 Abstractions

The total quantity abstracted from licensed sources of fresh waters in England and Wales in 1995 was 12,045Mm³ (33,000Ml/d) of which 13 per cent was from groundwaters. Potable supply accounted for 53 per cent of the total and the electricity supply industry abstracted 25 per cent for cooling purposes (Figure 3.13). There were marked regional differences in these proportions. The largest quantities for power generation were in the Midlands and Wales whereas potable supply accounted for the largest proportion in the Southern and Thames Regions where population is dense and the demands for other uses in these Regions were relatively low. Fish farming and cress farming accounted for 13 per cent of abstractions and other industries accounted for 7 per cent of abstractions. Agricultural uses (including irrigation) accounted for only one per cent with the largest quantities in the Anglian Region. By European standards, this percentage for agriculture is very low, and one of the lowest in Europe; it exceeds 50 per cent in the Netherlands.

Whilst these statistics give some appreciation of the needs of various activities for water, it is important to appreciate whether the use is consumptive or not, i.e. whether water is lost by evaporation or is returned to rivers, even if this is further downstream. Thus the use of water for fish farming is non-consumptive whereas the use of water for spray irrigation is consumptive. Potable supply is largely a non-consumptive use because about 70 to 80 per cent is returned via the sewer network, but a certain amount is lost by evaporation when water is used in garden watering. The returns from the sewer network tend to be at a distance downstream of the point of abstraction and in some cases, may be into different catchments. Abstractions for cooling in power generation are generally returned to rivers at the point of withdrawal or a short distance downstream, although usually at a lower quantity, and with little change in water quality, except for temperature.

Comparing these abstraction rates per person with those elsewhere in Europe shows some interesting differences. The quantity abstracted is about 642 litres/person/day in England and Wales. Equivalent figures for France are 1,800; for Germany 2,000; and for Norway 1,307. Industrial and irrigation uses tend to be higher in some parts of Europe than in England and Wales. The greater availability of water resources in the countries mentioned above may mean that consumptive uses are less of a threat although seasonal availability needs to be considered too. If only the quantity abstracted for potable supply is considered, then the relevant figures are 331 litres/person/day in England and Wales compared with 177 litres/person/day in Germany, 215 litres/person/day in France and 520 litres/person/day in Norway (Stanners and Bordeau, 1995). (The figure of 331 litres/person/day is much greater than the average domestic consumption of 140 litres/person/day, quoted in the section on household demands. This is because water abstracted for potable supply is also used for many industrial and commercial uses, and is based on the abstracted amount, not demands or consumption). Such differences between countries may reflect the different purposes for which potable supply is used within the countries, different charging schemes, and different rates of leakage between the point of abstraction and use, so they need to be interpreted with care. Water saving domestic appliances have been well developed and promoted in other countries which must have some impact on the figures, as will metering which is commonplace elsewhere.

Whilst groundwaters contribute only 13 per cent of the total amount of fresh water abstracted, they provide about 35 per cent of abstractions used for potable supply nationally, with this proportion rising to over 70 per cent in the Southern Region (Figure 3.14). Groundwaters are also an important resource for rural communities. There are about 1500 water

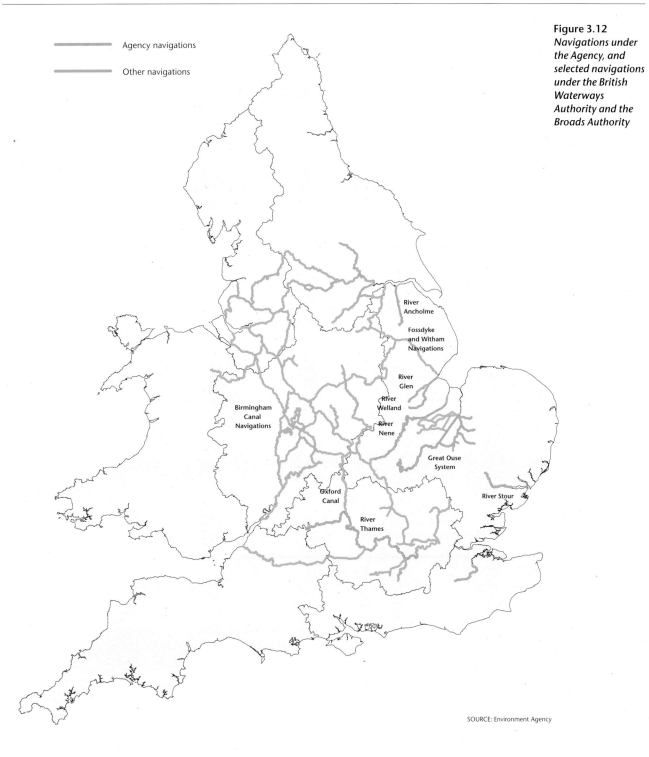

Agency navigations

Other navigations

Figure 3.12
*Navigations under
the Agency, and
selected navigations
under the British
Waterways
Authority and the
Broads Authority*

River
Ancholme

Fossdyke
and Witham
Navigations

River
Glen

River
Welland

Birmingham
Canal
Navigations

River
Nene

Great Ouse
System

Oxford
Canal

River
Stour

River
Thames

SOURCE: Environment Agency

Figure 3.13
Quantities of fresh water abstracted by purpose, 1995

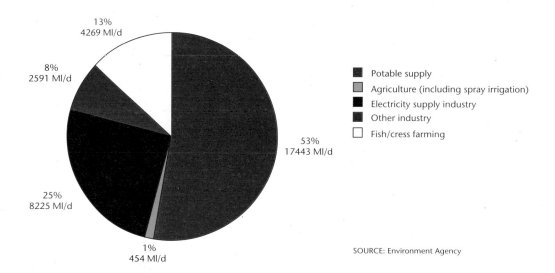

- Potable supply
- Agriculture (including spray irrigation)
- Electricity supply industry
- Other industry
- Fish/cress farming

SOURCE: Environment Agency

supply boreholes nationally or 2000 if springs are included.

Trends

The total quantity of water abstracted from fresh waters in England and Wales has fallen by about 16 per cent from 1971 to 1995, mainly because of the reduction in freshwater use for power generation, and by efficient water use by industry and the restructuring of economic activity away from heavy water-using sectors (e.g. chemicals, steel, textiles). Industrial abstractions alone fell by 60 per cent from 1971 to 1990 (Herrington, 1996). Quantities put into potable supply and agricultural uses, including spray irrigation, show the opposite trend with a growth of 27 per cent in potable supply since the early 1970s with an increase in consumption per person (Figure 3.15). The demand for irrigation water in the dry years of the early 1990s was three times the amount abstracted in the mid-1980s.

A further breakdown of potable supplies suggests that metered use has remained relatively stable over the last 30 years, but that unmetered domestic uses have increased from 85 litres/person/day in 1961 to 140

litres/person/day in 1991/92, although the greatest increase was in the first 10 years to 108 litres/person/day by 1971, the time when washing machines and improved bathrooms were being widely installed. Whilst domestic use was estimated to be 140 litres/person/day in 1991/92, the water supplied to unmeasured households was estimated to be 163 litres/person/day, the difference reflecting leakage from pipes (Herrington, 1996).

The increase in water supplied to domestic properties exceeds the rate of population increase and in part relates to a trend in the greater number of households and changing lifestyles. Domestic consumption in 1991 to 1992 in the south east was 7 litres/person/day (5 per cent) higher than the figure for England and Wales (Herrington, 1996). This is thought to reflect the drier climate of the south east and hence garden watering as well as greater wealth for household appliances. Domestic demand also rises in hot dry summers. Anglian Water Services put 8.3 per cent more water into the public water supply system in the drought year of 1995/96 compared with the previous year and South West Water supplied an increase of 5.9 per cent. Across England and Wales the picture was more variable, due to the lack of

Figure 3.14
Groundwater and surface water abstraction for public water supply, 1995

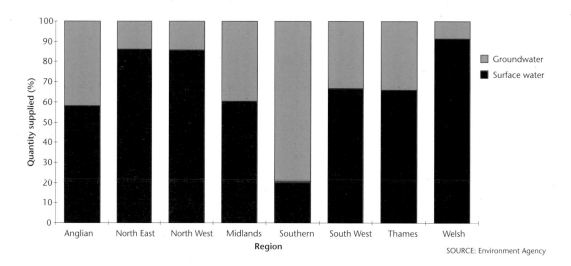

- Groundwater
- Surface water

SOURCE: Environment Agency

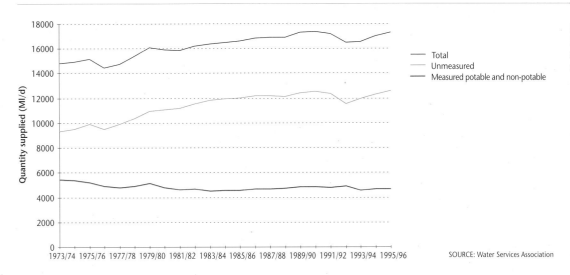

SOURCE: Water Services Association

Figure 3.15
Public water supplied, 1973/74 to 1995/96

availability of supplies to meet increased demand in north east England (Palutikof *et al.*, 1997).

Spray and trickle irrigation practices are predicted to increase significantly by 2020, especially in the drier south eastern part of the country due to the increased volatility of the weather, higher temperatures, and higher standards required by supermarkets for quality produce. At the moment, only 2.4 per cent of cropland in the UK is irrigated compared with 59 per cent in the Netherlands and 17 per cent in Denmark. In Europe, only Austria, Belgium and Finland irrigate a lower percentage of their total land than the UK. There are high evaporative losses inherent with spray irrigation, so that more water must be used to achieve the desired level of soil wetting. As a result of this, a recent report on Water Conservation and Supply (House of Commons Environment Committee, 1996) recommended that consideration is given to replacing spray irrigation systems with trickle or drip irrigation equipment which is more efficient. Trickle irrigation is currently exempt from licensing regulations and the Agency is considering whether it ought to be brought under licensing control. Other measures to spread the impact of irrigation are being brought into use. Winter storage reservoirs are encouraged wherever possible to take advantage of the higher winter runoff and the lack of water availability in the summer. Tradeable licence schemes and cooperation within a catchment are being explored. Farmers are also being encouraged to adopt best irrigation and growing practices to make the most of the water available.

Water abstracted from the freshwater environment will necessarily cause a reduction in flow at the point of abstraction and hence reduce the amount of flow naturally available in the rivers and aquifers. This is unavoidable and there is a need to know how much can be abstracted without causing unacceptable change to the downstream freshwater environment. When there is an exceptional shortage of rainfall and supplies are threatened, water companies can apply for drought orders or permits to abstract more water

from rivers than is permitted under 'normal' flow conditions. The effects of drought orders require careful monitoring to ensure that there is minimal damage to the aquatic environment. The number of drought orders per year since 1976 is shown in Figure 3.16, highlighting the large number during the 1989 to 1992 drought. There were more drought orders in 1976 and 1984 than in any one year of the 1989 to 1992 drought, but significant new resources, as previously shown in Figure 2.4, have come on line since then. Some Regions, for example the Anglian, the Thames and the Midlands have had fewer drought orders than in other parts of the country. These differences reflect local climate conditions, needs and effective resource planning in the past.

Leakage

Leakage from the distribution system is a particularly topical issue because evidence suggests that an average of 30 per cent and up to 40 per cent of water put into the distribution system by the large water companies is lost from supply by leakage from pipes (Figure 3.17). In England and Wales in 1995/96, about 4,979Ml/d were lost due to leakage. The range varied from 125 litres per property per day by Southern Water Services to 331 litres per property per day by Thames Water Utilities and Dŵr Cymru (Welsh Water). These figures ignore any leakage from customers' own pipes. This water is not permanently lost from the environment because it will eventually flow back to rivers or groundwaters but the time delay in this process implies that it is lost as a water resource and cannot be used. More water than necessary is therefore abstracted from the freshwater environment at times of stress. Furthermore, the water will not generally be returned to where it was abstracted from, causing local resource problems.

At a Water Summit held in May 1997, the government asked the Director General of Water Services, in consultation with the Agency, to set demanding leakage targets for the water companies so that this pressure on the environment is reduced, and for the water

Figure 3.16
Drought orders made, 1976 to 1995

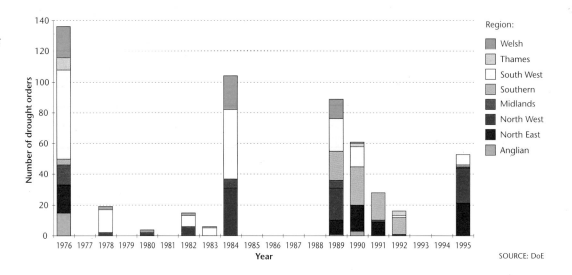

SOURCE: DoE

companies to provide a free leakage detection and repair service for supply pipes owned by domestic customers. The mandatory leakage targets set by OFWAT in October 1997 are to reduce leakage to 4,285Ml/d in 1997/98 and to 3,585Ml/d in 1998/99, 25 per cent below the leakage reported in 1992/93. These targets address the issue in the short-term, but the Agency looks forward to cooperating with OFWAT in considering the scope for reducing leakage further in the long-term. The government has also announced a review of the abstraction licensing system which will include consideration of economic instruments to achieve a more efficient allocation of water resources. The review is expected to be completed in early 1998.

Water Efficiency

Water efficiency is essential if the rising pressure from abstraction, at a time of climate change, is to be reduced. The droughts of 1984, 1988 to 1992, and 1995 have also been significant in raising awareness of the need to use water sensibly. The water charging system of the water companies is currently being reviewed and this could also be used to reduce the

pressure from abstractions. The NRA set out in a consultation report, *Saving Water*, the water saving potential of a number of water conservation options and showed that leakage control, lower volume flush toilets, more efficient washing machines and fitting flush controllers to urinals can all be cheaper than developing new resources for equivalent volumes of water. Furthermore, the amount abstracted for public water supply could be reduced by as much as 42 per cent if all demand management options are implemented. Although not necessarily always justifiable in terms of a water company's or individual's cashflow, once the full value of the environment is taken into account a great many of them are economically justified (NRA, 1995a).

New resources should only be developed if there is insufficient scope for deployment of existing resources to meet properly managed demand. As well as demand management measures, this includes bulk transfer arrangements, efficient operation of sources, and possibly redistribution of abstraction licences. There is a need to determine and apply the optimum package of demand management measures for each

Figure 3.17
Leakage rates of the large water companies, 1994/95 and 1995/96

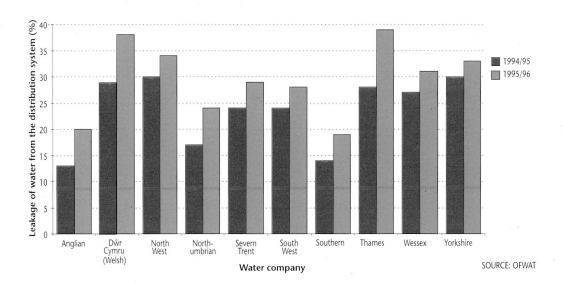

SOURCE: OFWAT

particular water supply area, taking into account the balance between availability of developed resources and the projected changes in demand (DoE *et al.*, 1996).

The *SavingWater* consultation exercise carried out by the NRA showed that there is general agreement that water conservation and demand management should play a more important role in water resources strategies and that there is a clear need for greater cooperation between companies, regulators, customers, and 'opinion shapers'. There was strong support for the adoption of water saving measures, although a third of respondents were opposed to an extension of water metering. The Agency will build on this exercise and the other reports published in 1996 and 1997, in developing its water resources policy (Environment Agency, 1997b).

3.4   Discharges

It is an offence – with certain exceptions – to cause or knowingly permit any poisonous, noxious, or polluting matter, or any solid matter, or any trade or sewage effluent to enter fresh waters in England and Wales. The principal exceptions are small ponds and reservoirs which do not supply water to other watercourses, although public water supply reservoirs are included. A defence against this general offence is for a person to possess, and be compliant with the conditions of a discharge consent issued by the Environment Agency or its predecessors.

Discharges to the freshwater environment may counteract the effect of abstraction to a certain extent by returning water to rivers, canals and groundwaters. Many of these return flows are a large distance downstream of the abstraction point though and may even return flows to a different catchment, and their quality may differ from the abstracted quality. This section looks at point discharges and diffuse discharges, as well as accidental or illegal discharges, known as pollution incidents.

Point Sources

There are more than 70,000 consented discharges to fresh waters ranging in size from flows over 150,000m³/day (less than 0.1 per cent of the total) to flows of less than 5m³/day (57 per cent of the total) although discharges below 5m³/day are mostly not consented (exempted). In general, large discharges have the potential to cause the largest impact, although the size of the discharge relative to the receiving watercourse is important. Discharges are consented to control their potential impact and are set to ensure compliance with water quality objectives, to protect public health, and to meet other local needs. About 20,000 have numeric limits (quality standards) imposed. Some five per cent of discharges exceed flows of 1,000m³/day. The regional split of these discharges is shown in Figure 3.18.

Most of these 70,000 discharges are from sewage-treatment works (82 per cent). Many of these are small, from private dwellings or similar, and only 1,600 serve population equivalents greater than 2,000, and about 700 serve population equivalents greater than 10,000. Figure 3.19 shows the location of STWs operated by the water companies based on size, which highlights the density in high areas of population. Nationally, over 10,000Ml/d are collected by water companies for treatment and Figure 3.20 shows the large difference in volumes of sewage collected per region. The figure shows how the contribution from unmetered properties is by far the greatest component of sewage collected for treatment. The quantities of sewage collected are increasing by about two per cent per year, consistent with water supplied (OFWAT, 1996b).

There are many privately-owned small STWs and commercial properties with STWs. Numerically there are 2,392 small STWs with consents not operated by the water companies compared with 4,054 operated by water companies, but the volume discharged by these small non-utilities STWs is relatively small and

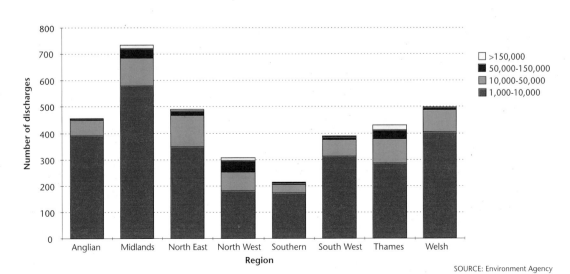

Figure 3.18
Number of large consented discharges (over 1,000m³/d) in each region, 1997

SOURCE: Environment Agency

Figure 3.19
Location of sewage treatment works and size of population served

Population equivalents

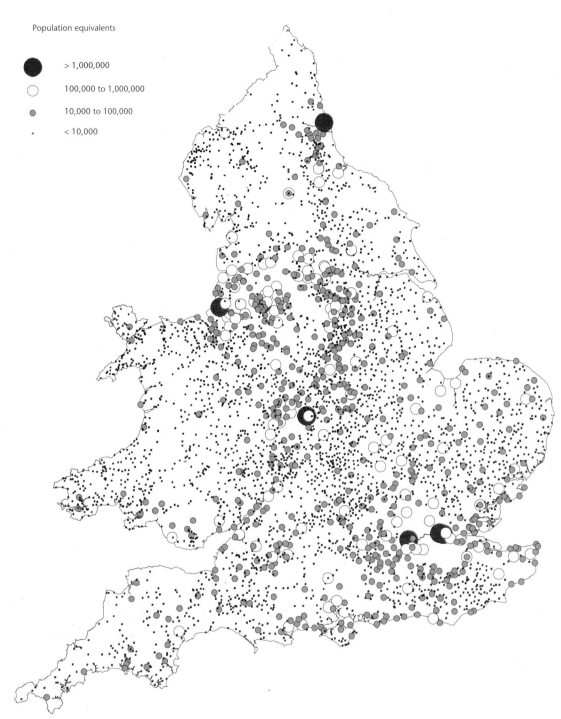

> 1,000,000

100,000 to 1,000,000

10,000 to 100,000

< 10,000

Sewage works owned by water companies and having numerical consents

SOURCE: Environment Agency

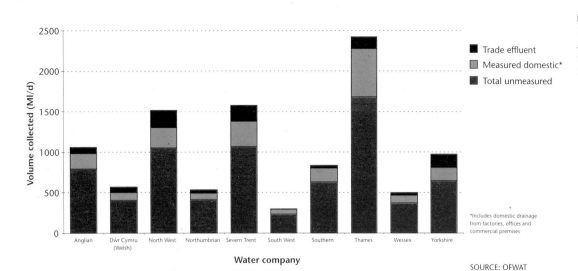

Figure 3.20
*Total volume of
sewage collected by
water companies,
1995/96*

SOURCE: OFWAT

usually less than 20 m³/day; in the Upper Thames catchment, the consented discharge volume from non-utilities STWs is less than two per cent of the volume discharged by STWs operated by water companies. Furthermore, these small works tend to discharge into rivers where the dilution available is over one hundred times the quantity discharged and hence, in general, their impact on the environment is small. Where surface watercourses are absent, discharges may be made onto or into land. Consents are based on minimising the risk of groundwater pollution, but the impact of historic discharges to ground is difficult to determine.

Only 12 per cent of discharges are from 'trade sites' which include power stations, airports, mineral works, fish farms and other industry but these trade inputs can have large polluting potential unless adequate treatment is provided. This low number may appear surprising. Whilst industrial processes produce large volumes of liquid waste, many discharge to sewer for treatment at sewage works because these can produce better effluents, by mixing industrial effluents with domestic effluents, than would be produced by the trader treating on site. As figure 3.20 shows, approximately 10 per cent of sewage collected by the water companies is trade effluent, varying from 16 per cent in Yorkshire to five per cent in the South West and Southern Regions. The quality of trade effluent discharged to sewer is consented by water companies, but these data are not available outside the companies. The water companies are both regulators of substances entering their sewers and they provide a commercial treatment service for those substances, a situation which is not ideal. It does not, in the long term, support sustainable use of resources and may well be inimical to waste minimisation. The Agency is concerned that the water companies' interest in trade effluent control appears to be far more focused on the commercial than the regulatory aspects of the business.

Treatment of sewage varies depending on the history of management, the needs of the receiving waters and

past legislation. In theory, discharges are consented with quality standards attached to minimise the effects of pollution on receiving waters. In practice, many consents are historic and the lack of investment in STWs lead to widespread failures to meet consent conditions in the 1980s. Since privatisation of the water industry in 1989 and expenditure by the water companies at that time, the situation has improved. In 1995, less than four per cent of STWs failed to meet their consent conditions whereas 10 per cent were failing in 1990, 17 per cent in 1988 and 23 per cent in 1986 (Figure 3.21). Thirty years ago, in 1964/65, nearly 60 per cent of sewage works failed their consents, mainly due to lack of adequate available treatment capacity. This situation arose because STWs had not been planned in advance to keep pace with housing and industrial development (Ministry of Housing and Local Government and Welsh Office, 1970). With the planned increase of 4.4 million homes between 1991 and 2016, there is a need to make sure that sewage-treatment facilities are adequate to protect fresh waters and public health.

The improvement in compliance with consents is one measure of the reduction of pressure on fresh waters caused by sewage works. It is also interesting to look at the actual reduction in organic load from STWs between 1990 and 1995. Nationally, Figure 3.22 shows that concentrations of BOD and ammonia averaged for all STWs and weighted for the size of population served, have reduced significantly over the period 1990 to 1995. The data for each Region are given in Table 3.4. This shows that BOD concentrations have reduced by between eight and 43 per cent, and ammonia concentrations have reduced by 17 to 47 per cent. There are significant regional differences; the 43 per cent reduction seen in BOD concentrations in the Welsh Region was from an initial value of 16.1mg/l, whereas the Thames Region with a 39 per cent reduction started with a much lower concentration at 8.5mg/l.

The differences in 1990 concentrations reflect historic practices to some extent. A survey of consent limits in

Figure 3.21
*Sewage treatment
works complying
with discharge
consents, 1986 to
1995*

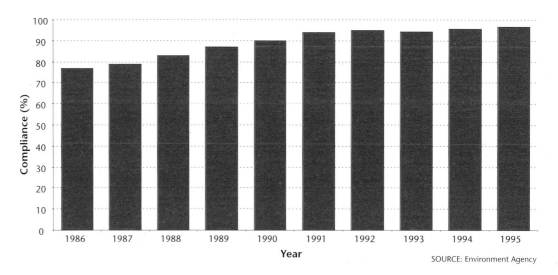

SOURCE: Environment Agency

1990 showed that only three consents in the North West Region and five in the North East Region had ammonia limits, compared with 285 in the Anglian Region. The same survey showed that the stringency of consents varied with the Thames and Anglian Regions having set tighter ammonia consents than the Welsh Region (NRA, 1990). These historic differences reflect regional needs. Population is less dense in the Welsh Region than the south east so the ratio between discharge and river dilution is greater in the former, leading to a historic need for tighter consents in the latter.

Sewers and sewage works are designed to accommodate a certain amount of flow. It would be uneconomic to size sewers and treatment works to be capable of dealing with all the flows that are ever likely to occur, so they are designed to deal with flows that occur for most of the time. Whilst the main component of sewer flow is domestic and industrial waste, many sewers were built at a time when drains from roads and other areas were also connected to the sewers. In these areas of 'combined' sewers, storm water from rainfall can lead to the capacity of the sewers being exceeded and overflows discharging directly from the sewers to watercourses. Furthermore, in the major urban areas, many sewers date back to Victorian times and the capacity of these is

insufficient to cope with the large volumes of wastewater generated now. As a consequence of this, storm sewer overflows which were designed only to deal with storm flows, now operate in dry weather conditions resulting in water quality problems.

Overall, the polluting load from storm overflows is generally much less than that from treated sewage because most of the flow is rainwater. It is, however, contaminated with sewage which can cause extremely high loads of pollution for a short period of time, especially during the 'first flush' of rain. Problems arise in some watercourses due to the consumption of oxygen by bacteria decomposing sewage derived material. Storm overflows can also cause aesthetic problems if the discharges are not screened, allowing litter in the form of rags, plastics, and sanitary products to be discharged. These are a health hazard and are unsightly on river banks.

The magnitude of the problem varies from place to place depending on how the sewerage network was designed in the past, the age of the system, and the geography of the area. New towns, for example, have separate systems for rainwater and so there should not be problems. Past designs reflected regional needs;

Figure 3.22
*Average
concentration of
BOD and ammonia
in discharges from
sewage treatment
works, 1990 to
1995*

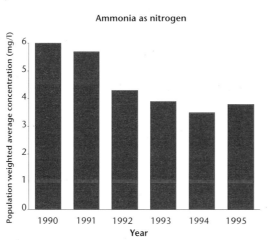

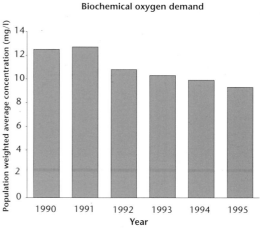

SOURCE: Environment Agency

Region	Mean[1] BOD in 1990 (mg/l)	Mean[1] BOD in 1995 (mg/l)	BOD reduction since 1990 (percentage)	Mean[1] ammonia in 1990 (mgN/l)	Mean[1] ammonia in 1995 (mgN/l)	Ammonia reduction since 1990 (percentage)
Anglian	6.8	5.3	22	2.5	1.8	28
Midlands	11.8	8.4	29	5.7	3.3	42
North East	20.1	15.7	22	9.8	5.2	47
North West	12.3	11.3	8	8.7	6.6	24
Southern	14.2	10.0	30	3.5	2.3	34
South West	11.6	9.1	22	2.9	2.4	17
Thames	8.5	5.2	39	3.7	2.8	24
Welsh	16.1	9.2	43	6.5	4.2	35
Total	12.5	9.3	26	6.0	3.8	37

[1] Weighted for the size of population that each sewage works serves

Table 3.4
The organic concentration of discharges from water company sewage-treatment works by region for 1990 and 1995

because the River Thames is abstracted to supply water to London, the network was designed to higher standards above the abstraction points to ensure limited contamination from overflows. Where the uses of rivers do not include abstraction for drinking water, the number of storm overflows tends to be greater.

The Anglian Region's data gives an idea of the number of point discharges from storm overflows compared with sewage works. The breakdown of 4,262 discharges that Anglian Water Services are responsible for is shown in Table 3.5:

Table 3.5
Number of some types of point discharges in the Anglian Region

Sewage-treatment works	1,083
Storm tanks (at sewage works)	338
Storm sewage overflows	1,285
Emergency overflows (e.g. from pumping stations)	1,024
Surface water sewers	376
Water treatment works	119
Others	37

This information gives an idea of the number and type of discharge points. Generally a small proportion of discharges cause most of the environmental problems, which are more likely to be related to the size of discharges than their number.

A further issue related to point discharges is that of 'misconnections'. This is the term given to plumbing in areas where there are separate sewers for sewage and rainwater but sewage outlets have been connected

to the storm water system. Recent surveys in the north east have found 10 per cent of properties with wrong connections, mainly from washing machines which have been connected to surface water sewers rather than foul sewers. These misconnections cause local contamination of watercourses, especially in heavily urbanised areas where watercourses are small compared with the amount of stormflow that they receive. Figure 3.23 shows the contamination caused by misconnections to two small watercourses in North London when rainfall was low and so surface runoff should be low. The highly variable biochemical oxygen demand and ammonia concentrations show contamination by sewage, with very serious consequences on dissolved oxygen concentrations. The solution is for sewerage companies to trace the misconnections but that is a labour intensive and difficult task in an area with so many households.

A study of groundwater pollution based on NRA data and information from waste regulation authorities, water companies and other published sources attributed pollution to different land uses. There were significant gaps in the information obtained, so these figures were heavily biased towards the activities regulated by the former NRA and those incidents where abstractions or surface waters had been affected by the groundwater contamination. However, it gives some indication of the pressure from land-use on groundwater quality (Environment Agency, 1996b).

The most frequent activity contributing to groundwater contamination is waste disposal, although half of the activities in this category relate to suspected contamination only (Figure 3.24). The effects are usually not serious for water supply. Landfill leachate can also pollute adjacent watercourses. The main contaminants are ammonia and chloride. Leachates may have oxygen demands

Figure 3.13
*Contamination of
two London rivers in
1995, due to
misconnections to
surface water
sewers*

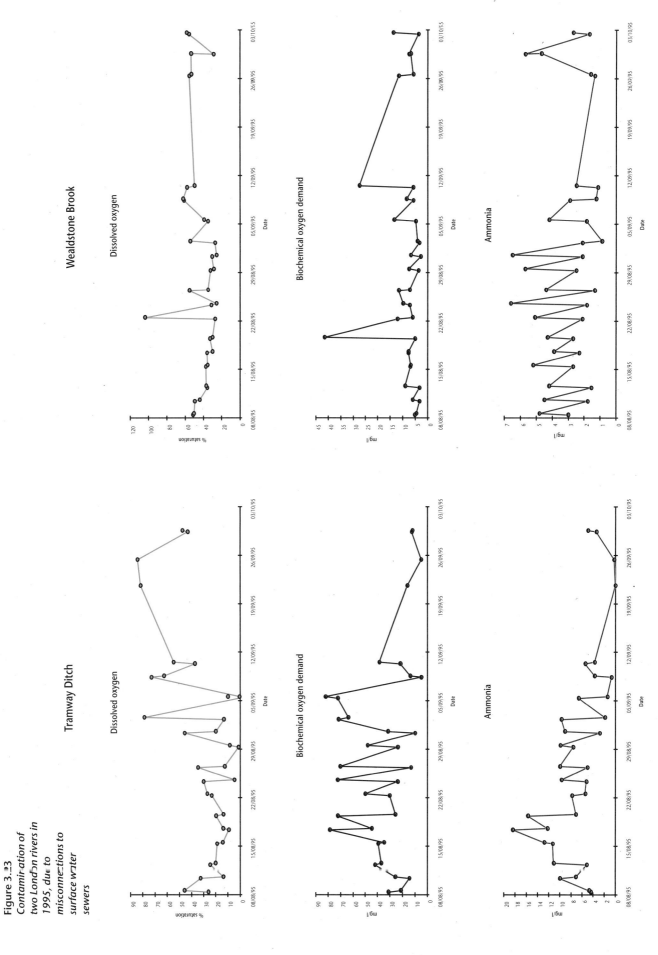

SOURCE: Environment Agency

(chemical) up to 152,000mg/l which could potentially cause significant pollution. Levels of hazardous substances are low in most cases, although pesticides and polychlorinated biphenyls have been found at a few sites (DoE, 1995c). Guidance on landfill design and operation aims to degrade wastes to stable forms within 30 to 50 years of tipping ceasing (DoE, 1995d). Many existing landfills constructed to previous standards are likely to leave a legacy of poor quality leachate for much longer than this. For new sites, the best approach should now be determined by a risk assessment based on the type of waste and the characteristics of the site. Total containment is now accepted as not attainable or sustainable, so the design must promote biological decomposition and allow flushing to remove the breakdown products. The leachate must be collected for treatment to the required standards prior to discharge to sewer, watercourse or land. Further details on the impact of contaminated land on groundwater and rivers are given in *Contaminated land and the water environment* (NRA, 1994c).

The other most frequently identified sources of groundwater contamination are chemical sites and metal workings although contamination from other sources, for example petrol stations are also thought to be widespread. The low number of sites within the military land-use category may be due to information for this activity not being readily available. The study also showed that there were significant concentrations of polluted groundwater sites beneath some of the major conurbations and industrial areas which are underlain by aquifers, suggesting that this type of land-use creates significant pressure on the freshwater environment. Groundwater pollution is particularly serious because of its long-term nature. It can take decades or centuries for pollutants to move through the ground, and effective clean-up of groundwater pollution is difficult and costly, and usually within the same long timescales. Prevention is better than cure.

Diffuse Sources of Pollution

The pressures from discharges described above relate to point discharges to the environment, most of which are consented although misconnections are essentially illegal discharges. As well as point discharges, fresh waters can become polluted by diffuse sources which occur when runoff from land surfaces becomes contaminated before entering rivers and aquifers, and when rainfall becomes contaminated before depositing. In urban areas, runoff from roads and paved areas is another source of contamination which can lead to chronic pollution in some urban watercourses. An overview of these pressures due to land-use are given here.

Agriculture can lead to diffuse pollution. In particular, fertilizers and pesticides can enter the water cycle from this source. Nitrate from agricultural land has been recognised as a major source of nitrate pollution in rivers since the 1970s and attempts have been made to reduce the pressure from this source in the last 10 to 20 years by changing the times of fertilizer application and planting times of cereals. Overall, nitrogen application rates have reduced steadily from about 145kg N/ha in 1985 to about 125kg N/ha in 1996. The application rates to arable crops averaged 147kg N/ha in 1995/96, and the application rates to grassland averaged 115kg N/ha (FMA, 1997).

There are about 450 pesticides approved for use, though trends in usage are affected by changes in the crops grown and husbandry techniques. The quantity of organochlorines used decreased in the early 1980s but the area treated increased, mainly because of the use of gamma-hexachlorocyclohexane (lindane) on the expanding area of oilseed rape. Lindane is also used as a wood preservative and in the textile industry. With many organochlorine pesticides now banned, the amounts used will continue to decline. Initial replacements such as the organophosphorus compounds are also declining and being replaced by synthetic pyrethroid insecticides.

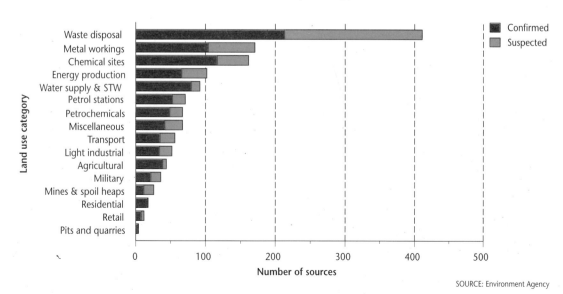

Figure 3.24
Activities causing contamination of groundwater, up to 1995

SOURCE: Environment Agency

There is a lack of treatment and disposal facilities for organophosphorus sheep dip pesticides (propetamphos, diazinon, and chlorfenvinphos) which are often detected in watercourses and cause pollution. Sheep which have been treated could also have an impact by paddling in streams. Concern with the effects of organophosphorus compounds on human health has led to the use of synthetic pyrethroids as sheep dips. The pyrethroid cypermethrin, for example, is less hazardous to humans than organophosphorus but is extremely toxic to aquatic life. It is suspected to have caused severe damage to several rivers in rural areas of Wales and northern England. These and other pesticides are also contained in effluents from the wool processing and textile industries which are not treated specifically to remove pesticides but discharged to rivers via sewage-treatment works. Some of these pesticides can also arrive on imported fleeces.

The application of fungicides to cereals commenced in the early 1970s and use has continued to increase. A similar increase has occurred in the use of herbicides. These dominate agricultural pesticide usage. Most modern pesticides are used in much smaller amounts than those they replace but this is only possible because they are much more effective. Residuals of a number of herbicides used on arable crops occur in ground and surface waters including atrazine, isoproturon, mecoprop and bentazone. Experiments at a farm in Herefordshire demonstrated that the movement of some pesticides from agricultural fields to receiving waters can take only a few hours following rainfall and short-term peak concentrations can be high. These high concentrations can kill aquatic life in local streams. A project showed that in the spring of 1989, 0.3 per cent of simazine applied eight days earlier to adjacent land was accounted for in the nearby stream. Although the mass of individual pesticide accounted for in the stream was only a small proportion of the total amount applied to the field, the effect could still be significant. The magnitude of the pressure on the river appeared to depend on the amount, the half-life of the pesticide applied, its solubility and toxicity, and the amount and timing of any following rainfall (NRA, 1995e). Concentrations in runoff to fresh waters vary from year to year depending on the weather and conditions at the time of application. Changes in formulations and care with application have led to reduced pressures in recent years (NRA, 1995c) but herbicides are still commonly detected at water supply intakes and have to be removed by treatment to protect drinking water.

Atrazine and simazine (herbicides) were banned from non-agricultural use in 1993, and in many localities there is a downward trend in the pressure from these pollutants on fresh water. Simazine is used on a variety of agricultural and horticultural crops. Atrazine is still used on maize, a crop that is expanding rapidly. This has resulted in atrazine being detected in surface waters in such areas and there is the potential for contamination of underlying aquifers depending on rock type. Pollution prevention campaigns by the Agency and water companies have been successful in ensuring that diuron, a common alternative to atrazine, has not increased dramatically in waters whilst atrazine concentrations have declined (see Figures 4.30 and 4.31 later).

Soil erosion is a natural process caused by the action of wind or water, but rates of erosion may be increased due to land management. Runoff from fallow fields or land where vegetation is incomplete may carry soil particles into watercourses causing contamination greater than which would occur naturally. A study of 12 susceptible catchments over the period 1989 to 1994 recorded erosion in 39 per cent of the fields monitored. It was observed on 50 per cent of fields sown with winter cereals and on 10 to 20 per cent of fields of potatoes, sugar beet and oilseed rape (Royal Commission on Environmental Pollution, 1996). There is a concern that overgrazing of permanent grassland due to increasing sheep stocking rates is exacerbating erosion in some upland areas. The pressure caused by soil erosion on fresh waters is two-fold. Firstly, phosphates, pesticides and other contaminants adhere to soil particles and can be carried in runoff into fresh waters. Secondly, soil entering watercourses causes physical changes and may block navigation channels, which increases the risk of flooding, and blocks spawning gravels which is thought to have contributed to a decline in salmon and trout numbers. In the South West Region, the Rivers Taw, Torridge, Tamar, Axe, Otters, Piddle, Frome and Avon have all been identified as systems where salmonid spawning and nursery territories have been affected.

The ploughing and cultivation of land close to the banks of watercourses can lead to bank erosion which leads to increased sediment loads in rivers and siltation of the river bed. Where the risks are high, buffer strips can be very effective in minimising soil loss. Encouraging farmers to seek advice on erosion control and to draw up farm management plans aimed at minimising the loss of soil from their land is required as is further work to establish the minimum effective width of buffer strips. Both these recommendations, if followed, should have benefits for the freshwater environment (Royal Commission on Environmental Pollution, 1996).

With the rapid expansion of fish farming in the past 20 years, contamination has arisen from veterinary products as well as from nutrient rich organic matter entering watercourses. Watercress farmers use zinc sulphate as an insecticide and this has created pressures on rivers in the Southern Region in the past.

A certain amount of diffuse pollution comes from the atmosphere. In particular, acid deposition arises as a result of reactions between water in the atmosphere and oxides of sulphur and nitrogen which are emitted when fossil fuels are burned. There are also contributions from ammonia emitted from livestock wastes. As well as being deposited in rain, acidity is deposited by low-level clouds, and by dry deposition. When these deposits are added to land or water, the acidic balance changes which can then affect aquatic life. The areas of highest nitrogen deposition correspond with the areas of highest rainfall (Wales, northern England) although there is increasing nitrogen deposition downwind of major conurbations due to traffic pollution. The highest depositions of sulphur compounds tend to be in areas of highest emissions, e.g. the Midlands.

Urban areas have a large amount of hard or paved surfaces. Runoff from these areas may become contaminated due to substances such as:

- particles (suspended solids) from construction sites, including road construction;

- chemicals used for de-icing at airports;

- oil, diesel and chemicals washed off road surfaces;

- herbicides used besides roads, railways and in urban parks.

The environmental impact can be minimised through good design of urban drainage. Many road systems are now designed with gully-pots, filter drains, or oil interceptors to catch these substances before they enter surface or groundwaters. These systems require an effective maintenance programme if they are to continue to catch the 'first flush' of high pollutant loading associated with the beginning of a storm. Drainage from urban areas should not damage freshwater resources if best management practices are followed, though there is a need for support and cooperation from a wide range of public and private organisations involved in urban development. By working together, it should be possible to ensure that drainage from roads and urban areas is designed in a cost effective and sustainable manner (Scottish Environmental Protection Agency et al., 1997). The use of de-icers at airports is regulated by the Agency and airport authorities operate to codes of practice to minimise discharges and pollution risks.

Diffuse and point discharges from abandoned metal and coal mines can have a significant, if localised, impact on the water environment. Throughout England and Wales there are many hundreds of discharges from abandoned mines affecting water quality to some extent and about 100 coal mines and 70 metal mines cause significant problems in Wales and northern and south west England. There is evidence of groundwater pollution due to mining in South Wales and a large area

of the chalk aquifer in Kent has been contaminated by minewater from Tilmanstone mine. They are, in the majority, a legacy of the past but mines abandoned in the last 10 to 20 years may present problems for the future. As mining operations are curtailed and pumping ceases, groundwaters return towards original levels. The water becomes contaminated as it rises through the previously mined strata, often resulting in new and difficult to predict outbreaks of mine drainage. These discharges can be extremely variable but normally have significant metal concentrations. Staining of the stream bed by reddish-brown deposits of oxidised iron may occur. They can also cause siltation of river gravels affecting the spawning areas of fish. Discharges from small metal mines in remote areas, which were abandoned several years ago, may still exert an influence on the water quality and biology of small upland streams.

Total Contaminant Loads

Data are not readily available on the total contaminant loads discharged to fresh waters, but data are available on the total contaminant load discharged by rivers to the sea. These data can be used to give some indication of the trend in contaminant loads to fresh waters over time and an indication of the pressure caused by fresh waters on the marine environment. The data are from the Harmonised Monitoring Scheme (HMS) set up by the former Department of the Environment in 1974, using a network of sites to measure the load of contaminants discharged by rivers to the sea. Between the late 1970s and the early 1990s, most sites showed reductions in copper, zinc, ammonia and lindane concentrations, and biochemical oxygen demand, whereas there were widespread increases in orthophosphate and chloride concentrations (Figure 3.25) (Institute of Freshwater Ecology, 1995).

Since 1989, the pattern for orthophosphate concentrations has changed and they now show a decreasing trend (Figure 3.26). There have been marked annual variations in the nitrogen load to the sea and current loads are not as high as in the late 1970s. Overall, the pattern is fairly stable. The loads of copper, zinc and lead have shown steady decreases since the 1970s with a more constant input since the early 1990s (Littlewood et al., 1997) (DETR, 1997).

North Sea Ministers made a commitment to reduce aquatic inputs of hazardous substances to the North Sea in the late 1980s (Appendix 1). A target was set to reduce by 50 per cent between 1985 and 1995, the inputs of 36 substances from rivers and direct discharges. Total inputs, including atmospheric, of dioxins, mercury, cadmium, and lead were to be reduced by 70 per cent. The UK set these targets for inputs to all its coastal waters collectively. A revised strategy for hazardous substances is being developed by the Oslo and Paris Commissions which should be put to the 1998 Ministerial Conference.

Figure 3.25
The percentage of Harmonised Monitoring Scheme sites which have improved or deteriorated between the late 1970s and the early 1990s for 13 determinands

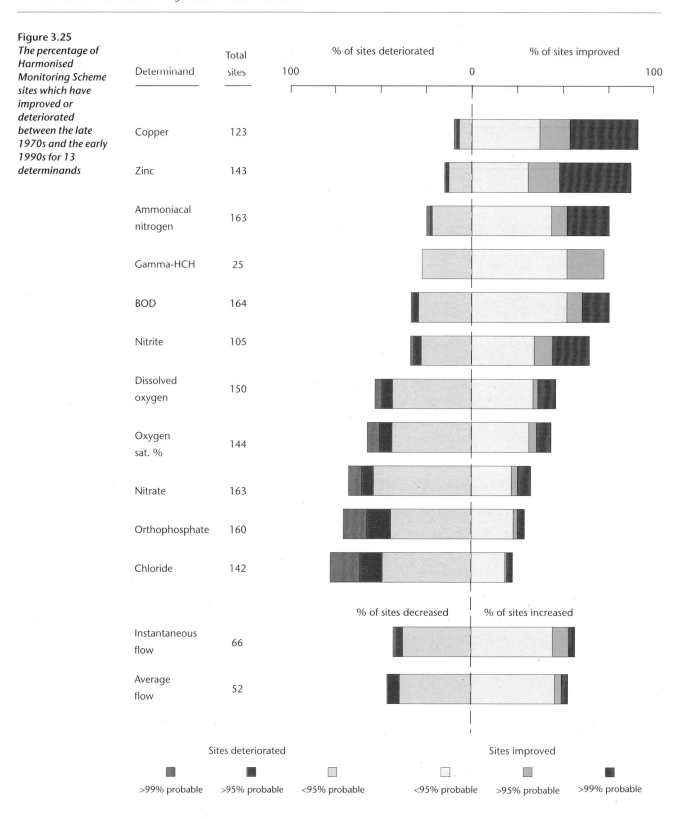

SOURCE: Institute of Freshwater Ecology

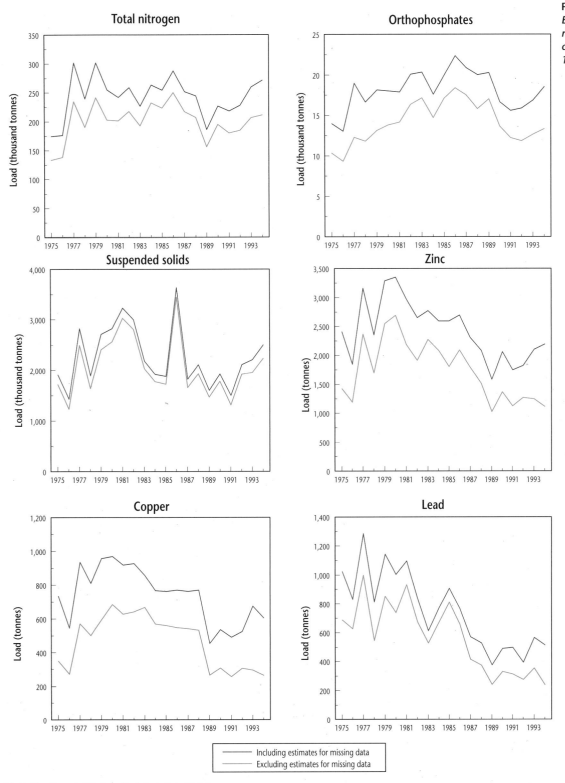

Figure 3.26
*Estimated total
riverine inputs to UK
coastal waters,
1975 to 1994*

Calculated from Harmonised Monitoring Sites by the Institute of Hydrology
for the Department of the Environment, Transport and the Regions

SOURCE: Institute of Hydrology/DETR

Data for riverine and direct inputs from the UK have been assessed. Where substances were not detected in a sample, the load estimates assume that the concentration was equal to the limit of detection. The data for 1995 indicate the load reductions achieved since 1985; mercury 77 per cent, cadmium 62 per cent, copper 49 per cent and lindane 61 per cent. These show load reductions in line with the overall targets set in the 1980s. Zinc has been reduced by 23 per cent showing that further progress appears to be needed. Zinc is used in many domestic products as well as in industry. The data for the UK as a whole show that a significant reduction (of 50 per cent or more) of waterborne inputs of 24 of the 36 substances has been achieved. Reductions exceed 45 per cent for three other substances. The data are given in full in the government's *Digest of Environmental Statistics* (DETR, 1997).

Pollution Incidents

Pollution incidents are short-term events or accidents which create a high temporary pollutant load in a water body. In contrast to the other continuous pollutant pressures in rivers, the elevated pollutant concentrations are usually diluted and dispersed within hours or days although they may persist longer in standing waters or sediments, and can have an impact for decades if groundwaters are affected. Many minor incidents have a local effect which may be difficult to detect, although repeated pollution can cause cumulative long-term damage to river life. Major incidents can require closure of abstractions, threaten human health and cause extensive biological damage, killing fish and invertebrate populations over many kilometres of river.

Damage to watercourses can result from physical effects on habitats, for example, high loads of suspended solids from construction sites may smother stream beds. Chemical effects occur through the spillage of substances which are directly toxic, such as paints, pesticides, and many industrial chemicals. Other organic substances which are relatively harmless in small quantities, such as milk, beer, sugar and more obviously sewage, have equally serious effects when large quantities are released into watercourses. This is caused by their biodegradation which uses up oxygen dissolved in the water, suffocating fish and other organisms. Oil is the most commonly observed substance polluting watercourses being easier to see than other substances.

The causes of pollution incidents usually relate to equipment and management which fall short of the required standards and best practice. There is then a greater risk of accidents and natural events (especially heavy rain) triggering an incident, although in some cases natural causes are difficult to avoid. The latter was exemplified in the 1995 drought when thunderstorms over Birmingham followed weeks of dry weather. The rain washed accumulated silt and standing water from urban drainage systems into the River Tame. The high organic content of the material caused a rapid depletion of dissolved oxygen, resulting in the death of thousands of fish, despite a major recovery exercise by the National Rivers Authority which limited even more damage. In 1996, 12 serious pollution incidents were due to natural events, with Anglian being the worst affected region where seven fish kills resulted from low flows and algal blooms. The worst incident led to 6,000 fish being killed at a Rutland fishery due to an algal bloom while 2,000 coarse fish were killed by low dissolved oxygen concentrations in the West Fen Catchwater in Lincolnshire.

The Agency uses a standard pollution incident classification system which discriminates major pollution incidents (category 1) from others (categories 2 and 3) and those which were reported to the Agency but were not substantiated by Agency staff (category 4). During 1996, more than 32,000 pollution incidents were reported, of which 20,150 (63 per cent) were substantiated. Over the last decade there has been an upward trend in reported incidents. They were 51 per cent higher in 1996 than in 1986, although less in 1996 than 1995. The number of incidents reported is influenced by a wide range of factors including public concern, awareness of the Agency's emergency hotline and relationships with the fire services. One other factor that may have lead to less incidents in 1996 than in the previous three years was the unusually dry weather. However, substantiated incidents have declined over the last two years to about the same number found in 1985 (Figure 3.27). The number of major incidents has fallen from 386 in 1991 to 156 in 1996 (Figure 3.28). The continued reduction in these incidents is welcome and indicates that pollution prevention, backed up by legal action against polluters, is having an effect.

Regional variations in the number of pollution incidents (Figure 3.29) seem to reflect the size of the region and the number of rivers per region; there is about one incident for every one to two kilometres of river per year. Population density does not appear to be a factor, with fewer incidents in the south east and high numbers in Wales. The split by type of pollutant is fairly consistent across the regions, though the 'Fuel and oils' and the 'Other' categories are noticeably higher in the Midlands Region, possibly reflecting the diversity of economic activity there. There is a higher proportion of incidents involving organic wastes (largely agricultural sources) in the South West Region. Nationally, sewage accounts for 26 per cent of incidents, fuel and oil a further 28 per cent, organic wastes 11 per cent (of which cattle slurry represents 44 per cent), and chemicals nine per cent.

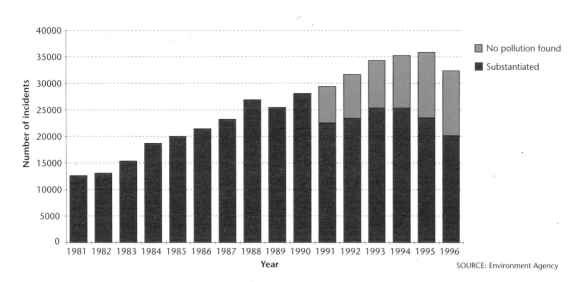

Figure 3.27
Number of pollution incidents, 1981 to 1996

SOURCE: Environment Agency

It is useful to consider the pressure caused by incidents based on the economic sector because this information helps to determine ways of reducing the pressure. Figure 3.30 splits substantiated incidents into sector and shows that agricultural pollution incidents are dominated by dairy farming, due to problems with slurry stores, yard drainage and runoff of farm waste applied to land. The total number of substantiated incidents has fluctuated in recent years, but major incidents due to agriculture have declined markedly from 99 in 1991 to 28 in 1996.

In the industrial sector, the construction industry is the most frequent polluter. Other important sources are engineering, the food industry, the chemical industry, and mining. Of the major incidents which occurred in 1996, 27 per cent arose from industrial sources, of which the biggest source was the construction industry (19 per cent). In the sewage and water industry, the main sources were water company surface water outfalls, combined sewer overflows, foul sewerage systems, and sewage-treatment works. The number of incidents from industry increased in the early 1990s from 2803 in

1991 to 6002 in 1993. Since 1993 the trend has been downwards and was 4025 in 1996.

The majority of transport related incidents originate from roads, mainly as a result of road traffic accidents. Spillages range from small amounts of petrol from cars, to large quantities of diesel from lorry fuel tanks and the loss of many tonnes of product from road and rail tankers, barges, ships and pipelines. Transport was reported separately for the first time in 1993 and showed an apparent increase in the number of incidents. By 1996 transport accounted for 28 per cent of all incidents. Rainfall runoff from roads and railways also carries pollutants such as silt, toxic metals, poly-aromatic hydrocarbons, oil, herbicides, salt and organic material. The levels of these substances are related to the volume of traffic, the pattern of rainfall and maintenance activities.

More than 5,200 (26 per cent) pollution incidents from 'other' sources were substantiated in 1996, of which 68 per cent could not be classified any further. Domestic and residential premises accounted for 24 per cent of these incidents.

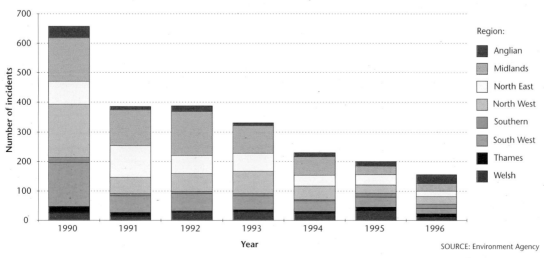

Figure 3.28
Number of major pollution incidents, 1990 to 1996

SOURCE: Environment Agency

Figure 3.29
*Regional numbers
of substantiated
pollution incidents
by source, 1996*

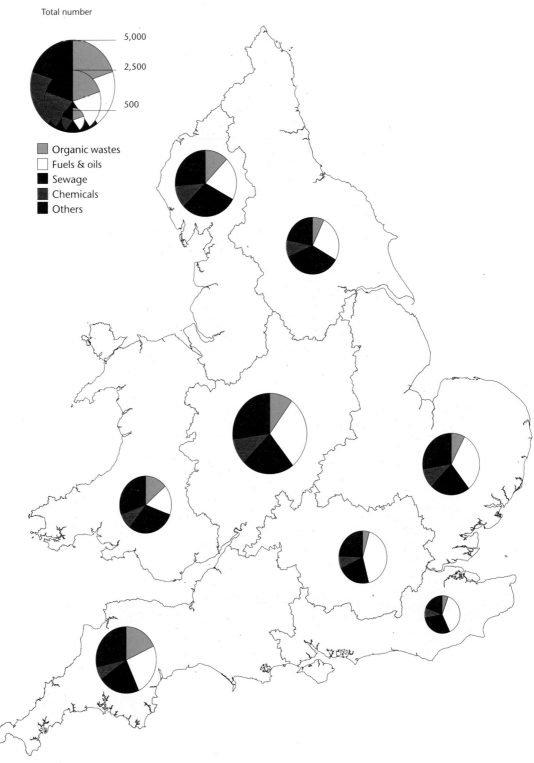

Total number

5,000

2,500

500

Organic wastes
Fuels & oils
Sewage
Chemicals
Others

SOURCE: Environment Agency

Figure 3.30
Substantiated pollution incidents by source, 1996

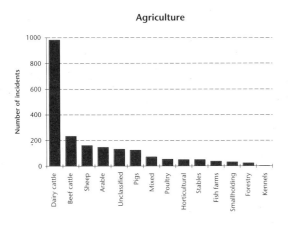

Agriculture

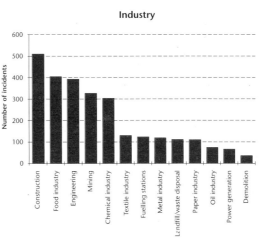

Industry

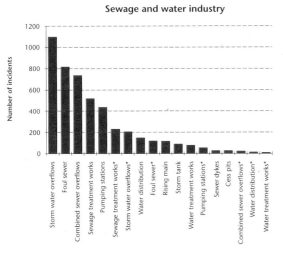

Sewage and water industry

*Private sewage and water industry sources

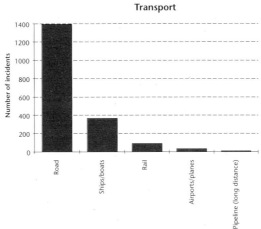

Transport

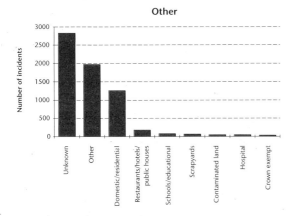

Other

SOURCE: Environment Agency

Table 3.6
Pressures on the freshwater environment

Pressure	Nature of pressure	Trend in pressure (+ increasing - decreasing = stable)
Climate change	Affects temperature, rates of evapotranspiration, rainfall and runoff. Likely to affect habitat, species, frequency of flooding, water demand, water stocks and distribution.	+ Awareness
Urbanisation (including transport and households)	Increase in paved areas gives rise to less infiltration and groundwater stocks, more rapid runoff, contamination from roads to surface waters, more storm overflows and loss of riverine habitats. Pesticides and fertilizers used in parks, homes, roadsides and gardens cause diffuse pollution. More roads imply loss of habitat. Car emissions contribute to climate change and acidification. 'DIY' misconnections affect river quality. Households demand for water increasing. Increasing number of households increases potential for sewage system overload. Development in floodplains increases risk of flooding and need for defence schemes. River engineering and other flood defence works to protect property can cause loss of habitats.	+ Road and urban runoff + Habitat loss by urbanisation + Flood defence schemes + Demand for water + Transport pollution incidents
Recreational activity	Fish stocking can affect fish populations, boating causes erosion of banks and streamside habitats, walking can disturb wildlife, and litter reduces aesthetic quality. The introduction of exotic flora and fauna compete with indigenous species, which can be lost, and may transmit diseases.	+ Recreational demands
Abstractions	Pressure created by need to meet potable supply needs, leakage from system, farming and industrial needs, and waste of water. Can cause low flow rivers and loss of wetland habitats and aquatic life as well as less dilution for consented discharges.	+ Domestic - Industrial + Farming
Sewage disposal	Discharges can affect river quality, but organic loads from treatment works have decreased since 1990. They are a source of nutrient input to rivers, especially phosphorus, although these are reducing too. Intermittent discharges from storm overflows cause episodic pollution, short spells of high toxic ammonia and aesthetic pollution.	- Sewage-treatment works - Storm overflows = Pollution Incidents
Farming	Excess fertilizers (especially nitrate), pesticides and slurry affect river and groundwater quality. Loads decreased since 1990, especially pollution incidents. Emissions of ammonia from livestock contribute to acidification and climate change. Drainage for productive land reduces wetland habitat. Demand for irrigation water increasing. Crop changes and overgrazing can affect siltation and colour of water.	- Pollution incidents - Fertilizers - Atrazine/Simazine = Land drainage + New pesticides, for example, pyrethroid sheep dips + Demand for irrigation water + Siltation
Industrial activity (including waste disposal)	Pollution caused from solvents (in groundwater), the textile industry (pesticides), and other toxic substances. Leachate from landfills (industrial and households), contaminated land, and storage of chemicals and oil cause groundwater pollution. Abandoned mines cause local problems to surface and groundwaters. Industry has high demand for cooling water, though some of this is returned downstream. Potential hazard from storage of oil and chemicals on sites - accidents lead to devastating effects. Emissions contribute to acidification, and climate change, which then impact on fresh waters.	- Water demand - Indirect discharges + Closure of mines +/= Waste disposal +/= Pollution incidents - Emissions causing acidification

3.5 Summary

Table 3.6 summarises the information presented in this chapter. It also provides further subdivision of the pressures by drawing together the information related to the major economic activities of farming and industry. The table draws out the pressures which are increasing that need attention, and shows where pressures have been successfully reduced.

4 The State of the Freshwater Environment

Measuring the state of the environment is a fundamental aspect of the Environment Agency's environmental management role. A sound scientific understanding of what the state of the freshwater environment is at any one time, and how it is responding to the many and varied pressures placed upon it, is critical to achieving this role. It provides the basis for assessing priorities for action, charting progress with respect to environmental management plans and targets, and producing information on the environment for all those that have an interest in it. It also provides an important part of assessing the rate of progress towards achieving the objective of sustainable development. Although vast amounts of data exist on the freshwater environment, there are many gaps and inconsistencies when the information base is considered as a whole. This is partly because there is no coherent national framework for measuring the state of the whole freshwater environment. There is a need to adopt an integrated view because some parts of the freshwater environment depend on other parts; an improvement in one aspect could be at the expense of deterioration in another aspect, so there is a need to look at the environment as a whole.

This section attempts to answer the question: "What is the general state of the freshwater environment and how is it responding to the pressures placed upon it?". This fundamental question gives rise to several further basic questions about how best to describe its state and changes to it. It can be broken down in the following way.

Assuming that the various types of land and water resources can be characterised, how are these resources changing over time?

How are the various (key) populations and communities of flora and fauna changing over time?

How is the quality of the environment changing over time, as judged by comparison with physical, chemical and biological standards?

How is the health of the environment changing over time?

How is the environment changing in the long-term as a result of both natural and human pressures, such as climate change?

How are aesthetically valued features (noise, landscape, amenities etc.) changing over time?

This framework is discussed in more detail in the Agency's consultation document, *Viewpoints on the*

Environment – Developing a National Environmental Monitoring and Assessment Framework (Environment Agency, 1997a).

Each of the above sets of environmental indicators may be affected by one or more pressures placed upon it, quite often with a natural pressure being exacerbated by a more-readily controllable human one. Irrespective of such cause and effect relationships (most of which are not fully understood), and bearing in mind that it is impossible to measure everything, this section presents a selection of the information available on the state of the freshwater environment in order to answer the questions posed and identify areas where more monitoring and surveillance is required.

4.1 Land Use and Environmental Resources

A reasonable first question to ask is, "how much fresh water is there?". To answer this, there are two aspects that need to be considered:

The amount of water (surface and groundwater). There are 1,100km^2 of standing water and 600km^2 of running water in England and Wales; and 1,700 bodies of standing water with a surface area greater than 4ha and 12,500 greater than 2ha. Most of these are in the north and west, although the Broads are important in East Anglia (DoE, 1993);

The amount and nature of the physical freshwater habitat. This is important because habitats support biodiversity and provide important services, both in terms of ecological processes and services to society. This aspect includes in-river habitats as well as wetlands. Human activities have modified physical habitats and an appreciation of these is needed too.

This section considers these aspects in more detail.

The Usable Quantity of Freshwater Resources

Estimating freshwater stocks is difficult due to the temporal and spatial variability of the hydrological cycle and the effects of human activities such as abstractions and effluent returns. The renewable freshwater resource of England and Wales is the amount of water moving in rivers, lakes and aquifers, originating from rainfall. The long-term average precipitation minus losses due to evaporation (known as effective rainfall) gives a measure of the natural runoff and infiltration and hence freshwater stocks.

Based on the average of 30 years effective rainfall data from 1961 to 1990, the characteristics of the water resources in England and Wales are:

- a total stock of 77,000Mm³/year on average;

- a stock of only 39,000Mm³/year in drought years;

- 1,470m³/person/year or 4,000 litres/person /day on average, which is very low by European standards, due to the population density in England and Wales rather than low effective rainfall;

- only 740m³/person/year or 2,000 litres/person/day in drought years;

distinct regional differences in the stock available with a west-east trend (highest in the west) reflecting climate (Figure 4.1).

The Welsh Region has the most abundant stocks at 18,700Mm³/year on average and 12,100Mm³/year during droughts. These equate to 17,100 litres/person/day and 11,100 litres/person/day respectively. At the other end of the scale, the Thames Region has 3,480Mm³/year on average, and 1,290Mm³/year during droughts, equating to 800 litres/person/day and 300 litres/person/day respectively.

In 1995, 12,045Mm³ were abstracted from fresh waters, about 16 per cent of the total available resource. This suggests that England and Wales are well

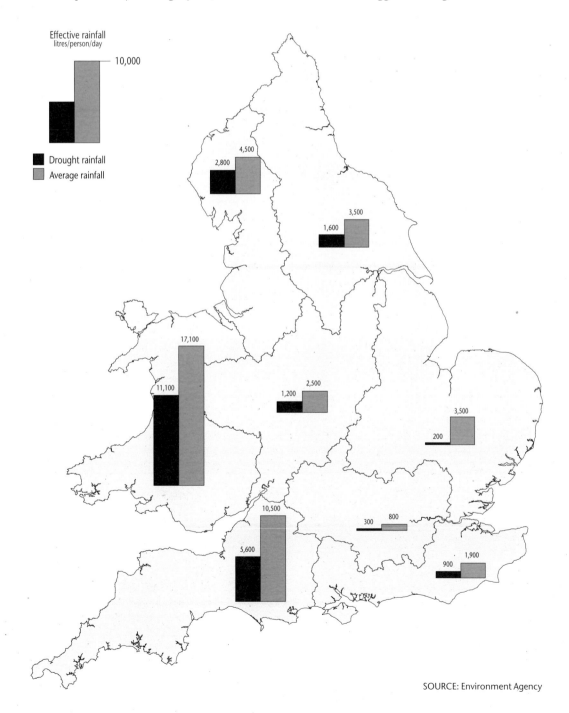

Figure 4.1
Average and drought effective rainfall in relation to regional population density

SOURCE: Environment Agency

63

Figure 4.2
The reservoir capacity of large water companies

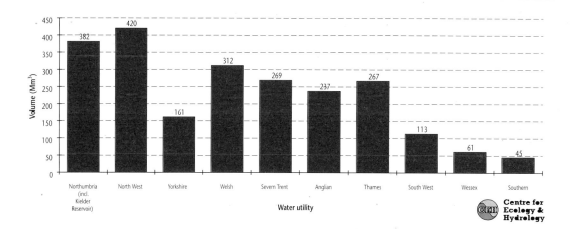

Centre for
Ecology &
Hydrology

endowed with freshwater resources when compared with other countries; 34 per cent of available resources are used in Germany and 32 per cent in Italy (OECD, 1994). Freshwater resources are not, though, spread evenly over space and time. The issue is therefore about the distribution of resources, in all the places and in all the quantities that the environment or people may want (UK Round Table, 1997a).

Actual river flow throughout the year will depend on the natural effective rainfall, the amount of water abstracted and discharged, and on a day to day basis will also depend on the proportion of flow coming from groundwater storage. This proportion, known as a baseflow index, varies across England and Wales, from over 0.7 in chalk and limestone areas (that is, 70 per cent of river flow comes from springs and groundwater storage) to less than 0.4 elsewhere. In areas with high baseflow index, there is a greater buffering capacity against reduction in river flows and less of a variation between extreme events. In areas with low baseflow, rivers are dependent on surface runoff which gives rise to rapid runoff (flashy flow) and a sudden decrease when rainfall ceases.

In order to meet public demands for water, when and where they are required and without undue depletion of rivers, water resources schemes (for example reservoirs) have developed over the past century or so.

Careful planning can ensure that water is abstracted during the winter months when river flows are high and the water is stored in reservoirs, so that sufficient water is available for the summer months. Almost 18 million people were affected by hosepipe or sprinkler bans in 1995 and in a few areas there was the threat of standpipes or rota cuts, perhaps suggesting a need for even more schemes. As annual and peak demands increase, there is a need for management of this demand or for increased storage. Water resources schemes include indirect reuse within catchments, storage by reservoirs, use of aquifers and artificial recharge of aquifers. These schemes need to be sized sufficiently to meet demands and to avoid over-exploitation of natural resources during times of low flow.

The usable reservoir volume for water supply in England and Wales totals about 1,560Mm³ reflecting the amount of stored water available. This is slightly less than the total capacity of reservoirs because of 'dead' water at the bottom. There are substantial regional differences, shown in Figure 4.2, reflecting the differing need for reservoirs which depends on the amount of alternative sources available such as groundwater. Reservoir stocks over the period 1988 to 1995 are shown in Figure 4.3 showing how depletion occurs in response to low natural resources in summer months and the greater depletion in the

Figure 4.3
Total reservoir stocks, 1988 to 1995

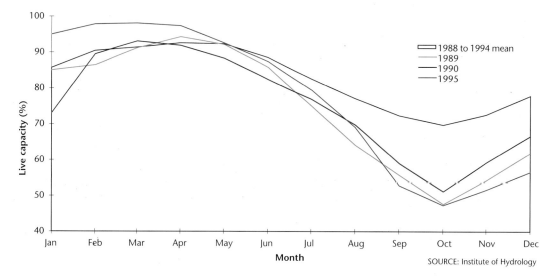

SOURCE: Institute of Hydrology

drought years of 1989, 1990 and 1995. Regional differences reflect the balance between demand and storage and Figure 4.4 shows 1996 reservoir storage for water companies' areas compared with the average storage volumes over the 1988 to 1994 period.

Aquifers provide a natural storage of freshwater resources and of the total amount of water abstracted, about 13 per cent is from groundwater. This figure rises to over 50 per cent in eastern, central and southern England. Of the water put into potable supply, 35 per cent comes from groundwater. Furthermore, a large proportion of rural populations depend on private water supplies and these are almost exclusively groundwater derived. The total amount of water stored within the entire area of chalk (an area of 20,694km^2, and the largest aquifer) produces about 21,000Mm^3 (for comparison, Kielder Reservoir is one per cent of this) (Centre for Ecology and Hydrology, 1996). Whilst this may represent the total storage, the amount available for abstraction cannot exceed recharge if overall depletion is to be avoided. It also needs to be less than recharge to avoid environmental damage. Figure 4.5 compares quantities abstracted from aquifers with rates of replenishment and shows that nationally,

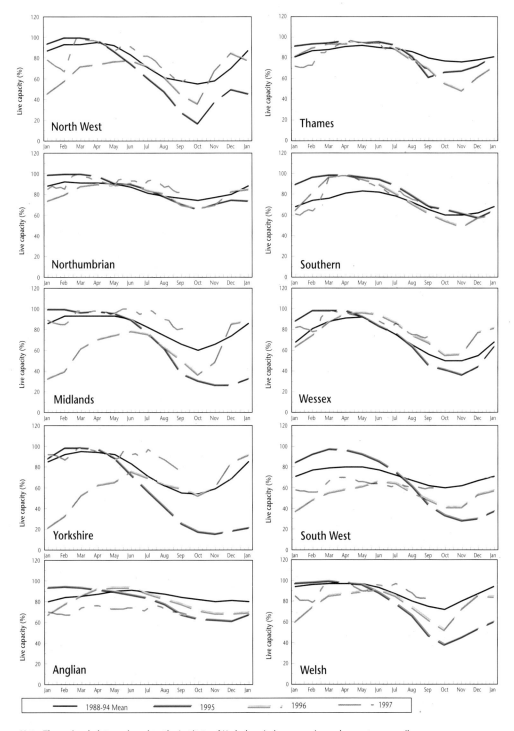

Figure 4.4
A water company guide to combined reservoir stocks in 1996 and 1997 compared with an average year and the 1995 drought year

Note: The regional plots are based on the Institute of Hydrology index reservoirs, and are not necessarily representative of the total stocks available in each water company area.

SOURCE: Environment Agency

replenishment appears to exceed use, although there are many local areas where this is not the case. Understanding sustainable yields of aquifers is difficult. Furthermore, not all recharge is available for abstraction and the baseflow contribution to rivers must be maintained. In coastal regions, the seaward flow of groundwater must continue in order that saline intrusion is prevented.

Withdrawal of water from natural resources at a rate faster than it can be replenished naturally can lead to low flows in rivers and the loss of wetland habitats. Groundwater stocks which are over-exploited lead to low flows in particular. Groundwater must be managed as a sustainable resource. In some areas, sustainable yield may have been exceeded and aquifers have depleted storage, low flows have occurred in rivers and wetlands have been affected. East Ruston Fen, a Site of Special Scientific Interest in Norfolk, is an example of a wetland affected by groundwater abstraction. In response to these problems, groundwater licences are no longer issued in areas where groundwater levels are not sustainable, and the Environment Agency is developing better methods of recharge and sustainable yield estimation, though there still remains considerable uncertainty over aquifer storage parameters.

About 30 rivers, fens and lakes have been recognised nationally as suffering from low flows or low water levels due to over-use, and other sites are being considered (Figure 4.6). There are 28 Sites of Special Scientific Interest which are affected by abstraction and a further 21 Sites of Special Scientific Interest for which information is being assembled for consideration. Eight of these are riverine Sites of Special Scientific Interest, the others include fens, commons, lakes and meadows (English Nature, 1997b). The abstractions are licensed but many of the rivers are 'low flows' due to the effect of groundwater abstraction on springs and seepages which should maintain the base flow in rivers. Action has been taken

to reduce abstractions in about 10 of these catchments where low flows had been previously recognised, for example Rivers Ver, Pang and Darent, and flows are now recovering. The number of rivers currently affected or at risk of over-exploitation may be as high as 100 (Hunt, 1996), but a basic problem lies in definitions and how the effects of natural variability in climate can be disassociated from the effects of over-use. The Agency is working with English Nature to determine the extent of the problem. Rivers and Sites of Special Scientific Interest where priority action is needed will be considered in the next periodic review of water company investment.

In some urban areas which overlie major aquifers, for example London, Birmingham and Liverpool, groundwater levels were drawn down by the extensive and heavy abstraction of water which occurred in heavily industrialised areas, dating in some cases back over 150 years. This has caused the water levels over wide areas to be drawn down substantially (for example, levels in a borehole in Trafalgar Square fell by 65m between 1846 and 1963). Since the 1960s, groundwater abstraction in the centre of cities has reduced for several reasons such as economic recession, improvements in the water efficiency of manufacturing processes, the relocation of industry from city centres to out-of-town industrial areas, and reliance on mains water. This has led to groundwater levels rising in these areas.

Rising groundwater may cause problems. These include ground movements due to the rewetting of clays which have dried out over many decades, flooding of basements which have been excavated while the groundwater levels were depressed, and the flooding of tunnels which then require dewatering. There may be chemical problems too. As water levels rise, the contaminants in the unsaturated zone may remobilise, pollute the groundwater and eventually pollute the surface water that this maintains. Furthermore, contaminated groundwater cannot be pumped out into

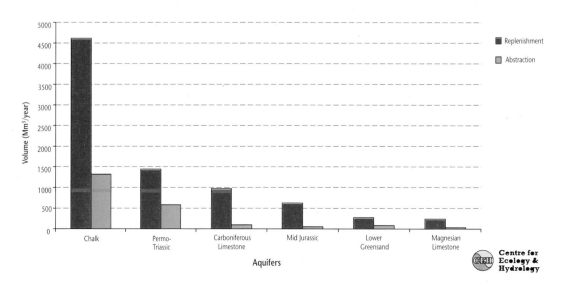

Figure 4.5
Average abstraction from and replenishment of major aquifers

surface waters without some treatment so dewatering becomes difficult. It has also been suggested that some foundations have not been designed to withstand reaction with rising groundwater, particularly where groundwater has become acidic. Many of these problems are postulated rather than existing because in some instances, water levels have some distance to rise before they interact with such features. The Agency is monitoring groundwater levels and is currently involved in considering ameliorating measures under London and Birmingham.

There is widespread concern that climate change has caused natural freshwater stocks to be more variable and more volatile, due to the occurrences of droughts in many of the recent summers and stress on the public water supply system. Flow data are useful in showing the frequency and severity of the problem. The flow records from eight representative sites have been used to compare the monthly mean river flows from 1988 to 1996 with the thirty-year monthly mean, maxima and minima, although only one site has been adjusted to take account of abstractions

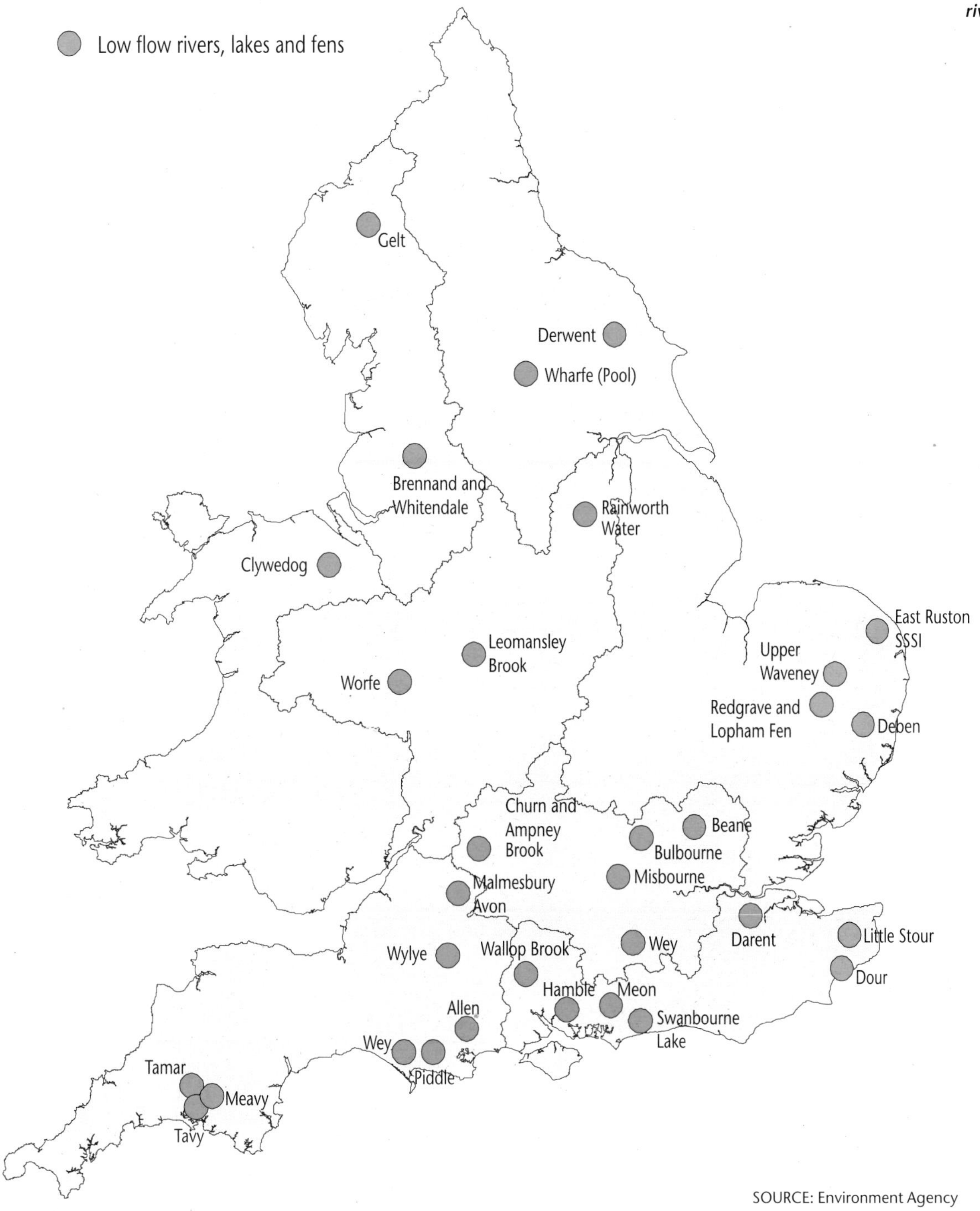

Figure 4.6
Location of low flow rivers, 1997

Low flow rivers, lakes and fens

Gelt

Derwent

Wharfe (Pool)

Brennand and Whitendale

Rainworth Water

Clywedog

Leomansley Brook

Worfe

East Ruston SSSI

Upper Waveney

Redgrave and Lopham Fen

Deben

Churn and Ampney Brook

Beane

Bulbourne

Misbourne

Malmesbury Avon

Wylye

Wallop Brook

Wey

Darent

Little Stour

Dour

Hamble

Meon

Allen

Swanbourne Lake

Wey

Piddle

Tamar

Meavy

Tavy

SOURCE: Environment Agency

(naturalised) (Figure 4.7). Several patterns can be seen in the flows of the last nine years:

sites in the east and south east (the rivers Witham and Thames) have many years with long periods of time below average;

the drought of the early 1990s caused low flows across the country;

the winter drought of 1991/1992 was particularly severe in the south west (the Tamar);

the low flows of 1995 and 1996 are most evident in the north and west, but less severe than in the early 1990s in the south and east;

many sites record a long-term minimum monthly flow during this period but only one or

Figure 4.7
Monthly average river flows of eight selected rivers, 1988 to 1997, compared with their 1961 to 1990 averages, minima and maxima

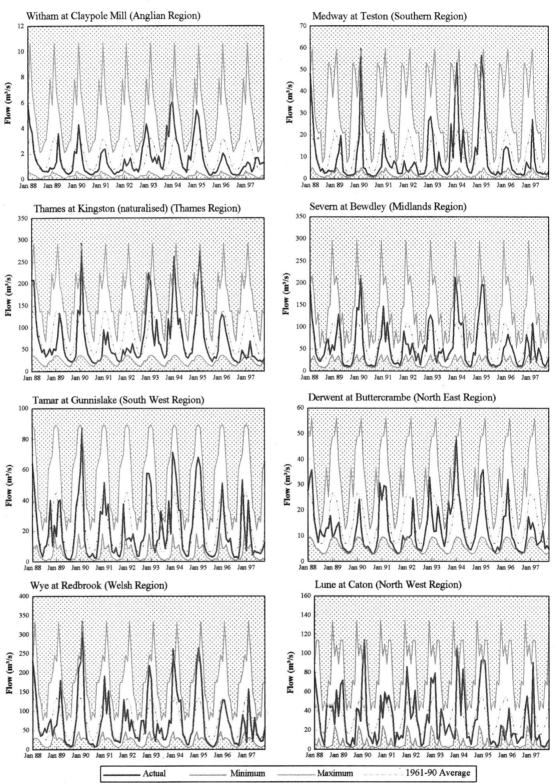

SOURCE: Environment Agency

two sites show a long-term monthly maximum with some places (the Witham and Derwent rivers) being very much short of the long-term maximum.

Figure 4.8 shows the deviation from the average and it is clear that summer flows have been about 50 per cent below average at many sites in the last decade, putting pressure on water resources in meeting the needs of abstractors and river ecosystems.

Figure 4.9 depicts groundwater levels for the last five years compared with the 30-year average groundwater levels at eight selected sites. It shows regional differences reflecting the type of aquifer and rainfall amounts and the response to abstraction. The plots show how groundwater levels vary significantly over the year although this varies with rock type, the greatest variation occurring in the oolitic limestones. Over the past five years, most sites have recharged to maximum levels at some stage, although for a large proportion of

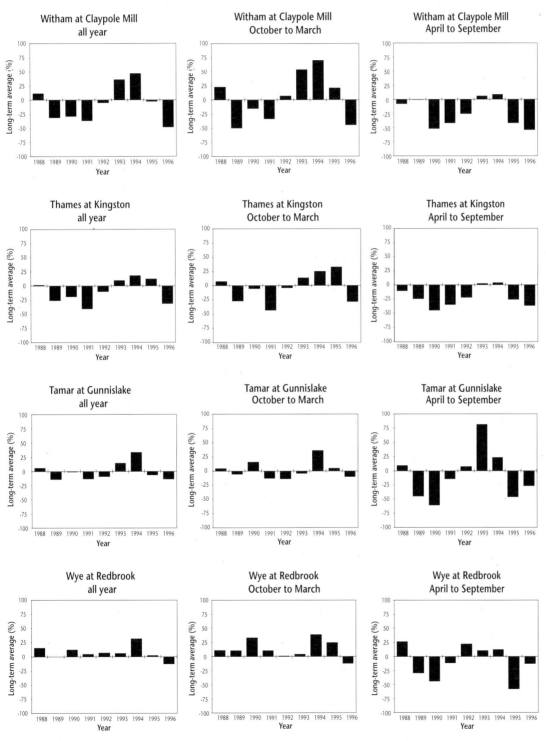

Figure 4.8
Annual winter and summer river flows, 1988 to 1996, as a percentage of the 1961 to 1990 long-term average

SOURCE: Environment Agency

**Figure 4.8
(continued)**
Annual winter and summer river flows, 1988 to 1996, as a percentage of the 1961 to 1990 long-term average

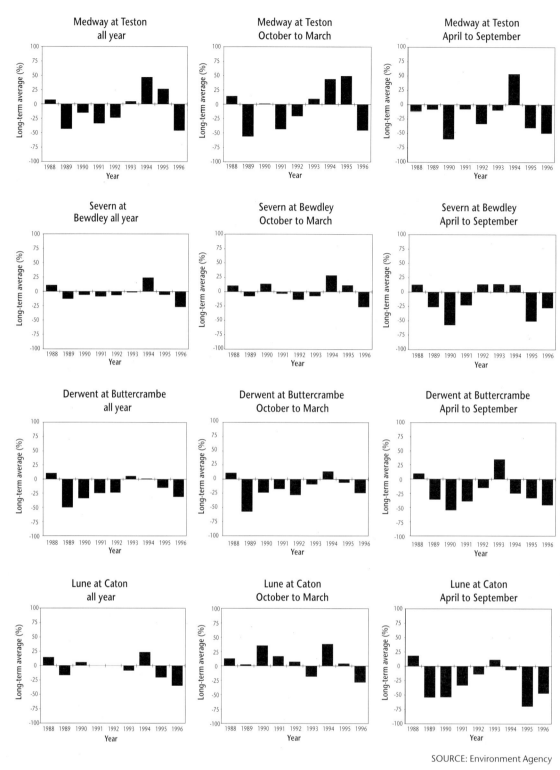

SOURCE: Environment Agency

time they have been below average, with some sites being consistently well below average (Swinnow Wood in the Sherwood Sandstone). Groundwater levels largely reflect the rainfall variability with 'normality' being more evident in the west and south west.

The variability of flows seen between 1988 and 1996 continued in 1997. The summer was rather wetter than average, especially in the south east, but only eight of the 30 months from April 1995 to October

1997 had above average rainfall and only three of those months were in the winter recharge period. In 1997, the drought focused on the east and south east, and the rainfall deficit led to a serious depletion of groundwater stocks. In October 1997, most aquifers were well below average and those in the south east were below their October historic minima. River flows suffered from the lack of baseflow. Such conditions led the water companies to develop drought contingency plans in August 1997.

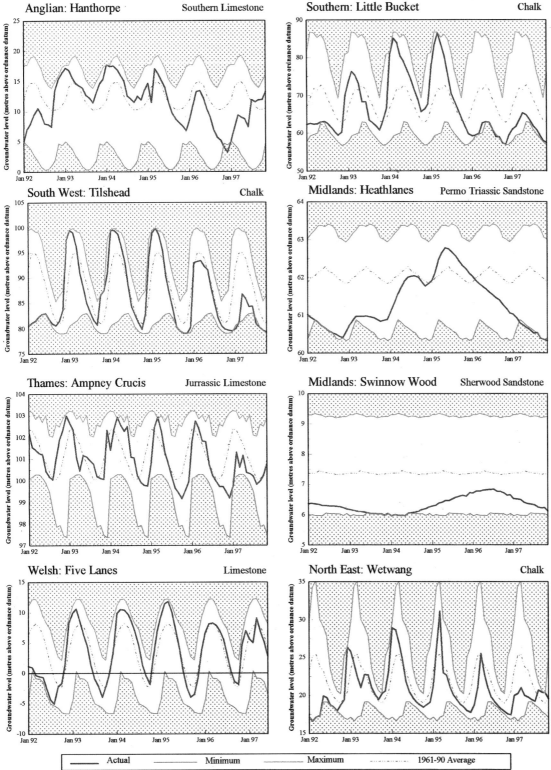

Figure 4.9
Groundwater levels at eight selected sites, 1992 to 1997, compared with their 1961 to 1990 averages, minima and maxima

SOURCE: Environment Agency

Figure 4.10
Area inundated by floods of 100-year return period level in absence of flood defences

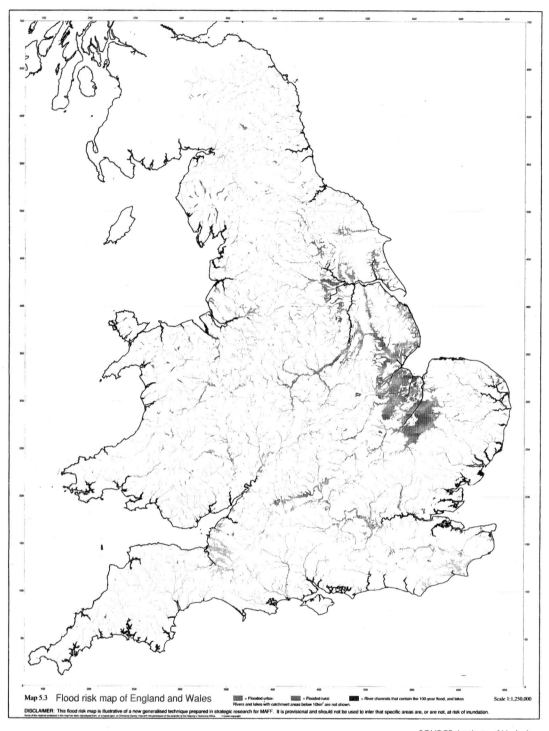

Map 5.3 Flood risk map of England and Wales

DISCLAIMER: This flood risk map is illustrative of a new generalised technique prepared in strategic research for MAFF. It is provisional and should not be used to infer that specific areas are, or are not, at risk of inundation.

SOURCE: Institute of Hydrology
Crown copyright

The Adequacy of Flood Defences

Flooding is a natural phenomenon and part of the natural fluvial cycle. Society's use of the environment has required the control of flooding in order to protect life and property. Figure 4.10 shows an estimate of the areas that would be inundated by floods of the 100-year return period level in the absence of flood defences. The map also identifies the urban areas that would be at risk. The results indicate that 10,683km^2 of land would be at risk, of which 611km^2 is built-up, roughly equivalent to the size of the West Midlands conurbation. These figures represent 7.1 per cent of the land area of England and Wales and 6.8 per cent of its built-up area respectively (Morris and Flavin, 1996). Flooding could be a risk to developments in these zones unless flood defences are maintained and there are about 34,000km of defences maintained for flood protection and land drainage purposes. In the past four years, the length of flood defence structures improved or built has exceeded 1,100km. It is estimated that nearly six million people live within the natural boundaries of river or coastal floodplains, so flood defences are essential to maintain quality of life.

Building flood defences changes natural river processes. The Agency has produced a document *Policy and Practice for the Protection of Floodplains* which advises planning authorities on the implications of development proposals in relation to flood risk issues and environmental impact. The aim of the policy is to encourage sustainable development, which takes account of natural processes and avoids committing future generations to unnecessary flood risks and a damaged environment (Environment Agency, 1997g).

River management activities over the centuries, for purposes ranging from navigation, and the use of water for mills, as well as for land drainage, have led to habitat loss and changed the natural flow regimes of many rivers. The extent of these changes has been estimated from a River Habitat Survey, which is now described.

Freshwater Habitats

A survey of river habitats was carried out over the three year period, 1994 to 1996. This was the first national programme for monitoring the quality of riverine habitats and it has been applied in Scotland and Northern Ireland too. The scheme provides a national reference network of sites consisting of three sites in every 10x10km square, and a method of assessing habitat quality (NRA, 1996a). It includes an assessment of the extent to which habitats have been modified (Appendix 2). The results show that of the sites visited:

river habitat types vary according to natural topography;

38 per cent of sites were semi-natural;

20 per cent were predominantly unmodified by humans;

42 per cent were obviously, extensively, or heavily modified (Figure 4.11);

wetlands, covering more than a third of the area at a site, were found at only 1.3 per cent of sites nationally (Figure 4.12);

vegetation choked channels affected 11 per cent of sites, mainly in the south and east of England (Figure 4.13).

Figure 4.14 plots the extent of habitat modification across England and Wales. This shows how the Thames Valley, areas around and to the north of the Wash, the Humber, Cheshire Plains and Somerset Levels have the greatest number of modified sites.

There have been other selective assessments of habitats. Fifteen wetlands are known, or thought to be, currently affected by high rates of abstraction or to be at risk, although there may be as many as 100 wetlands at risk of drying out or deteriorating from over-exploitation (Hunt, 1996). Many of these sites are also designated as Sites of Special Scientific Interest, e.g. East Ruston Fen. These will be considered by the Agency in its review with English Nature, mentioned previously.

The Fenlands in East Anglia have been drained over the past 300 years to provide good flat land for arable cultivation. The impact on the loss of habitat is clear from Table 4.1:

Table 4.1 *Area of fenland habitat, 1637 to 1984*

Year	Fenland habitat (sq km)
1637	3380
1825	2400
1934	100
1984	10

Source: English Nature

Such change in fenland area has affected species, for example, the Large Copper butterfly was associated with fens until the middle of the last century. Wet grassland habitats have also declined mainly due to the shift from haymaking to high intensity agriculture. Since the 1930s, 64 per cent of wet grassland in the Thames Valley, 48 per cent of Romney Marsh and 37 per cent of the Norfolk and Suffolk Broads have been lost. Other work suggests annual loss rates of 4.4 per cent in lowland wet grassland in Humberside although only 0.2 per cent in Cumbria (English Nature, 1997a). It is also estimated that there has been an annual loss of 5.5km^2 of swamp, marginal and inundation habitats between 1947 and 1980, with an estimated average annual loss of between 0.2 and 0.6km^2 of reedbed every year between 1945 and 1989 (RSPB, 1996).

Blanket mires and raised mires in Britain depend on water inflows exceeding outflows so that peat forms. In recent years, they have been particularly vulnerable to pressures from agriculture, afforestation and mechanised peat milling, a process that can remove 500mm of peat in a single year. Naturally, the rate of peat growth is about 1mm per year so the extraction rate is clearly greater than its creation (Heathwaite, 1995).

Wetlands are, therefore, subject to natural pressures and pressures from a variety of human activities. These are summarised in Table 4.2 (Buisson and Bradley, 1994).

One way of protecting reedbeds, fens and other wetlands is the formation of a water level management plan which aims to balance and

Figure 4.12
The distribution of wetland sites, 1994 to 1996

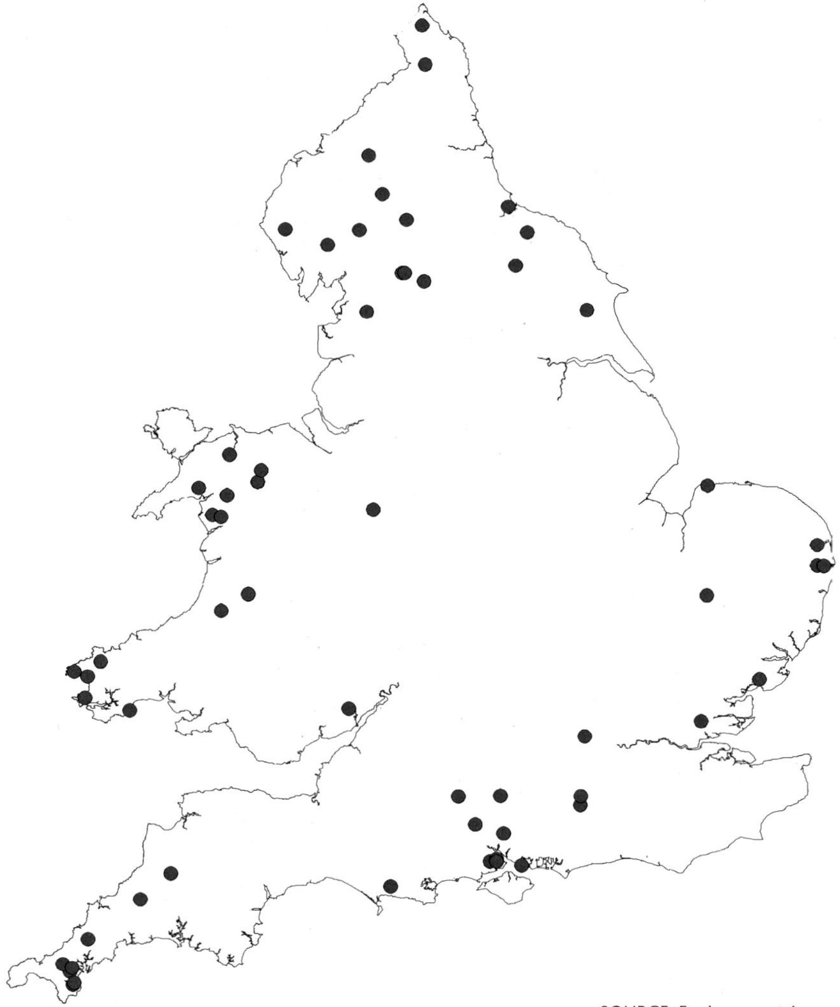

SOURCE: Environment Agency

Figure 4.11
Regional distribution of river habitat scores, 1994 to 1996

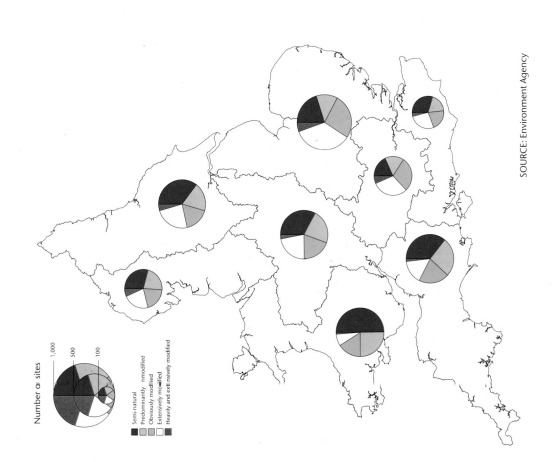

SOURCE: Environment Agency

Number of sites

1,000
500
100

Semi-natural
Predominantly unmodified
Obviously modified
Extensively modified
Heavily and extensively modified

Figure 4.14
*River habitat scores,
1994 to 1996*

- ● Semi-natural
- ● Predominantly unmodified
- ● Obviously modified
- ○ Extensively modified
- ● Heavily and extensively modified

SOURCE: Environment Agency

Figure 4.13
*The distribution of
river channels
choked with
vegetation, 1994 to
1996*

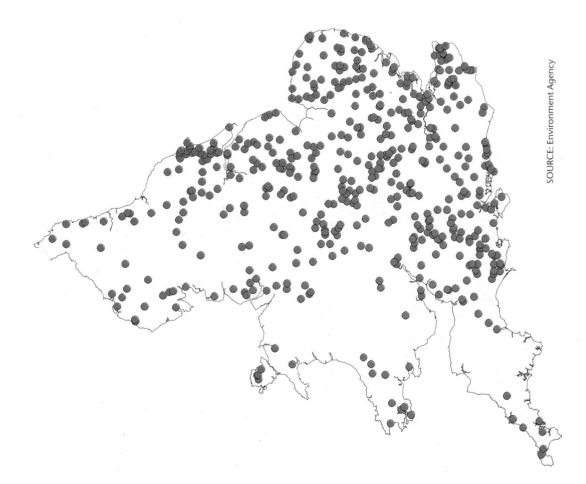

SOURCE: Environment Agency

75

integrate the needs of agriculture, flood defence and conservation (although priority is being given to Sites of Special Scientific Interest). A Plan is a written statement by the operating authority which contains an agreed procedure for the management of water levels. Where possible, the management promotes conditions favourable to wintering and breeding birds, and for characteristic ditch and meadow plants and invertebrates. The Agency is currently responsible for 382 water level management plans (Figure 4.15), Internal Drainage Boards for 131, and Local Authorities for 90, as of June 1997. As responsibility for the plans will change between operating authorities before the completion date is reached, these figures are indicative only and cannot be taken as final. The Agency has completed 65 plans and is preparing a further 88. Interim management statements have been issued for 165 and are being prepared for 18 sites. They are an important input to any Local Environment Agency Plans which cover the same areas.

Streamside habitats were investigated as part of the 1990 Countryside Survey of the former Department of the Environment. This showed that they supported a number of species rare in other types of habitat and were therefore important for plant diversity. From 1978 to 1990 there was evidence of a loss of species from streamsides, apparently related in part to drying out. This underlines the importance of riparian zones and the need to monitor and protect them.

Although some ponds are permanent features, most are temporary. They nevertheless provide a distinctive habitat and many rare species are found in them. Once a common and central feature of English village life, the number of ponds has been continually declining. It is estimated that in 1880 there were about 800,000 natural ponds in England and Wales but by 1990 the number had declined to no more than 180,000 and possibly less, and the rate of decline seems to be increasing (Rackham, 1986; DoE, 1993).

The decline in the number of ponds and wetlands has to some extent been offset by a large increase in the number of flooded gravel pits and reservoirs, which provide open water and marginal wetland habitats for birds. Since 1930, the number of great crested grebes has trebled due to these new habitats. There is also an increasing number of ponds in gardens, providing some habitat for freshwater species in urban areas.

The headwaters of rivers provide important habitats for juvenile fish and macroinvertebrates, many species of which are only found in these waters. An assessment of 49 small streams in four catchments found that only 47 per cent have very good biological quality. A substantial number showed signs of habitat degradation thought to be caused by drought, acidification, siltation, and contamination of sediments due to diffuse pollution (NRA, 1993).

Table 4.2
Causes of wetland loss

Cause		Wetland Type		
		Flood Plain	**Marsh**	**Peatland**
Human activities	Drainage	C	C	C
	Dredging	-	P	-
	Built development	C	C	-
	Pollution	C	C	-
	Mineral extraction	P	-	C
	Groundwater abstraction	P	C	-
	Sediment starvation	C	C	-
	Hydrological alteration	C	C	-
	Subsidence due to mining	C	C	-
Natural causes	Subsidence	-	-	P
	Drought	C	C	P
	Storms	-	-	P
	Erosion	P	-	P
	Biotic effects	C	C	-

Source: Buisson and Bradley, 1994

Key: C = Common and important cause

　　　 P = Present but not a major concern

　　　 - = Absent or exceptional

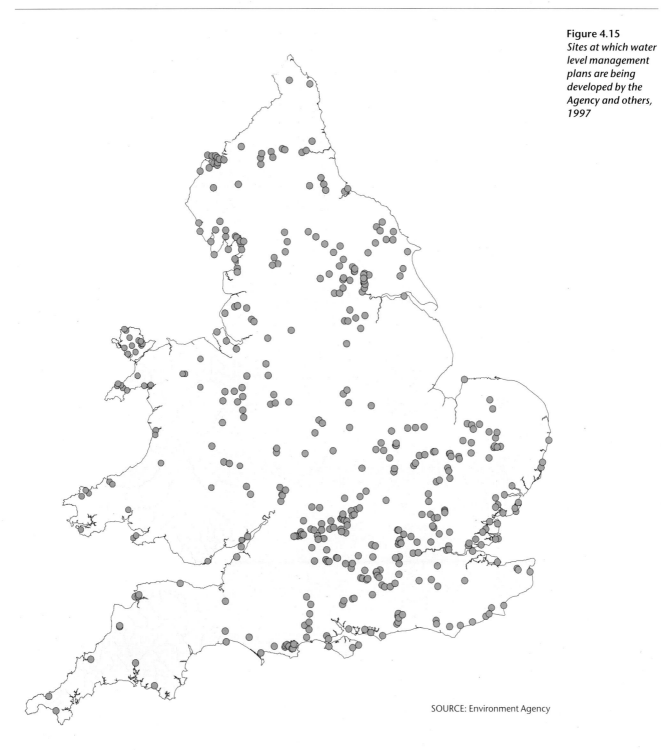

Figure 4.15
Sites at which water level management plans are being developed by the Agency and others, 1997

SOURCE: Environment Agency

4.2 The State of Biological Populations and Communities and of Biodiversity in Fresh Waters

Biodiversity is the variety of life forms that exists around us. It encompasses the whole range of mammals, birds, reptiles, amphibians, fish, insects and other invertebrates, plants, fungi and micro-organisms. The importance of biodiversity is summed up in the following quotation:

"Our Planet's essential goods and services depend on the variety and variability of genes, species, populations and ecosystems. Biological resources feed and clothe us and provide housing, medicines and spiritual nourishment....The current decline in biodiversity is largely the result of human activity and represents a serious threat to human development" (DoE, 1994).

Seven freshwater habitats have shown significant changes and these changes cause concern (Table 4.3). Many of the habitats are threatened by agriculture, drainage and pollution and the UK Biodiversity Action Plan seeks to find ways of restoring the balance (DoE, 1995). This section looks at the biodiversity of the freshwater environment, by reference to aquatic plants and major animal groupings, to identify the current state of populations and trends.

Aquatic Plants

The aquatic flora of England and Wales is relatively rich, largely due to the wet maritime climate. The British Isles have 21 of the 22 European species of pondweeds (*Potamogeton*) and nine of the 11 species of spearworts and crowfoots (*Ranunculus* subgenus *Batrachium*). Over the past 50 years, there have been some major changes in the distribution of aquatic plants. For example, frogbit (*Hydrocharis morsus-ranae*), sharp-leaved pondweed (*Potamogeton acutifolius*) and long-stalked pondweed (*Potamogeton praelongus*) are much less common now than in the 1950s (Preston and Croft 1997). Frogbit is still ubiquitous in the Somerset Levels but it has decreased markedly in the Fens and Romney Marsh where it was very common in 1964. The change is due to the conversion of grazing land to arable farming after which small ditches have been overgrown by other plants or destroyed all together. Furthermore, the increased use of fertilizers has caused a change in the nutrient status which is reflected in these communities. Another species on the decline, the sharp-leaved pondweed, has been declining over a much longer time period. In this case, it was last seen in some counties in the late 18th century, Gloucestershire in 1870 and Surrey in 1965; modern farming methods cannot therefore account for this decline.

Table 4.3
The status of key freshwater habitats in the UK Biodiversity Action Plan

Habitat	Distribution	Important biological features	Pressures
Chalk rivers	35 in southern and eastern England	Plants Invertebrates Trout populations	Nutrient enrichment Siltation Low flows
Mesotrophic lakes	Mainly in the north and west	Plant communities Rare fish: –vendace (*Coregonus albula*) –schelly (*Coregonus lavaretus*)	Nutrient enrichment Non-native fish species Macrophyte damage by boats
Eutrophic standing waters (natural)	Lowlands	Plant communities Breeding and wintering waterfowl Coarse fish populations	Nutrient enrichment Abstraction Recreation
Aquifer fed, naturally fluctuating standing water bodies	Wales (1 site) East Anglian Fens (5 sites)	Aquatic mosses Plant communities Invertebrates, amphibians	Abstraction/drainage Climate change Nutrient enrichment
Reedbeds	5,000 ha, many small and fragmented	Invertebrates Wetland birds	Land drainage Drying out by abstraction Nutrient enrichment
Fens	Largest in Broadland, eastern England	Plant and invertebrate communities	Land drainage Drying out by abstraction Recreational activity Nutrient enrichment
Grazing marsh	300,000 ha, fresh and brackish	Breeding waders Wintering wildfowl Ditch plants and invertebrates	Land drainage and flood defence works Nutrient enrichment

Plant species' declines since 1930 are most significant for wetlands and grasslands reflecting the loss of habitat described in Section 4.1 (Ratcliffe, 1984). A study of the impact of 150 years of drainage and land use change found that of 526 floral species studied, 20 to 33 per cent have become locally extinct, more than 50 per cent have declined and only 34 increased in number, these being mainly exotic species (Mountford, 1994).

The non-native and exotic plant species, giant hogweed, Japanese knotweed and Himalayan balsam occur in patches, most noticeably in South Wales, East Devon, Merseyside, London and pockets in East Anglia (Environment Agency, 1998a). Several lakes are affected by Canadian pondweed and between 1980 and 1995, the Australian swamp stonecrop invaded 530 water bodies in England, including many ponds of high conservation value in the New Forest (English Nature 1997). At least four other non-native species

which were rare 50 years ago, are now widespread. These are New Zealand pigmyweed, St. John Nuttall's waterweed, least duckweed and parrot's feather. All were thought to have been introduced into garden ponds which later became naturalised. The least duckweed was first recorded in 1977, so that in only 20 years it has spread significantly throughout east England (Preston and Croft, 1997).

Trees form an important part of the bankside vegetation in many places and their roots help to stabilise the banks. One of the most abundant bankside trees, the common alder (*Alnus glutinosa*) can suffer from a lethal disease by a fungus of the genus *Phytophthora*. This fungus invades the stems and roots of trees. Various investigations made during 1994 to 1996 have shown that the disease is widespread. Figure 4.16 shows the distribution recorded in an Agency survey in 1995 and 1996. In another survey

Figure 4.16
The distribution of Phytophthora in alders, 1995 and 1996

Phytophthora in alders

○ Disease present

● Disease extensive

SOURCE: Environment Agency

79

of rivers over 8m wide, 1.2 per cent of alders were found to have been killed by this disease between 1994 and 1995, and 2.2 per cent between 1995 and 1996. In terms of an estimated total population of 580,000 alders on rivers this size, this suggests that some 18,000 trees became diseased or died during 1994 to 1996 (Gibbs et al., 1996). No quantitative information is available for smaller streams but on some of these, hundreds of trees are known to have died.

Although the disease was not described until 1993, there is no doubt that it has been present in England and Wales for several decades. The possibility exists that it is a native fungus which has been rendered damaging by changes in the environment. An annual doubling in the number of diseased trees is alarming. If this rate continues, half the riverside alders in the area covered by the survey of rivers over 8m wide (300,000 trees) would be dead by the year 2000. However, insufficient is known about the disease and its links with environmental factors, so further surveys and research are needed (Forestry Commission and Environment Agency, 1997).

Macroinvertebrates

The Agency samples rivers for macroinvertebrates, and bases one of its water quality classification schemes on them (see Section 4.3). The data from 6,039 river sites in England and Wales sampled in 1995 have been analysed to derive geographic and frequency distributions for the macroinvertebrate groups, most at family taxonomic level. The sites were chosen as representative of the reaches in which they are located. Most of the sites were at easily accessible locations, usually at the downstream end of a river reach. Headwaters and springs were under-represented, and few watercourses with flows of less than 0.3m^3/s were included, although these ecologically important habitats are being studied separately. Seventy-six families were identified but only 54 occurred in sufficient numbers to justify frequency distributions for the classification schemes. The others may be considered as rare or local and hold biodiversity value for that reason.

The analysis revealed several distribution patterns between different groups. These may be due to water quality or habitat preference, or because the geographical distribution of species is influenced by climate, altitude and other physical or natural water chemistry factors.

One snail family (Lymnaeidae) and diving and whirligig beetles (Dytiscidae) show widespread and fairly uniform distributions. A non-native snail (Hydrobiidae), worms (Oligochaeta), freshwater shrimps (Gammaridae), a mayfly family (Baetidae) and non-biting midges (Chironomidae) are widespread but uneven in distribution. Figure 4.17 shows the distribution of freshwater shrimps. This uneven distribution may be due to the higher abundances which can occur with these families, depending on habitat availability and the degree of organic enrichment.

A mayfly family (Caenidae) and the water hog louse (Asellidae) are widespread. The former, which is less pollution tolerant than the latter is more rare in the most industrialised areas. The latter is distributed in lowland areas naturally and is not found in the uplands of northern England, Wales and the south west. Other families which are geographically biased include snails (Valvatidae) and damselflies (Coenagriidae). These occur more commonly in the lowland rivers of the south and east of England and Figure 4.18 shows the distribution of the snails. The dragonfly family (Calopterygidae) has a similar distribution but extends its range more into the South West Region. These differences in natural distribution show why a range of families are needed to assess the state of macroinvertebrate populations.

Families requiring the cleanest waters occur in northern England and the south west, for example stonefly families (Heptageniidae and Leuctridae). Freshwater shrimps appear to be found abundantly in areas of chalk and limestone and many snails may have this preference because they need the calcium to build shells. The riffle beetle (Elmidae) is widespread, occurring abundantly in upland waters, and far less so in the lowland regions where riffle areas with turbulent flows are scarce, and hardly at all in the main industrialised areas (Environment Agency, 1997c).

The Agency is responsible for managing an action plan for several of the invertebrate species specified in the UK Biodiversity Action Plan (see Table 4.7). Information on these species is patchy and cannot be gleaned from the family-level information used in water quality assessment procedures. If a narrow distribution of a family of macroinvertebrates is found, any species in that family is assumed to have that narrow distribution and it is flagged up as needing special attention. Rare species within families with a wide distribution are not neglected, but with the information available on nationally-rare families, a start can be made on assessing the biodiversity within rivers.

A reference data set of 614 sites has been used as a basis for evaluating the conservation status of macroinvertebrate taxa in streams and rivers (Wright et al., 1996). Of 637 taxa found at the reference sites, 15 are designated as being under threat. The data set will also help in the assessment of the conservation status of a wider range of taxa and sites than previously possible. Some 227 taxa occurred only at one per cent or fewer sites and 75 were found at just one site. The majority of species with a rare frequency of occurrence at the reference sites were beetles (Coleoptera) and two-winged flies (Diptera),

Figure 4.17
The distribution of Gammaridae (freshwater shrimp), 1995

Average Abundance per 10 km square

Key to Symbols

· > 0
· > 0.5
· > 1.0
• > 1.5
• > 2.0
● > 2.5
● > 3.0
● > 3.5

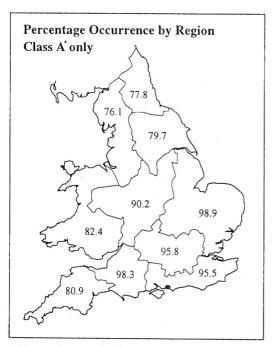

**Percentage Occurrence by Region
Class A* only**

77.8
76.1
79.7
90.2
98.9
82.4
95.8
98.3   95.5
80.9

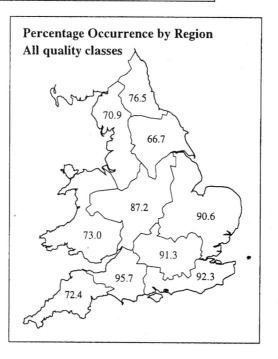

**Percentage Occurrence by Region
All quality classes**

76.5
70.9
66.7
87.2
90.6
73.0
91.3
95.7   92.3
72.4

* Very good water quality class

SOURCE: Environment Agency

Figure 4.18
*The distribution of
Valvatidae (snail),
1995*

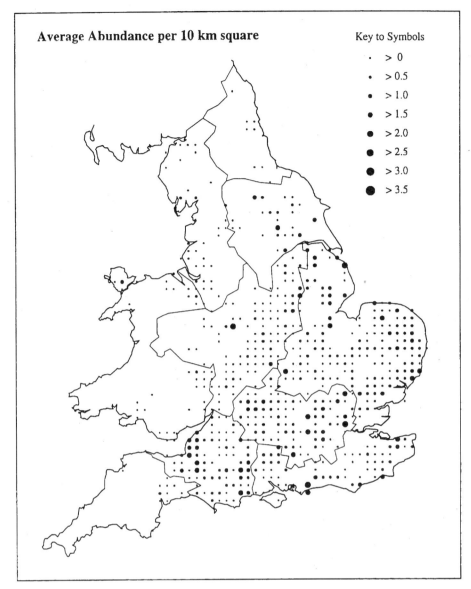

Average Abundance per 10 km square

Key to Symbols

· > 0
· > 0.5
· > 1.0
● > 1.5
● > 2.0
● > 2.5
● > 3.0
● > 3.5

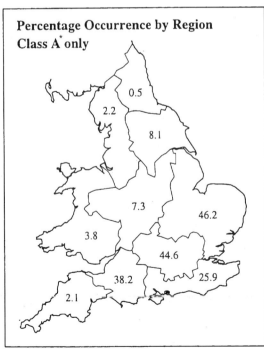

Percentage Occurrence by Region
Class A* only

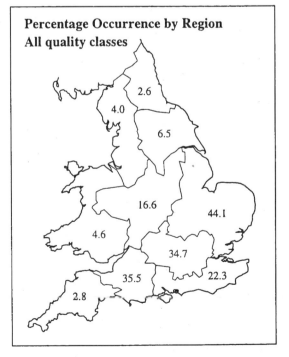

Percentage Occurrence by Region
All quality classes

* Very good water quality class

SOURCE: Environment Agency

Major group	Percentage occurrence (number of sites)				Number of threatened taxa
	5-100 (31-614)	<5-1.1 (7-30)	1.0-0.3 (2-6)	0.2 (1)	
Flatworms (*Tricladida*)	6	2	0	1	
Snails (*Gastropoda*)	17	5	4	3	2
Bivalve molluscs (*Bivalvia*)	9	5	6	2	1
Worms (*Oligochaeta*)	25	11	12	3	
Leeches (*Hirudinea*)	6	6	2	0	
Crustaceans (*Crustacea*)	5	1	3	2	
Mayflies (*Ephemeroptera*)	22	10	4	1	3
Stoneflies (*Plecoptera*)	20	4	3	0	
Dragonflies (*Odonata*)	4	2	6	1	
Bugs (*Hemiptera*)	6	6	10	6	
Beetles (*Coleoptera*)	18	22	37	27	4
Alderflies (*Megaloptera*)	2	1	0	0	
Lacewings (*Neuroptera*)	0	2	0	0	
Caddis flies (*Trichoptera*)	46	24	21	7	4
Two-winged flies (*Diptera*)	80	39	41	22	1
Seven unidentified groups	2	2	3	0	
TOTAL	268	142	152	75	15

Table 4.4
The frequency of occurrence of macroinvertebrate taxa within each major taxonomic group found at 614 reference sites

Source: Wright et al., 1996. Copyright John Wiley & Sons Limited.
Reproduced with permission.

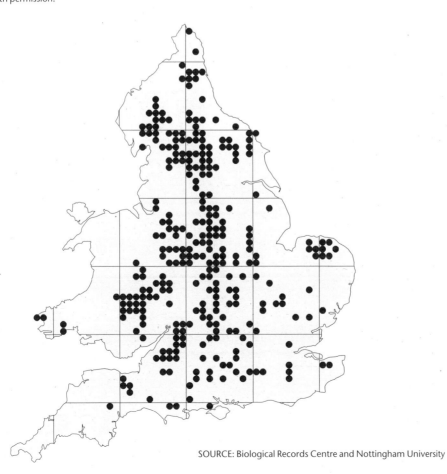

SOURCE: Biological Records Centre and Nottingham University

Figure 4.19
The distribution of native crayfish by 10km squares, 1990 to 1995

Figure 4.20
Total rod and net catches of salmon and sea trout, 1951 to 1995

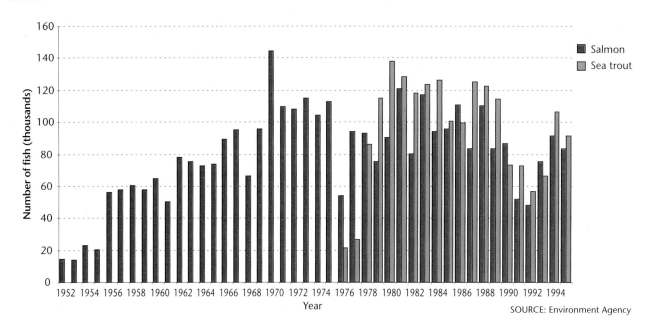

SOURCE: Environment Agency

of which 27 and 22 respectively occurred at a single site (Table 4.4).

There is a native species of crayfish, the freshwater white-clawed crayfish (*Austropotamobius pallipes*), which is up to 10cm long and occurs in a variety of freshwater habitats. A Biodiversity Action Plan has been prepared for this relatively conspicuous macroinvertebrate. It is eaten by some fish species and can be an important dietary component for otters. Native crayfish are threatened by the American signal crayfish (*Pacifastacus leniusculus*), which have escaped from farms and been deliberately introduced since the 1970s to meet culinary demands. Signal crayfish out-compete the native species and carry crayfish plague, a fungal disease. Native crayfish are found extensively in northern England and Wales but populations are more sparse in other regions (Figure 4.19). The areas where crayfish are abundant have generally been designated 'no-go' areas for signal crayfish, that is signal crayfish farming is not permitted in these areas.

Fisheries

There are 38 species of freshwater fish native to Great Britain of which two are rare, three vulnerable, and three endangered (DETR, 1997). Some significant changes to the status of recreational fisheries in England and Wales have occurred in recent years. Salmon catches have declined in some rivers, contributory factors being the impact of netting, both along the coast and on the high seas, climatic changes, and changing land use. For trout fisheries there appears to be a decline in wild populations whereas stocking of rivers is on the increase, bringing with it the concerns about genetic integrity. The popularity of

fishing for trout in lakes is greater than before and more artificial trout lakes have been created to meet the demand for this type of fishing. Similarly, there has been an increase in the number of specially created stillwater coarse fisheries operating on a day-ticket basis. In the wild, the coarse fish populations of the river systems are generally thought to be stable.

The Agency's Regions undertake programmed and reactive survey work on fish populations but there is a lack of national data on fish populations and national reporting is based mainly on the number of salmon and migratory trout caught. 'Catch' data are based on reports made by rod and net licence holders. They are therefore subject to variation and catches themselves have a variable relationship with stock size because of many factors such as low flows and fishing effort. Ways of countering this are being developed, but in addition there is an urgent need for more comprehensive and robust methods to report fish stock status. The emerging Fisheries Classification Scheme will be a principal vehicle for this and is being supported through a nationally consistent monitoring programme for salmonids and coarse fish.

Total national catches (by rod and net) for salmon and sea trout are given in Figure 4.20 although the absence of data for some regions precludes the collation of national totals in many years. The principal influence on catches in the 1995 season was the drought which resulted in low flows throughout England and Wales for most of the fishing season. Overall rod catches of salmon and sea trout in England and Wales were markedly lower than those reported in 1994 but were about average for the past five years. The 1995 salmon catches were similar to those in the

Figure 4.21
*Rod catches of
salmon and sea
trout in the River
Tees, 1965 to 1995*

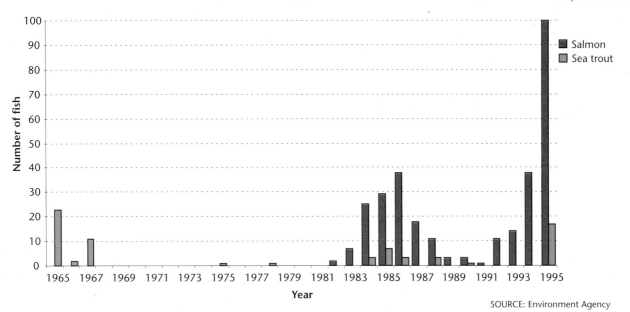

SOURCE: Environment Agency

previous drought, 1989 to 1991. Net catch data are incomplete though the figures to date are slightly higher than the five-year average. Thus, net catches were apparently less affected by the drought than rod catches.

Salmon and migratory trout are subject to oceanic and estuarine conditions which may cause natural changes in populations linked to conditions over which society has little control. The survival and growth of salmon in the North East Atlantic is giving cause for concern. Salmon which have spent several winters at sea and which return during the spring (known as 'springers') are low in number and may still be declining. It is therefore particularly important that management in fresh waters optimises production and survival in this phase of the life cycle over which society has some control. Effective progress in this respect also requires the continued control of high seas fishing by other countries.

Poor water quality limits the quality, or even the existence of fisheries in some waters, and pollution incidents can have devastating effects. Significant improvements have been made over recent years in the quality of some rivers which have been fishless for long periods due to industrial and sewage pollution. An example of a recovering river is the Tees (Figure 4.21) which demonstrates what has been and can be achieved with appropriate investment. Early this century the fish stocks were eradicated by gross industrial pollution. The main problem area was the tidal stretch, where poor water quality presented a barrier to migrating fish and supported few coarse fish species. The recovery of the Tees has been brought about through the tightening of existing discharge

consents, the setting of new consents and the transfer of sewage-treatment works outfalls, as well as the decline of heavy industry in the Tees Valley area. A restoration programme has also introduced one million salmon parr to the river. The 1995 reported salmon catches were the highest since the records began and the sea trout catches, without stocking, were the largest since 1965. In addition, 22km of fresh water impounded by the Tees Barrage since December 1994 now support good populations of coarse fish.

Other rivers are exhibiting a decline in salmon and sea trout numbers; the Hampshire Avon is an example (Figure 4.22). This figure clearly demonstrates the decline in the number of spring salmon over the past 25 years. Total stocks were reduced to low levels by the effects of the prolonged drought from 1988 to 1992, which resulted in a significant loss of juvenile habitat. High mortality was also suffered by smolts which reached the sea in 1989 and 1990. There is also concern that in this case, increased siltation of spawning gravels, thought to be due to soil erosion from changing farming practices, has led to the decline. Studies on the River Torridge have also found high concentrations of fine sediment in spawning gravels and a study on the River Piddle in Dorset showed that the source of sediments tends to be from cultivated areas. The full extent of siltation affecting spawning areas is not yet known but the Agency, in conjunction with others, is currently carrying out research to bring together all the evidence. Rich invertebrate communities in such rivers also suffer from siltation. Low flows exacerbate the problem since high winter flows should flush silt out of the river gravels. Acidification in the headwaters of the

River Wye and other west coast rivers has led to a significant reduction in effective breeding areas for salmon and trout.

The main causes of wild trout habitat degradation in the UK are thought to be acidification in Wales and the Pennines, agricultural pollution in the south west, low flows in the chalk streams of the south east, and drainage schemes over much of the rest of England. As a consequence of habitat degradation or overfishing or both, the vast majority of lowland trout fisheries now tend to rely on stocking to provide fish for angling with consequences for genetic integrity (Royal Commission on Environmental Pollution, 1992). There is a need for much better information on the state of wild trout populations.

A Strategy for the Management of Salmon in England and Wales was launched by the NRA in February 1996. This identifies priority objectives and a consistent framework to manage stocks. The objectives for the future management of this resource are to:

> optimise the number of salmon returning to home water fisheries;

> maintain and improve the fitness and diversity of salmon stocks;

> optimise the total economic value of surplus stocks;

> meet the necessary costs of managing the resource.

The Agency will implement this strategy by means of Local Salmon Action Plans drawn up by the year 2000 for all principal salmon rivers, through consultation with local interest groups. These plans will set spawning targets and fishing controls, identify factors limiting salmon populations and outline a programme of improvement works in order to maximise catches. Specific habitat improvements to protect salmonid populations include gravel cleaning, creation of buffer zones, screening abstraction intakes and the construction of fish passes. In 1995/96 over 200 fish habitat schemes were completed. Apart from managing external impacts on fisheries, the catch and release of migratory salmonids is also encouraged by the Agency in an attempt to maximise the numbers of spawning fish. The numbers of anglers returning their catches to the river have roughly doubled between 1993 and 1995, to over 3,000 salmon and 11,000 sea trout.

The lack of data collected in a nationally consistent manner to permit a coordinated analysis of salmonid species also applies to other fish species, including coarse fish and eels. This is being addressed by developing monitoring and classification systems which will be applied over the next few years. A coarse fish management strategy which consolidates the work being undertaken nationally on these species will be subject to consultation early in 1998. A strategy will also be developed for resident and migratory trout.

There is concern in some places about the introduction of non-native and exotic fish species. English Nature (1997) quote an example of the non-native ruffe eating the eggs of vendace (a type of fish only found in large deep lakes) in Bassenthwaite. Vendace occur only in one other locality in England, Derwent Water, and are listed on the UK Biodiversity Action Plan. Zander were first introduced to the Great

Figure 4.22
Rod and net catches of salmon and sea trout in the Hampshire Avon, 1954 to 1996

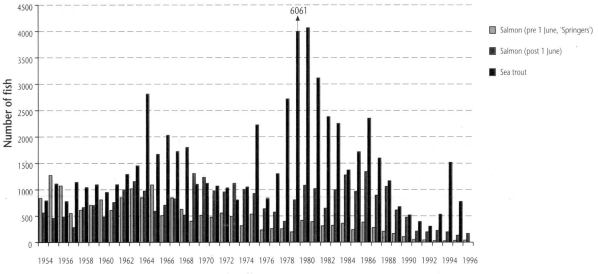

Ouse in 1963 and reduced populations of their prey species, roach and bream. They have since spread to other catchments across the country. Since 1978 there has been an increasing trend for still water fisheries to be stocked with wels catfish and non-native strains of carp. Exotic species are of particular concern because they may carry disease. In the late 1980s, imported fish were probably responsible for transmitting 'spring Viraemia' disease of carp which killed up to 100 per cent of some resident populations. Stocking with bottom feeding fish (for example carp and bream) has also led to eutrophication of several lakes by disturbance of bottom sediments. Although the Agency has responsibility for consenting fish introduced into inland waters which are not fish farms, the primary responsibility for fish diseases in England and Wales falls to the Ministry of Agriculture, Fisheries and Food. The introduction of the Fish Health Directive, EC 91/67, has placed increasing pressures on the organisations responsible for preventing the spread of serious fish diseases. Control of illegal fish introductions is best achieved through an educative and cooperative approach.

In addition to vendace, allis and twaite shad are the subjects of Biodiversity Action Plans. Both shad species migrate into rivers to spawn. The twaite shad has declined and been lost to previous spawning rivers and now only remains in the Wye, Usk, Severn and Tywi. There are no English or Welsh rivers where allis shad are known to spawn. The actions needed include studies to confirm the status and requirements of each species, and management to protect them from fishing and habitat destruction where necessary.

Waterway Birds

Of 22 primary bird habitats, six are dependent on fresh waters (RSPB, 1996). Surveys of waterway bird populations for the past 20 years have been carried out on over 130 stretches of rivers or canals, each about 5km in length. Observers mapped their sightings of 19 bird species on the river bank during nine to 10 visits during the mid-March to mid-July breeding season. The number of birds reported for these 19 species in 1993 is given in Table 4.5, together with the trend in numbers since 1974.

Looking over the whole record since 1974 (Figure 4.23), the decline of the yellow wagtail is evident and its spatial distribution is also declining, with fewer records in the north and west and a concentration of the remaining populations in eastern England. There does not appear to be any association between this decline and rainfall conditions in West Africa which have affected other migrants at times, for example the sedge warbler (Marchant and Balmer, 1994). Cold weather conditions and the unusually high number of severe winters in recent years appear to have affected some species, e.g. kingfisher and grey wagtail.

Three species have shown significant increases in population size between the 1992 and 1993 surveys; mallards (9 per cent), grey wagtails (46 per cent) and whitethroats (32 per cent). The increase in mallards is the cause of local concerns because many village ponds are perceived to be overpopulated and the pressure from mallards affects the aesthetic characteristics of the areas. Part of the reason for the increase in mallards is due to ready food being provided by people feeding the ducks, and some parishes are considering culls. The increase in whitethroats is notable because the 1992 survey also showed a 54 per cent increase and this species is now at its highest since the surveys began. It is not possible to determine links between populations and the stock and quality of fresh waters, but it is encouraging that some species are increasing and most populations remain stable. More information is really necessary to be certain of this.

Nationwide, a survey carried out in 1990 indicated that the British swan population had increased by some 37 per cent since the previous survey in 1983. The number of swans on the River Thames was very high in the 1920s and 1930s, with 250 cygnets being marked (between London and Henley) in 1921. During most of the 1920s and 1930s, strenuous efforts were made to reduce the numbers, mainly by removing all but two eggs from each pair. This was not very effective, largely because the population in the Thames Valley as a whole was increasing due to the proliferation of suitable waters, especially gravel pits. Post-war numbers started very high, but then started to decline; the number of cygnets fell to 150 in 1951 and then to very low levels in the late 1960s and the lowest ever of 22 cygnets in eight broods in 1984. Studies to try to find the cause of the decline were carried out by the Edward Grey Institute and lead-poisoning, by the ingestion of angling weights, was found to be the major cause of mortality. In 1987 the sale and use of these weights was banned and since then the number of swans has increased markedly. There were 27 broods of 101 cygnets between Sunbury and Henley in 1996. In that year 566 fully grown swans were counted between Sunbury and Abingdon, including 56 pairs with 189 cygnets. While there can be no doubt that the withdrawal of the use of lead was a major factor in the recovery of the population, other factors have helped as well. The run of fairly mild winters has been good for cygnet survival and a number of very efficient swan rescue services save the lives of many swans each year. The biggest single problem remains the interface between swans and anglers; although the numbers dying from lead poisoning is now very much reduced, the number of tackle injuries remains very high (Perrins, 1997).

There has been an increase in the number of some exotic species including Canada goose, whose droppings may lead to eutrophication in small lakes

Table 4.5
Waterways bird surveys

	1993 total	No. survey plots	Trend since 1974 (= is stable, - is decline, + is increase)	Comments
Mallard	1894	101	+ Doubled.	Commonest.
Moorhen	839	89	= Stable.	Second most abundant.
Sedge Warbler	448	60	- Slight decline	Migrant – decline linked to W African rainfall.
Coot	413	53	+ Doubled.	
Reed Bunting	322	59	- Stable since 1983, though this level is 50 per cent 1977 level.	
Pied Wagtail	256	70	- Slight decline.	May be linked to winter weather (cold).
Oystercatcher	223	30	= Increased to 1986 then stable.	
Whitethroat	221	57	+ Increasing	
Lapwing	180	41	= Increased to 1985, now decreased. Minimums in 1992/93.	
Grey Wagtail	158	66	- Slight decline.	Linked to harsh winters.
Common Sandpiper	154	29	= Stable but minimums in 92/93.	
Mute Swan	114	55	= Stable, maximum in 92/93.	
Dipper	114	37	= Stable.	
Tufted Duck	105	30	= Variable.	
Redshank	88	19	= Stable but may be decline?	
Kingfisher	65	55	- Decreased markedly 1978 to 1979, 1981 to 1982, 1991.	Susceptible to severe winter weather. Recovers well.
Curlew	64	28	+ Shallow increase since 1979.	
Little Grebe	49	19	= Stable.	
Yellow Wagtail	37	23	- Strong decline; 25 per cent of the 1976 level.	Linked to African conditions?

Source: British Trust for Ornithology

and ponds and cause bacterial contamination. The geese may also cause aesthetic problems on some grassy areas adjacent to water. The problem can be particularly intense in urban parks, and methods of deterring their numbers are necessary. The goosander is a relative newcomer and was only a rare winter visitor 100 years ago; it was first found nesting in England in 1941. Since then, in spite of persecution because of possible effects on fish stocks, it has continued to expand its range. Other species, native to specific locations, are extending their ranges. The red-breasted merganser has also only nested in England since 1950, and their impact on fisheries is a concern to anglers (Holden *et al.*, 1994). Cormorants, essentially a coastal species, have recently moved up rivers in winter and started to breed inland; their effect on freshwater fish stocks, particularly in still waters has led to concerns. The Agency is contributing

to a research project, coordinated by MAFF and DETR, which is investigating the impact of fish-eating birds on a number of types of fishery and ways of reducing that impact. The project is due for completion in 1999.

Mammals and Amphibians

Water voles, *Arvicola terrestris*, were common and conspicuous waterside mammals but a survey in 1989 to 1990 indicated that they were absent from two-thirds (67 per cent) of the sites where they were recorded in 1900 to 1939 (Figure 4.24; Strachan & Jefferies, 1993). This serious decline is thought to have been caused by the disturbance and loss of riparian habitats and predation by the non-native mink. For water voles, a Biodiversity Action Plan has been prepared and English Nature and the

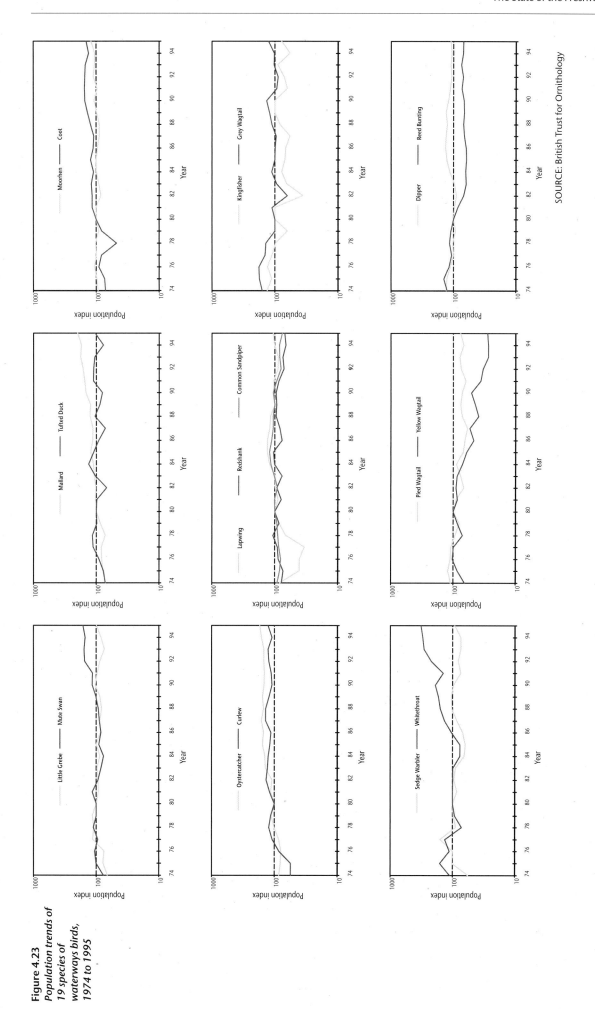

Figure 4.23
*Population trends of
19 species of
waterways birds,
1974 to 1995*

SOURCE: British Trust for Ornithology

Environment Agency have agreed to jointly fund the production of a *Water Vole Habitat Management Handbook*. An Agency research project is investigating the effects of land use, habitat and mink on water vole presence in eight catchments. This understanding is needed to show where management of habitat and mink can improve conditions for water voles. An important part of the programme is the provision of training for groups wishing to become involved in water vole work.

The otter, *Lutra lutra*, is a good indicator of overall river quality. Otters declined in many regions of England in the middle to later part of the 20th century probably due to several reasons including water pollution,

habitat damage and hunting (Figure 4.25). A national survey from 1991 to 1994 of alternate 50km grid squares across England indicated significant recolonisation by otters since the previous surveys (The Vincent Wildlife Trust, 1996). The percentage of sites occupied had risen from 5.8 per cent in 1977 to 1979, to 9.7 per cent in 1984 to 1986 and 23.4 per cent in 1991 to 1994. A more extensive survey in Wales covering the larger rivers and all 10km grid squares showed that 53 per cent of sites had evidence of otters in the 1991 to 1994 period. The population expansion was generally from Wales, south west and northern England to the east and south. This recovery appeared to be related to the legal protection of otters,

Figure 4.24
The distribution of 10km squares found to be occupied by water voles during 1989/90

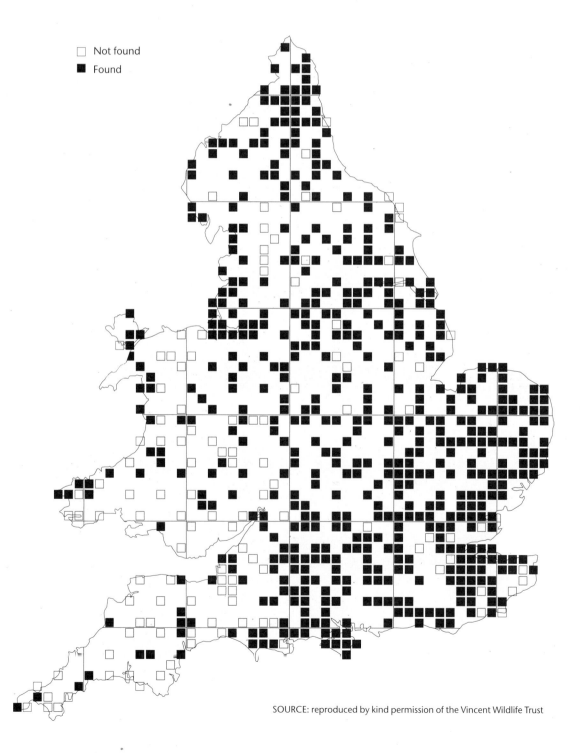

SOURCE: reproduced by kind permission of the Vincent Wildlife Trust

to habitat restoration and to controls on the use of the organochlorine pesticides dieldrin and aldrin, although there was no scientific proof (see section 4.4). Otters are still absent or sparse in many areas and require the provision of improved habitat for breeding and resting. The Agency is the contact point for the otter Biodiversity Action Plan. It has carried out many projects to improve riparian habitats for otters, by tree and shrub planting, fencing and constructing artificial holts. The MAFF grant aided habitat scheme water fringe option and management of riparian areas in woodland, as required in the *Forests and Water Guidelines*, should also help to promote the establishment of suitable habitat.

Fresh waters provide an essential part of the habitat requirements for amphibians. These animals are relatively well recorded, receiving much attention in local and national surveys. They are generally easy to observe because they spawn in waterbodies in the spring and newts can be counted by torchlight at night. Table 4.6 gives details from surveys taken up to 1995.

The common frog is still widespread throughout England and Wales despite the loss of breeding habitat and some evidence of a decline in numbers. Two questionnaire based surveys in 1970 suggested that frogs and toads had decreased slightly during the 1940s

Figure 4.25
The rivers and watersheds of England known to be occupied by otters, 1991 to 1994

———— Recovering wild populations

———— Released/reinforced populations and their progeny

SOURCE: reproduced by kind permission of the Vincent Wildlife Trust

Species	Records	Squares	Spatial coverage
Common frog (*Rana temporaria*)	13697	2432	Widespread
Common toad (*Bufo bufo*)	6930	1594	Widespread
Great crested newt (*Triturus cristatus*)	6131	921	Common except South West, North West and Wales
Smooth newt (*Triturus vulgaris*)	5751	1144	Widespread
Palmate newt (*Triturus helveticus*)	2681	927	Mainly Wales, South West and South East
Natterjack toad (*Bufo calamita*)	283	98	Rare
Edible frog (*Rana esculenta*)	119	48	South East
Marsh frog (*Rana ridibunda*)	112	41	South East

Source: Joint Nature Conservation Committee and Institute of Terrestrial Ecology, 1995.

and 1950s and suffered considerable declines throughout the 1960s. Garden ponds were the only habitat in which numbers increased. Both the frog and the toad decreased markedly in breeding sites on agricultural land in the early 1960s thought to be due to loss of suitable wetlands due to sites being filled in, drained or physically modified. Road mortality was also considered to be a factor and declines were significantly related to human population density (Cooke, 1972). The majority of the green frogs (edible and marsh) can be traced to introductions since the 1830s (edible frog) and the 1880s (marsh frog).

The common toad is also widespread across England and Wales but it is less frequently seen than the common frog. Many recordings are on roads, demonstrating the vulnerability of this species as it migrates to and from its traditional breeding sites. This problem has been tackled by a *Toads on Roads* project managed for the DETR by Herpetofauna Conservation International Limited. Over 400 sites are registered with this project to increase awareness and provide warnings to traffic.

The natterjack toad is now rare and has declined considerably over the last century due to habitat loss. It usually spawns in shallow water making it vulnerable to drying out of these pools in the spring or early summer, although the decline has also been linked to the acidification of ponds on heathland sites in south east England (Beebee *et al.*, 1990). The great crested newt is also on the decline with 42 per cent of the populations in the London area lost in 20 years, possibly due to habitat loss.

Rare and Vulnerable Species

The diversity of species cannot be separated from habitat diversity. In England and Wales, 27 rivers, 83 lakes, 75 gravel pits and reservoirs, 23 canals and 410 wetlands are designated as Sites of Special Scientific Interest, with fairly good coverage across all regions. Of these, 33 are designated as Wetlands of International Importance under the 1971 Ramsar Convention. Some 30 freshwater habitats are Special Protection Areas for birds under the EU Directive on the Conservation of Wild Birds (79/409/EEC), and a number of sites are due to be designated in the period 1998 to 2004 as Special Areas of Conservation under the Habitats and Species Directive (92/43/EEC). These are sites which support rare, endangered or vulnerable species of plants or animals (other than birds) or which support outstanding examples of habitats, characteristic of the region. The Agency must help to maintain the integrity of proposed Special Protection Areas and Special Areas of Conservation by ensuring no deterioration in conservation status is caused by Agency-consented activities. The Agency has worked with English Nature and the Countryside Council for Wales to identify any consents causing concern. Nationally, there are 41 sites where Agency-consented activities are being reviewed and a further 119 sites where investigative work is planned.

The Biodiversity Action Plan identifies 402 species which are rare, threatened or vulnerable (DoE, 1994). Of the 116 for which action plans have already been prepared, 47 are directly dependent on fresh waters, and for 12 of these the Environment Agency is the contact point for enquiries and information, and for 10 is the lead partner, that is, responsible for managing the action plan (Table 4.7). These species have been selected because they are most threatened or rapidly declining. For example, the Southern damselfly has declined by 30 per cent in the UK since the 1960s, and the fen orchid which used to occur in 30 sites, now only appears in four.

The action plans that are being developed specify targets to maintain and improve status where possible.

Mammals

Water vole[1]	*Arvicola terrestris*	Otter[1,2]	*Lutra lutra*

Birds

Aquatic warbler	*Acrocephalus paludicola*	Bittern	*Botaurus stellaris*

Reptiles and amphibians

Great crested newt	*Triturus cristatus*	Natterjack toad	*Bufo calamita*

Fish

Allis shad[2]	*Alosa alosa*	Pollan	*Coregonus autumnalis*
Twaite shad[2]	*Alosa fallax*	Vendace[1,2]	*Coregonus albula*

Insects

A ground beetle	*Bembidion argentoleum*	Large copper butterfly	*Lycaena dispar*
Southern damselfly[1]	*Coenagrion mercuriale*	A longhorn beetle	*Oberea oculata*
A leaf beetle	*Cryptocephalus exiguus*	A ground beetle	*Panagaeus crux-major*
Black bog ant	*Formica candida*		

Other invertebrates

Snail[1,2]	*Anisus vorticulus*	Depressed river mussel[1,2]	*Pseudanodonta complanata*
White-clawed crayfish[1]	*Austropotamobius pallipes*	Shining ram's horn snail[1]	*Segmentina nitida*
Sandbowl snail	*Catinella arenaria*	Narrow-mouth whorl snail	*Vertigo angustior*
Medicinal leech	*Hirudo medicinalis*	Round-mouth whorl snail	*Vertigo genesii*
Freshwater pearl mussel[2]	*Margaritifera margaritifera*	A whorl snail	*Vertigo geyeri*
Glutinous snail[1,2]	*Myxas glutinosa*	Desmoulins' whorl snail	*Vertigo moulinsiana*
A freshwater pea mussel[1]	*Pisidium tenuilineatum*		

Flowering plants

Ribbon-leaved water plantain[1,2]	*Alisma gramineum*	Holly-leaved naiad	*Najas marina*
Creeping marshwort	*Apium repens*	Slender naiad	*Najas flexilis*
Starfruit	*Damasonium alisma*	Shetland pondweed	*Potamogeton rutilus*
Fen orchid	*Liparis loeselii*	Three-lobed water-crowfoot	*Ranunculus tripartitus*
Floating water plantain	*Luronium natans*	Yellow marsh saxifrage	*Saxifraga hirculus*

Ferns

Killarney fern	*Trichomanes speciosum*		

Lichens

River jelly lichen[1,2]	*Collema dichotomum*		

Mosses

Derbyshire feather-moss	*Thamnobryum angustifolium*	Slender green feather-moss	*Hamatocaulis vernicosus*

Liverworts

Marsh earwort	*Jamesoniella undulifolia*	Norfolk flapwort	*Lophozia rutheana*

Stoneworts

Mossy stonewort	*Chara muscosa*		

1 The Environment Agency is the 'contact point' for enquiries and information.

2 The Environment Agency is the 'lead partner' for this species, responsible for managing the action plan.

Sites are managed to protect existing populations and include measures such as water level management, nutrient reductions (for example phosphate stripping at sewage-treatment works to protect vendace in Bassenthwaite) and pond management. Landowners' awareness and cooperation is vital for suitable land management and pond protection. In many cases, knowledge of the present distribution is incomplete so surveys are required to show where they occur (for example allis shad, river jelly lichen) and to identify suitable sites for re-introduction (for example great crested newt, natterjack toad, freshwater pearl mussel, several of the plant species). Research is needed to understand the requirements of some species, like aquatic warbler, shining ram's horn snail. Other management plans include re-creation of habitats, for example reedbeds for bitterns, and monitoring programmes are essential to show progress against targets.

4.3 The Quality of Fresh Waters as Determined by Compliance with Standards, Targets and Classification Schemes

There are many different environmental quality standards in existence that relate both to the protection of human health, such as water abstracted with the intention of potable supply, and to the protection of the environment itself, such as quality required to protect fish life. The standards are often expressed in terms of the concentration of a particular substance which must not be exceeded, according to set statistical compliance criteria. These standards may arise from EC Directives, national legislation or international agreements. There are also classification schemes which are non-statutory but provide a way of comparing quality through time, and spatially. Classification schemes are used to assess whether the principle of maintaining or improving water quality is being achieved. This section looks at compliance with statutory and non-statutory standards as well as trends in classification schemes.

EC Directives on Dangerous Substances

In accordance with the EC 'Dangerous Substances' Directive 76/464/EEC, the Agency monitors surface waters receiving List I (Black List) substances from point source discharges containing these substances. Such sources include all industrial plants liable to handle and discharge these substances and all significant discharges of these substances from sewage-treatment works. There are over 2,000 consented discharges for cadmium, 752 for mercury, 123 for hexachlorocyclohexane (HCH, also known as lindane), and less than 100 for each of the remaining List I substances. The number of monitoring points is less than the number of discharges because several discharges may share environmental monitoring points. 'Background' sites are also monitored for List I

substances at places unaffected by discharges and known as National Network (reference) sites. Sampling is monthly and results are reported annually against environmental quality standards (EQSs); these are statutory standards for List I substances (Appendix 3).

The results for the sampling sites below discharges and reference sites are plotted for cadmium, HCH, and mercury in Figure 4.26. EQS failures for List I substances in 1995 were limited to 1.3 per cent of the sites sampled. The most frequent failures were for HCH (10 sites) and cadmium (five sites). HCH failures were mainly associated with the wool processing industry, in the north east, due to residues on imported fleeces. HCH is also used to treat seeds and as a domestic wood preservative, and the Agency has advised MAFF and the Health and Safety Executive on the need for restrictions on its use to comply with the EQS. Cadmium failures in the Midlands Region related to a trade discharge which is under investigation. The others, in the South West Region, arose from minewaters which are subject to remedial action. Mercury failed at one site in the North West Region and the source discharge has been relocated to resolve the problem. The other List I substances exceeded EQSs rarely and concentrations at most sites are one or two orders of magnitude below the EQS, and often below the limit of analytical detection.

The Agency also monitors surface waters receiving List II (Grey List) substances against operational EQSs. The monitoring of List II substances will increase in April 1998 in light of the Surface Waters (Dangerous Substances) (Classification) Regulations, 1997 (SI 2560) (Appendix 3). About 1,200 sites are monitored for List II substances, and 4.6 per cent failed the operational EQS for one substance or more in 1995. EQS failures are dominated by copper, zinc and pH (Figure 4.27). The South West, Midlands, North East, and North West Regions show most failures. Of the copper failures, 41 per cent are derived from trade discharges or sewage effluent in which copper from domestic pipes is a significant source. Other sources of copper failures were mine drainage (21 per cent) and contaminated land leachate (13 per cent). Zinc and pH failures were most frequently due to water from mine workings (75 per cent and 79 per cent respectively). The cluster of zinc and pH failures in south west England were due to china clay extraction for which most consents have been tightened and discharge controls have been improved. Other failures for zinc and for most other substances were related to known point discharges (40 per cent of all failing sites) or contaminated land (nine per cent). The total picture for sources of List II failures is given in Figure 4.28. The management actions taking place to resolve the causes of failure, mainly reviewing discharge consents, are also summarised in the Figure.

The Agency monitors more sites for more pesticides than are designated under the Directive and as

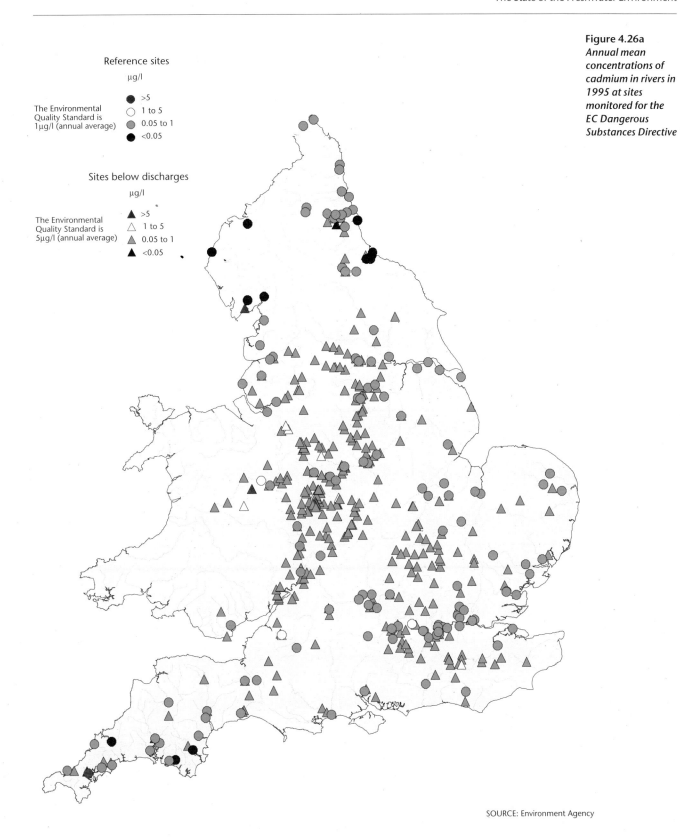

Reference sites

µg/l

- ● >5
- ○ 1 to 5
- ● 0.05 to 1
- ● <0.05

The Environmental Quality Standard is 1µg/l (annual average)

Sites below discharges

µg/l

- ▲ >5
- △ 1 to 5
- ▲ 0.05 to 1
- ▲ <0.05

The Environmental Quality Standard is 5µg/l (annual average)

SOURCE: Environment Agency

Figure 4.26b
*Annual mean
concentrations of
total HCH in rivers
in 1995 at sites
monitored for the
EC Dangerous
Substances
Directive*

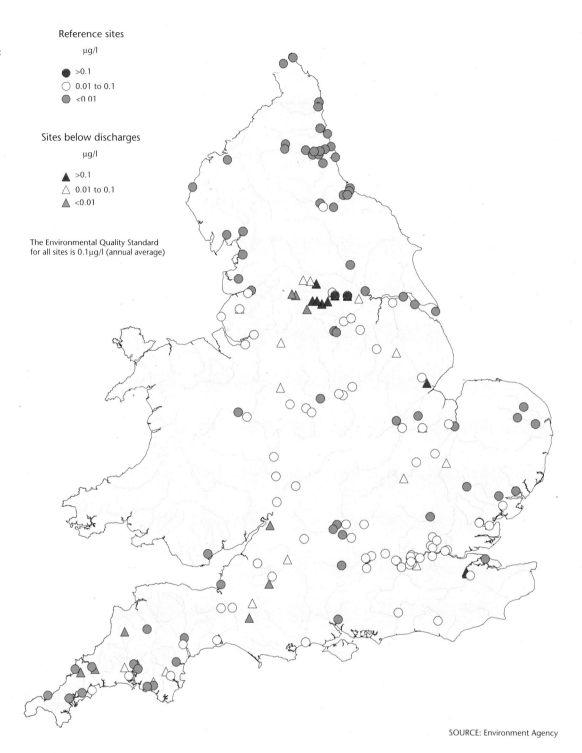

Reference sites
µg/l
● >0.1
○ 0.01 to 0.1
● <0.01

Sites below discharges
µg/l
▲ >0.1
△ 0.01 to 0.1
▲ <0.01

The Environmental Quality Standard
for all sites is 0.1µg/l (annual average)

SOURCE: Environment Agency

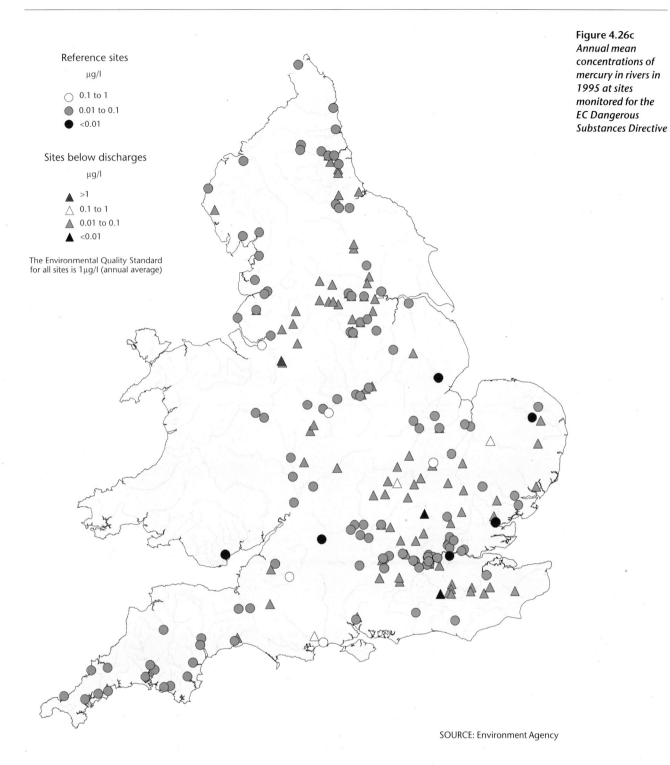

SOURCE: Environment Agency

Figure 4.26c
Annual mean concentrations of mercury in rivers in 1995 at sites monitored for the EC Dangerous Substances Directive

Reference sites

µg/l

○ 0.1 to 1
⬤ 0.01 to 0.1
● <0.01

Sites below discharges

µg/l

▲ >1
△ 0.1 to 1
▲ 0.01 to 0.1
▲ <0.01

The Environmental Quality Standard for all sites is 1µg/l (annual average)

Figure 4.27
River sites exceeding operational environmental quality standards for List II substances (non-pesticides) in 1995

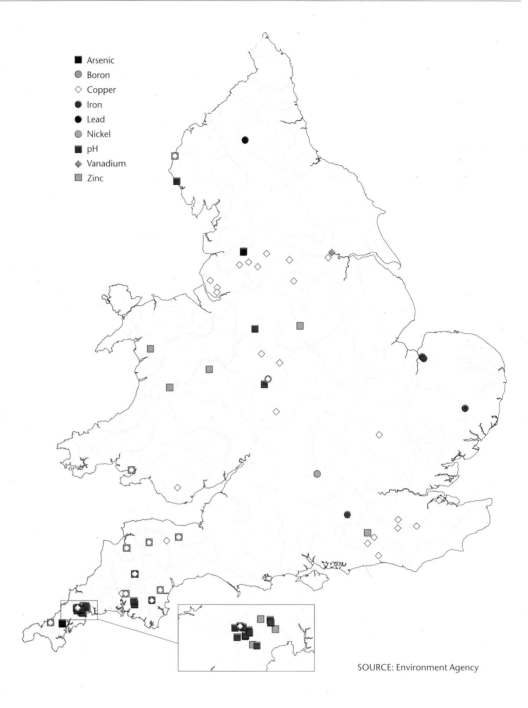

Arsenic
Boron
Copper
Iron
Lead
Nickel
pH
Vanadium
Zinc

SOURCE: Environment Agency

Figure 4.28
Sources of List II substances failing operational environmental quality standards and corresponding management actions, 1995

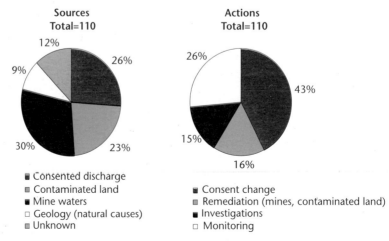

Sources
Total=110

12%
9%
26%
30%
23%

Actions
Total=110

26%
43%
15%
16%

■ Consented discharge
■ Contaminated land
■ Mine waters
□ Geology (natural causes)
■ Unknown

■ Consent change
■ Remediation (mines, contaminated land)
■ Investigations
□ Monitoring

Some sites fail more than one standard. The source of each failure has been included in this figure   SOURCE: Environment Agency

reported above. Monitoring of pesticides in groundwaters was undertaken for 124 pesticides at 580 sites in 1995, and for 158 pesticides at about 2,000 surface water sites. Over 450 pesticides are approved for use but it is too expensive to monitor for all of them. Those which are most likely to find their way into fresh waters are given priority. The monitoring results have been assessed against relevant statutory EQSs and proposed EQSs where there are no statutory standards in force. About eight per cent of surface water sites exceeded the statutory or proposed EQS for at least one pesticide. Comparison of the data with List I EQSs shows the HCH failures mentioned

above, six more HCH exceedances, six of dieldrin and three others (total DDT, ppDDT and hexachlorobenzene) (Figure 4.29). The number of failures is greater than under the Directive monitoring because the sites monitored under the Directive only relate to known point sources. Most pesticide runoff is diffuse. Exceedances are clustered around the Aire catchment in the north east. Comparison with EQSs proposed by DETR shows that cyfluthrin (an insecticide), permethrin (an insecticide) and PCSD (a moth proofing agent) caused most exceedances (Figure 4.29). The majority of failures were associated with the textile industry in the Pennines and the

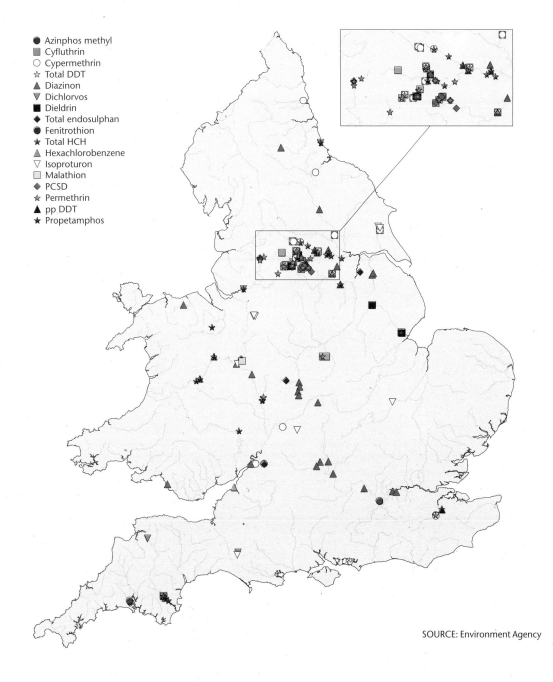

● Azinphos methyl
■ Cyfluthrin
○ Cypermethrin
☆ Total DDT
▲ Diazinon
▽ Dichlorvos
■ Dieldrin
◆ Total endosulphan
● Fenitrothion
★ Total HCH
▲ Hexachlorobenzene
▽ Isoproturon
■ Malathion
◆ PCSD
★ Permethrin
▲ pp DDT
★ Propetamphos

Figure 4.29
River sites exceeding standards for pesticides, 1995

SOURCE: Environment Agency

Figure 4.30
Pesticides most frequently exceeding 0.1ug/l in rivers, 1992 to 1995

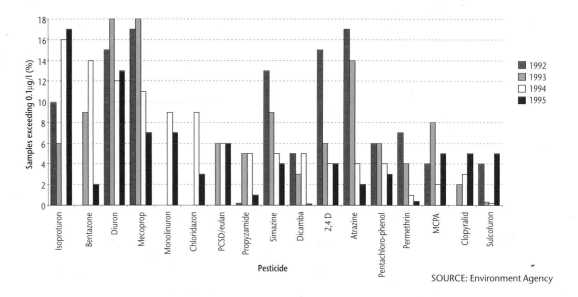

SOURCE: Environment Agency

Figure 4.31
Pesticides most frequently exceeding 0.1ug/l in groundwaters, 1992 to 1995

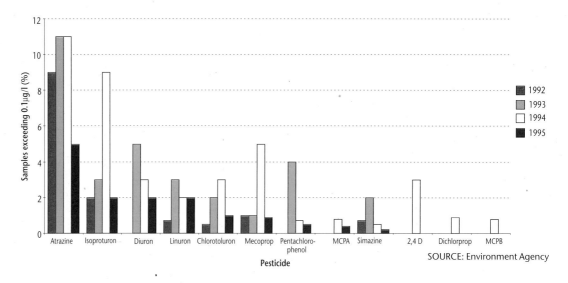

SOURCE: Environment Agency

Agency is working to resolve these problems. The sheep dip pesticides diazinon, propetamphos and cypermethrin, and isoproturon (a herbicide for crops), cause non-statutory EQS failures throughout the Regions, though the Midlands and the North East are most affected.

Pesticide contamination for each of the years 1992 to 1995, is given in Figures 4.30 and 4.31, for surface and groundwaters. These show the percentage of samples exceeding 0.1µg/l, the limit set for individual pesticides in the EC Drinking Water Directive. It is not directly applicable to fresh waters but because waters are abstracted for potable supply, it is a useful indicative limit in some cases, although some pesticides which fail EQSs do not appear in these figures because the EQSs are much more stringent than the 0.1µg/l indicative limit. They reveal the frequent occurrence of agricultural herbicides such as isoproturon and mecoprop in surface and groundwaters, and that atrazine and simazine in surface waters and groundwaters have declined since their ban from non-agricultural use in 1993, although atrazine continues to appear in groundwaters.

Declines in concentrations are expected to be slow because of the long residence times in groundwaters. The continuing use of atrazine on maize is of concern in some areas.

EC Directive on Water Quality Suitable for Freshwater Fish

The EC Freshwater Fish Directive (78/659/EEC) aims to protect and improve water quality in order to support fish life. Regulations were made in UK law in 1997. About 19,500km of rivers and canals are designated under this Directive, either as salmonid waters (suitable for salmon and trout) or as cyprinid waters (suitable for roach, bream, chub). Standards are specified for chemical substances and physical conditions. The salmonid standards are tighter than those for cyprinid waters, reflecting their need for cleaner water. The imperative standards include temperature, dissolved oxygen, pH, ammonium and zinc but there are also guideline values for many substances (Appendix 4). Derogations may be applied to waters which fail the Directive as a result of exceptional weather or special geographical conditions, and where it can be shown that it has no effect on the balance of fish populations. The Directive only considers water quality aspects required by fish and does not require an assessment of fisheries themselves. Compliance with the Directive does not guarantee healthy fish populations because there are many other factors, both natural and man-made such as habitat and flow regime, that affect fisheries.

There are a large number of salmonid waters in the north of England, Wales and the south west, and the rivers of lowland England generally comply with cyprinid status. Failures with standards occur in isolated patches (Figure 4.32). The Agency reports compliance with the Fish Directive annually to the DETR. In 1996, out of a total of 2,288 stretches, 150 (6.5 per cent) were non-compliant, covering 1,220.6km and a further 28 were given derogations.

Figure 4.32
River stretches designated under the EC Freshwater Fish Directive and those failing the standards in 1995

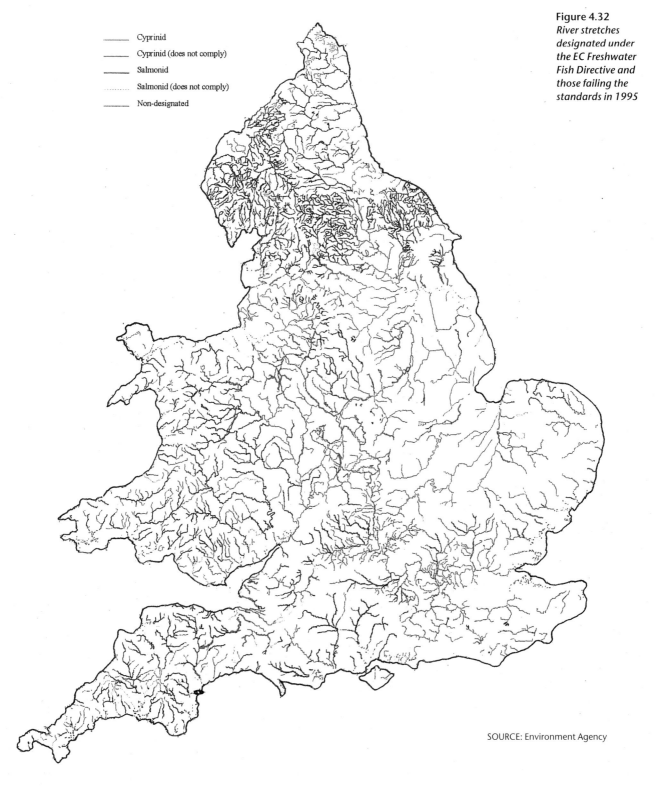

Cyprinid

Cyprinid (does not comply)

Salmonid

Salmonid (does not comply)

Non-designated

SOURCE: Environment Agency

Figure 4.33
*Reasons for failure
of the EC Freshwater
Fish Directive and
corresponding
management
actions, 1996*

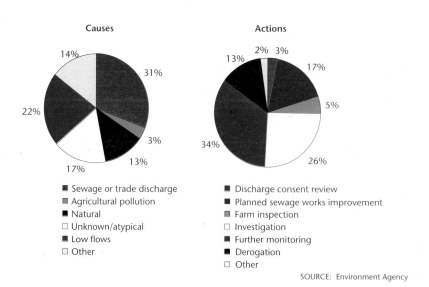

SOURCE: Environment Agency

Five determinands accounted for all failures: dissolved oxygen at 44 per cent of failing sites, total ammonia at 28 per cent of sites, un-ionised ammonia at 11 per cent of sites, pH at 15 per cent and zinc at one per cent (a few sites failed on more than one determinand). Low flows exacerbated by the 1995 and 1996 drought were considered the principal cause for 22 per cent of failures to comply with the Fish Directive (Figure 4.33). The reduced flows caused low oxygen concentrations and reduced the dilution of pollutants. Increased nutrient concentrations and temperatures allowed the build up of algal populations causing pH to exceed the upper limit at some sites. Low flows were particularly significant in the Southern, South West and North East Regions in 1995 and 1996.

Sewage or trade discharges accounted for 31 per cent of failures. By 1999, there are planned improvements in effluent quality by the water companies at 17 per cent of failing sites. Discharge consent reviews are being undertaken for three per cent of the failures and further investigations are planned at 26 per cent of the sites. Agricultural pollution was the main factor for three per cent of failures and the Agency has targeted farm inspections in just over half of these catchments. Where the cause of failure was unknown and atypical of past results, monitoring will continue and action will be taken if a recurrent problem is found.

Surface Water Abstraction Directive

The EC Directive on the quality of surface water abstracted for potable supply (75/440/EEC) specifies mandatory limits for 21 substances and guideline values for 31 substances. These apply at designated sites where water is abstracted for potable supply, and the level of treatment applied to the abstracted water must be consistent with the minimum requirements specified in the Directive for waters of the relevant class. It is the duty of the Agency to implement the requirements of the regulations made, and the

Directions given, by the Secretary of State in respect of these Directives, including the sampling and monitoring regime which reflect that in the Directive 79/869/EEC. The Agency reports compliance to the DETR for more than 450 sites which have been designated by the Secretary of State (Figure 4.34).

Some 136 sites failed the standard for one or more substances in 1996 although there were no failures at any sites for nine of the 21 substances. The most frequent failures were for dissolved hydrocarbons, colour, copper, dissolved iron, nitrate and polyaromatic hydrocarbons. This apparently high level of failure does not cause concern for several reasons. The analytical methodology for dissolved hydrocarbons is not very robust at detecting failures, the sampling rate at many sites is low which means that a single poor sample records a failure, and natural sources cause many of the hydrocarbon, colour and iron failures. In all cases, there is treatment after the abstraction point (and the sampling site used for the Directive) before the water is put into public supply to ensure that the standards required in the Drinking Water Directive (80/778/EEC) are met at the customer's tap. The standards and methodologies linked to this Directive will be reviewed as part of the proposed new Water Framework Directive.

Nitrate Limits in EC Directives

The EC Directive on the quality of surface water abstracted for potable supply (75/440/EEC) specifies a mandatory limit for nitrate of 50mg/l (11.3mg/l expressed as N) to be met by 95 per cent of samples. The EC Directive relating to the quality of water intended for human consumption (80/778/EEC) also specifies the same limit which applies to drinking water at the tap as set out in the Water Supply (Water Quality) Regulations (SI 1989 No1147) although in this case, it is a maximum admissible concentration. Two other Directives, the Urban Waste Water

Treatment Directive (91/271/EEC) and the Nitrate Directive (91/676/EEC) refer to the nitrate limit specified in the Surface Water Abstraction Directive as relevant criteria in identifying specific areas for further action, usually pollution control measures.

There are over 450 sites designated under the Surface Water Abstraction Directive where this nitrate limit applies. Nitrate concentrations in groundwater used for potable supply need to be kept below the 50mg/l standard if costly treatment or blending is to be avoided. Nitrate data from about 750 boreholes are collected by the Agency from water companies on a routine basis. Where surface waters or groundwaters

exceed or are at risk of exceeding the 50mg/l limit, then Nitrate Vulnerable Zones have been designated in accordance with the EC Directive on the control of nitrate pollution from agricultural sources (91/676/EEC). There are 68 designated Nitrate Vulnerable Zones in total covering an area of 600,000ha of which six are surface waters zones, comprising nine catchments, and the rest are groundwater zones. Within these zones there are over 140 boreholes used for abstraction purposes.

Nitrate Vulnerable Zones were designated in 1996 and there is a requirement for Action Programmes to change agricultural practices in these areas to reduce

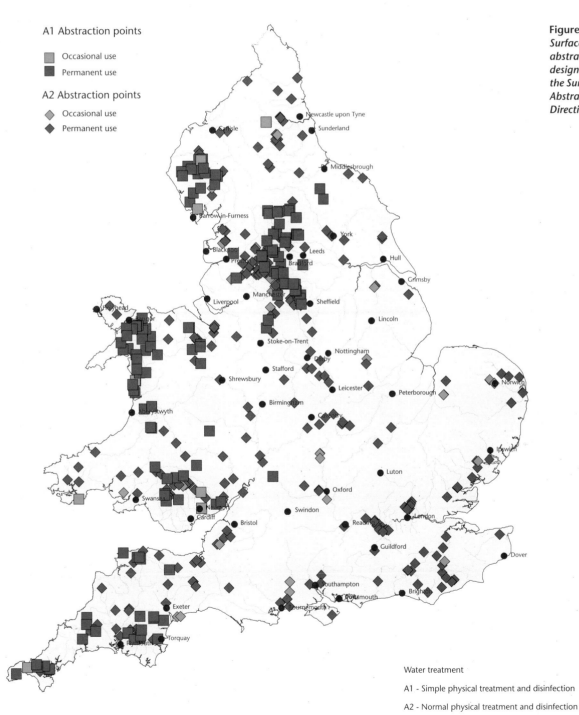

A1 Abstraction points

  Occasional use
  Permanent use

A2 Abstraction points

  Occasional use
  Permanent use

Figure 4.34
Surface water abstraction points designated under the Surface Water Abstraction Directive

Water treatment

A1 - Simple physical treatment and disinfection

A2 - Normal physical treatment and disinfection

SOURCE: Environment Agency

Figure 4.35
Nitrate Vulnerable Zones as designated in 1996

SOURCE: MAFF

nitrate runoff and nitrate leaching. These programmes will commence in 1998. A scheme of grant-aid for improvements to storage of livestock manure has been introduced where changes are needed in Nitrate Vulnerable Zones. The Nitrate Vulnerable Zones are mainly in the Midlands, East Anglia and the north east where the greatest amount of arable farming takes place. The largest Nitrate Vulnerable Zones are catchments upstream of surface water abstractions, but most zones are smaller areas, designated to protect groundwater sources, either individually or in groups where whole aquifer protection is required (Figure 4.35). Three Nitrate Vulnerable Zones are also designated as Sensitive Areas (Nitrate) under the Urban

Waste Water Treatment Directive. Where there are sewage-treatment works with a population equivalence exceeding 10,000 in these Sensitive Areas (Nitrate), then there is a requirement for further treatment (more stringent than secondary) as specified in the Urban Waste Water Treatment Directive. This requirement applies in three river systems in the Anglian Region, in the catchments of the Waveney, Great Ouse and Blackwater Nitrate Vulnerable Zones where public supply abstractions exhibit elevated winter nitrate concentrations. As a result of the designations, nitrogen reduction requirements in the discharge consents of eight large sewage-treatment works will come into effect by the end of December 1998.

Figure 4.36
*Nitrate
concentrations in
selected
groundwaters,
1980 to 1996*

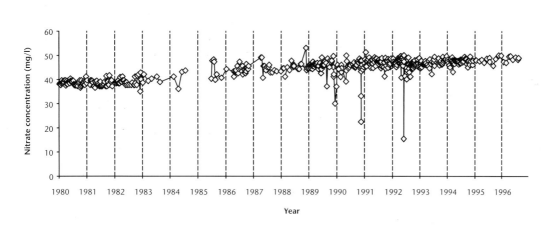

a. Tom Hill borehole in the Midlands Region, in the Permo-Triassic sandstone

Data for 1985 to 1989 measured as total oxidised nitrogen

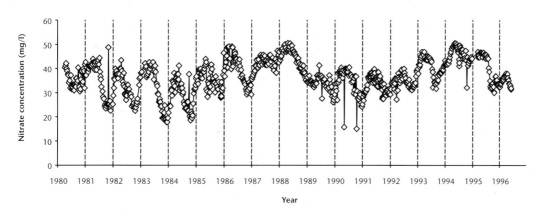

b. Branston Booths borehole in the Anglian Region, in the Jurassic limestone

SOURCE: Environment Agency

Prior to these Directives, the UK government was also concerned about high nitrate concentrations in groundwater. Where these exceeded or were at risk of exceeding 50mg/l, Nitrate Sensitive Areas were set up. Ten were designated in 1990 and a further 22 in 1994, covering a total of 35,000ha of eligible agricultural land. Within these areas, farmers are compensated by MAFF for voluntary restrictions to their fertilizer usage and farming practices which go well beyond good agricultural practice. All these Areas are now also within Nitrate Vulnerable Zones.

The concentration of nitrate in groundwater depends on the aquifer type as well as farming practice, and Figure 4.36 shows the 16-year trends in a typical sandstone and limestone aquifer. Unconfined aquifers tend to respond more rapidly to nitrate changes than confined aquifers where it may take several decades for surface water to move through the aquifer. Similarly, aquifers such as limestone, where the

majority of the flow is through fissures, tend to respond more rapidly to rainfall than sandstone aquifers. The nitrate concentrations show a steady increase in the sandstone aquifer whereas variability within each year is greater for the limestone aquifer without any obvious long-term trend.

Nitrate concentrations in rivers fluctuate more rapidly than groundwaters, exhibiting a strong seasonal pattern (Figure 4.37) with greater concentrations at times of high runoff, as demonstrated by a scatter plot (Figure 4.38). Concentrations can be particularly high when heavy autumn rain falls after dry summers and when there has been a build up of nitrogen in the soil. These have caused short term exceedances of the limit at many river abstraction points.

Evidence from a long-time series of test results for the lower River Thames show that nitrate concentrations have increased substantially since the 1940s but that

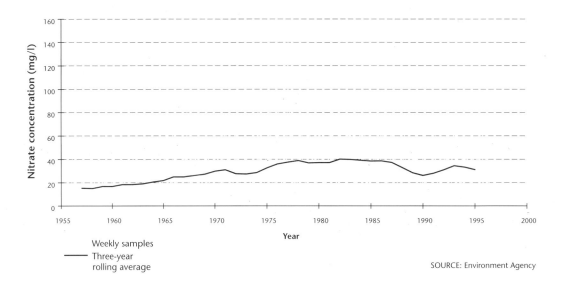

Weekly samples
Three-year rolling average

SOURCE: Environment Agency

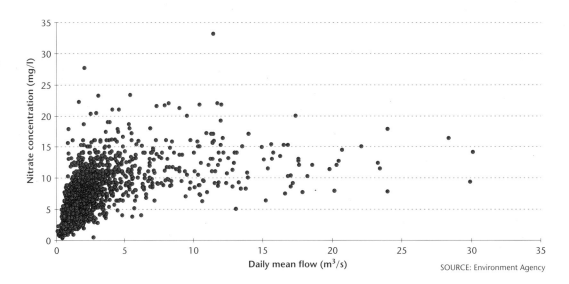

SOURCE: Environment Agency

they are fairly stable now (Figure 4.39). (The data in Figure 4.39 have been flow-weighted to dampen the effects of seasonal variation.) This pattern is expected to be fairly common across the country, as endorsed by Figure 4.37. However, nitrate concentrations are still increasing in some groundwaters due to the lag time for pollutants to move through aquifers with implications for rivers. Sites where nitrate concentrations are still increasing are given in Section 4.5. The change since the 1940s is due to changing agricultural practices. This results not just from increased application of nitrate-rich fertilizer, but also from ploughing established grassland and from the trend towards new crops with higher nitrate requirements such as oil seed rape. River nitrate concentrations show initially low levels during the stable agricultural practices prevalent in the 1930s before the Second World War (Figure 4.39). With the need for greater food production, nitrate concentrations rose steeply with the ploughing of grassland and subsequent intensification of agriculture during and after the Second World War. Further increases occurred in the 1960s with the

greater use of nitrogenous fertilizers. There are a few inconsistencies in later years. For example, the decrease in 1973 was probably caused by the energy crises of that time.

The UK Government's commitment to the Paris Convention and the International Conference on the North Sea Task Force includes the monitoring of nutrient inputs to the sea. The total nitrogen load discharged to the sea from England and Wales over the period 1990 to 1995 has varied between 179 thousand tonnes in 1992 to 274 thousand tonnes in 1993. The largest single input was from the River Trent into the Humber estuary followed by the River Severn and the River Thames, reflecting the size, nature and land-use of the catchment areas draining into these rivers. The inputs from individual estuaries have remained fairly constant in all but the Wash, where there appears to be a trend of increasing nitrogen load (NRA, 1995b). But this conclusion is tentative due to difficulties in estimating loads accurately. (Littlewood *et al.*, 1997)

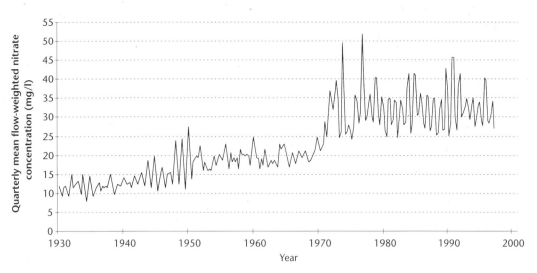

Figure 4.39
*Nitrate
concentrations in
the River Thames at
Walton, Surrey,
1930 to 1997*

SOURCE: Onstad and Blake, and the Environment Agency

Radioactivity

Radioactive substances may be present in fresh waters from natural sources or from human activity. Natural sources include cosmic ray bombardment producing radionuclides in the atmosphere which are subsequently transferred to the earth's surface, but the main natural source is leaching of radioactive substances from rocks and soils into groundwater. The human dose from natural background radiation averages 2.2mSv per year (Hughes *et al.*, 1993). Anthropogenic sources include routine discharges of liquid radioactive wastes to the environment from nuclear establishments, hospitals, research and industrial processes. Routine discharges may only be made in accordance with authorisations issued under the Radioactive Substances Act 1993. Other uncontrolled sources include atmospheric fall-out from nuclear weapons testing and accidents (such as occurred at Chernobyl in 1986).

Because exposure to radiation can come from both external and internal sources simultaneously, the standards relating to radiation are those of total dose received. The standard for humans is 1mSv per year from all anthropogenic sources. In order to protect the human population, all discharges are controlled on the basis of how radionuclides could result in exposure to radiation of members of the public and what this would mean in terms of dose. There are therefore no standards for individual radionuclides in the environment in England and Wales (although there are standards for them in any discharges, which are very carefully monitored). In order to give some level of comparison, reference can sometimes be made to the World Health Organisation's (WHO) guideline value for potable water of 0.1Bq/l for gross alpha and 1.0Bq/l for gross beta from all sources, natural and anthropogenic (WHO, 1993). These values are low and can be exceeded by naturally occurring radiation in some locations. The values represent concentrations below which water can be considered potable without

any further radiological examination. Tritium is a low energy emitter not detected by gross beta measurement and is reported separately.

Monitoring of radioactivity in the freshwater environment is undertaken by the Environment Agency. The Agency manages a programme on behalf of the Department of the Environment, Transport and the Regions and in collaboration with water companies to monitor radioactivity in water used as public drinking water sources (Newstead *et al.*, 1994). The Agency also monitors a wide range of rivers, ponds, lakes and reservoirs principally in the vicinity of nuclear sites in support of its regulatory functions under the Radioactive Substances Act (Environment Agency, 1996c). Measurements are also made by MAFF in support of their monitoring of radioactivity in freshwater fish and other foodstuffs (MAFF, 1995). Other monitoring is undertaken by nuclear site operators to check for migration of radioactivity into local surface and groundwaters. In addition to gross alpha and gross beta activity, a wide range of radionuclide specific measurements are made under these monitoring programmes. The results are reported annually by the relevant organisations.

The concentrations of gross alpha activity, gross beta activity and tritium reported for 1995 are shown in Figure 4.40 for sites in England and Wales. Results for gross alpha and gross beta activities for fresh waters used as sources of drinking water are all below the WHO's guideline values. Half of the results for alpha activity are below the limit of detection of 0.02Bq/l and the other half are within a narrow range of 0.03 to 0.07Bq/l. Positive values above the limit of detection for gross beta activity of 0.05Bq/l were recorded for all but the deep groundwater source. These positive values are also within a narrow range of 0.05 to 0.54Bq/l. These variations reflect local geology with higher values containing evaluated levels of radioactive potassium-40 leached from rocks in hard water areas. All tritium results for these waters are consistent with

SOURCE: Environment Agency

Figure 4.40
*Gross alpha, beta
and tritium activity
in certain surface
waters abstracted
for public supply
and in the vicinity of
nuclear sites, 1995*

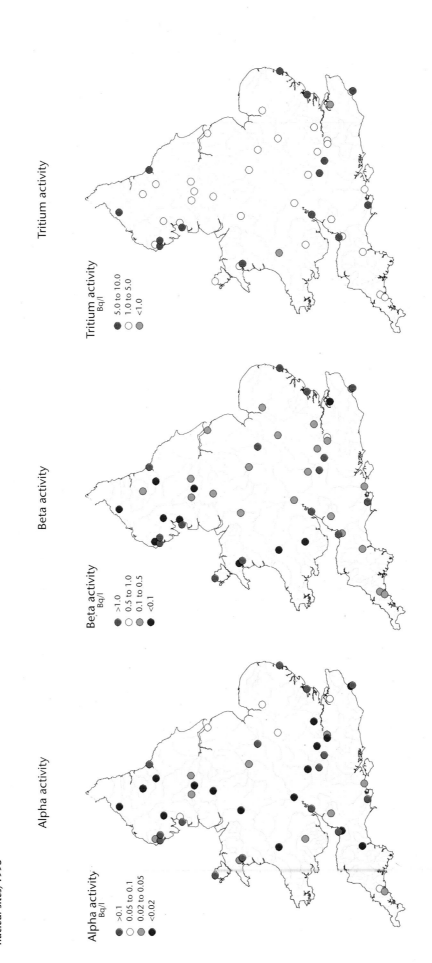

Tritium activity

Tritium activity
Bq/l
- 5.0 to 10.0
- 1.0 to 5.0
- <1.0

Beta activity

Beta activity
Bq/l
- >1.0
- 0.5 to 1.0
- 0.1 to 0.5
- <0.1

Alpha activity

Alpha activity
Bq/l
- >0.1
- 0.05 to 0.1
- 0.02 to 0.05
- <0.02

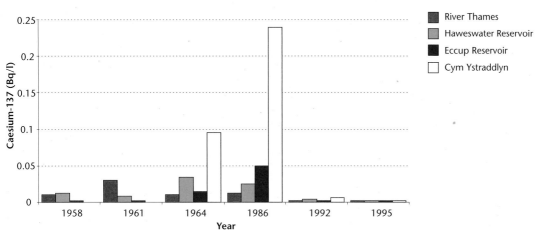

SOURCE: Environment Agency

Figure 4.41
Caesium-137 in waters at four sites in England and Wales, 1958 to 1995

the expected background range of one to ten Bq/l. Some variations within this narrow range are exhibited. Deep groundwaters, which are isolated from surface deposition, are generally the lowest and large surface reservoirs have the highest values.

The only measurable variations over time in surface water samples have been in caesium-137, strontium-90 and iodine-125, the first being most abundant. Results for caesium-137 in river waters at four sites in England and Wales from 1958 to 1995 are given in Figure 4.41. The peak in 1964 is related to fall-out from atmospheric testing of nuclear weapons during the late 1950s. The peak in 1986 was caused by atmospheric fall-out from the Chernobyl accident in that year. Concentrations have subsequently declined to very low levels.

Gross alpha and gross beta activities, marginally in excess of the World Health Organisation's guideline values, and elevated tritium results are reported for some small streams and ditches close to certain nuclear sites. In these cases elevated concentrations may also be found in sediments which can give rise to enhanced gamma radiation dose-rates at the margins

of the stream or ditch. These situations can arise from authorised discharges of low level radioactive waste waters to local streams, or rainwater washout of radioactivity from authorised atmospheric emissions. Other potential sources include off-site migration of contaminated groundwaters and runoff storm waters contaminated by on-site incidents. The reported elevated levels of radioactivity in water and sediment and any associated enhanced gamma dose-rates are kept under regular review by the Agency and are considered to be radiologically insignificant (Environment Agency, 1996c).

Radioactive substances in fresh water and sediments can transfer to fish and aquatic plants. Radionuclide specific results from MAFF's monitoring in the vicinity of certain nuclear sites are detailed in Table 4.8 for a range of fish and plants. Concentrations of radiocaesium in all species of freshwater fish are less than 1,000Bq/kg. They are kept under regular review by MAFF and are considered to be radiologically insignificant (MAFF, 1995). For example, in the vicinity of Harwell on the River Thames, the radiation dose to anglers in 1993 from fish consumption and principally from sitting on the river bank was 0.01mSv

Site	Material	Caesium-137 for 1995	Caesium-137 for 1996
Trawsfynydd (lake)	brown trout	140±1.4	180±1.8
River Thames near Pangbourne	pike	0.59±0.06	0.54±0.09
River Thames near Pangbourne	water lily	0.14±0.04	0.09±0.07
Grand Union Canal near Amersham	pike	0.34±0.07	0.24±0.06
Grand Union Canal near Amersham	water lily	0.03±0.02	0.03±0.02
Devoke Water	brown trout	74±1.7	79±0.8
River Thames near Harwell	pike	7.1±0.1	5.0±0.1
River Thames near Harwell	water lily	1.6±0.1	0.99±0.07
River Thames near Harwell	mud	570±4.7	470±4.4

Table 4.8
Radioactivity concentration (wet) in environmental materials close to five nuclear sites in England and Wales, 1995 and 1996 (Bq/kg).

Source: MAFF, 1996, 1997

Figure 4.42
Radiocaesium in brown trout in Ennerdale Water, Cumbria, following the Chernobyl accident, 1986 to 1995

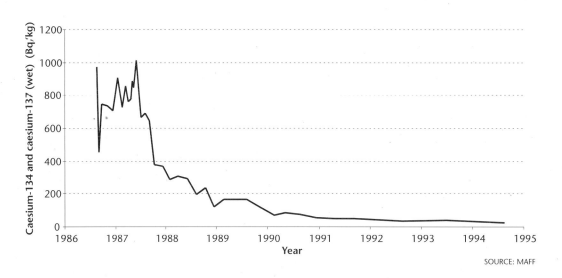

SOURCE: MAFF

or one per cent of the dose limit of 1mSv per year. Figure 4.42 shows the decline in radiocaesium, originating from Chernobyl fall-out, in brown trout from Ennerdale Water in Cumbria. In recent years the rate of decline has reduced and it is likely that levels have now become more stable.

Classification of Water Quality in Rivers and Canals

The Agency has a national method for classifying the water quality of rivers and canals, known as the General Quality Assessment scheme (GQA). This is designed to provide an accurate and consistent assessment of the state of water quality across England and Wales and changes in this state over time. It replaces previous classification schemes that were applied differently across England and Wales. The scheme consists of separate 'windows', to cover a range of ways of describing water quality. The Chemical GQA describes quality in terms of three chemical measurements (ammonia, dissolved oxygen and biochemical oxygen demand) which detect the most common types of pollution, including discharges of treated organic wastes from sewage-treatment works, agriculture and industry. It allocates one of six grades (A to F) to each stretch of river. The Biological GQA is another measure of quality based on monitoring the invertebrates which live on the bed of the river. It also allocates one of six grades (a to f) to each stretch. Additional windows for nutrients (orthophosphate and nitrate) and aesthetics are still being developed. Full details are given in Appendix 5. The scheme replaces a former scheme developed by the National Water Council which reported every five years (Quinquennial Survey). This reporting cycle has continued.

There were about 8,000 sites assessed, representing some 40,000km of rivers and canals, on samples taken from 1993 to 1995, the last Quinquennial Survey. The chemical results show:

91 per cent of rivers are Very Good to Fair (grades A to D);

eight per cent of rivers are Poor (grade E);

one per cent of rivers are Bad (grade F);

40.2 per cent (13,300km) of rivers improved since 1990;

12.6 per cent (4,200km) of rivers deteriorated since 1990;

there was a net upgrading of 28 per cent between 1990 and 1995.

The spatial distribution is shown in Figure 4.43 and the regional differences are summarised in Figure 4.44. Most grade A and B rivers occur in the South West and Welsh Regions, and the greatest proportion of lower graded rivers are in the North West and North East Regions, especially around the urban conurbations of Greater Manchester and West Yorkshire. The results demonstrate that river quality has improved nationally, although these figures relate to a change in grade recorded rather than a statistically significant change in grade. There is a statistical chance that the grade assigned to individual river stretches will be in error. When only statistically significant changes in grades are considered (at the 95 per cent confidence level), then one per cent (225km) show deterioration and nine per cent (3,400km) show improvement, a net improvement of eight per cent (Figure 4.45).

Based on samples taken in 1995, the biology results show:

93 per cent of rivers are graded Very Good or Fair (grades a to d);

five per cent or rivers are Poor (grade e);

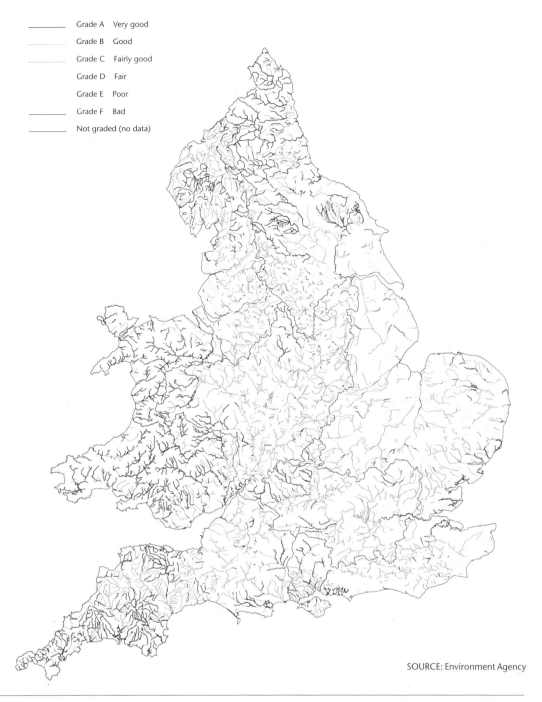

Grade A   Very good
Grade B   Good
Grade C   Fairly good
Grade D   Fair
Grade E   Poor
Grade F   Bad
Not graded (no data)

SOURCE: Environment Agency

Figure 4.43
*General Quality
Assessment for
chemical river
quality, 1993 to
1995*

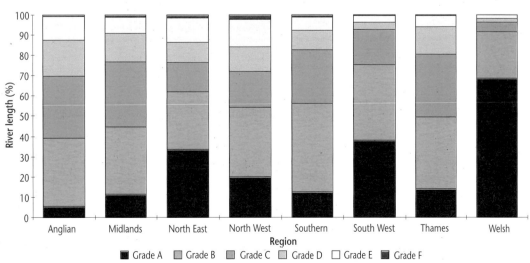

Figure 4.44
*General Quality
Assessment for
chemical river
quality by region,
1993 to 1995*

SOURCE: Environment Agency

two per cent of rivers are Bad (grade f) (Figure 4.46);

38.4 per cent (11,511km) improved since 1990;

12.8 per cent (3,851km) deteriorated since 1990;

there was a net upgrading of 26 per cent between 1990 and 1995.

The regional distribution of biological quality is summarised in Figure 4.47, which clearly shows that the South West, Southern and Welsh Regions have the highest proportion of grade a and b rivers, and a similar pattern as for the chemical classification. Biologically Poor and Bad quality rivers are mainly in the urban areas, and rural areas show better quality generally but there are some very large differences too. For individual reaches, only two per cent (526km) showed a drop in grade that was significant at the 95 per cent confidence level, nine per cent (2,655km) showed an improvement in grade (Figures 4.48 and 4.49).

Whilst the overall picture from the chemical and biological GQA is similar, locally there are distinct differences. Twenty per cent (8,000km) of the total river length assessed differs by more than two grades between chemistry and biology. Of this length, almost half has a quality where chemistry is good but biology is poor. A direct correspondence between the biological and chemical grades is not expected because the classification schemes are independent and measure different features of the environment. Although biology grades generally mirror those in chemistry, there is a tendency for there to be more places in the south and east where biology is significantly better than chemistry, and more places in the north and west where the opposite holds true (Figure 4.50). It is thought that this reflects several factors.

The chemical grade is based on three determinands (biochemical oxygen demand, dissolved oxygen and ammonia) whereas there are other substances, for example, metals and pesticides, that affect the biology. Hence the biology gives an integrated assessment of the effect of all pollutants. In some cases chemical water quality may be good but river sediments, upon which the animals live, may be contaminated and may remain so for many years. The biology will reflect any such sediment contamination whereas the chemistry will not. But there are other factors to consider too. Physical river management such as abstractions, culverting, impoundment and dredging will affect chemistry and biology to different extents. The consequences of predation and disease could reduce biological quality.

Figure 4.45
Significant changes in chemical river quality between 1990 and 1995

Significant upgrade
Significant downgrade
No significant change

SOURCE: Environment Agency

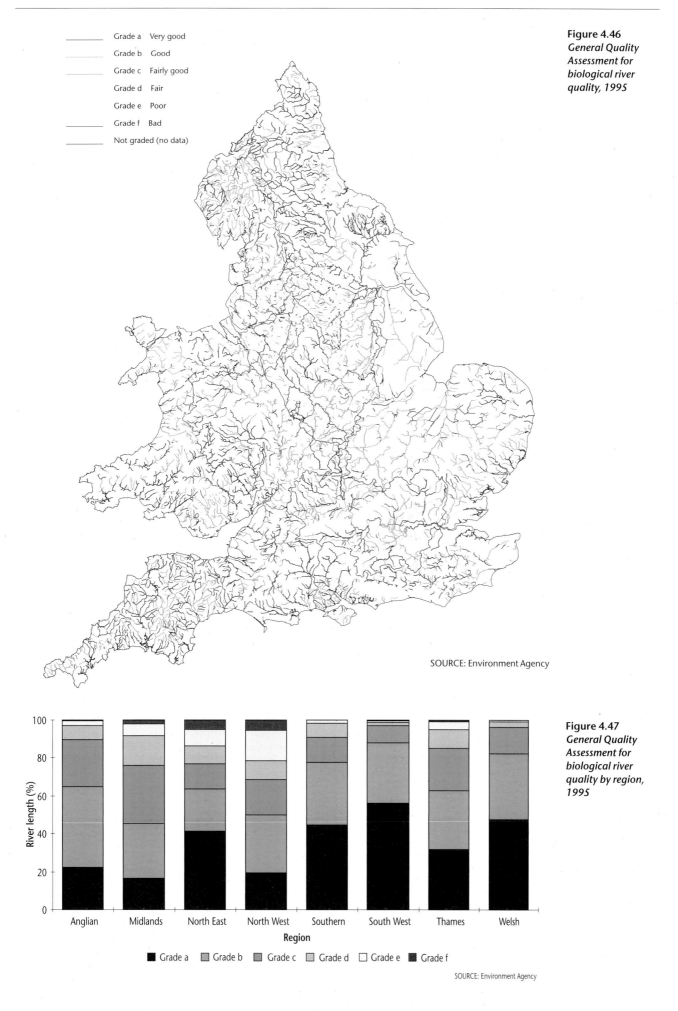

Grade a   Very good
Grade b   Good
Grade c   Fairly good
Grade d   Fair
Grade e   Poor
Grade f   Bad
Not graded (no data)

Figure 4.46
*General Quality
Assessment for
biological river
quality, 1995*

SOURCE: Environment Agency

Figure 4.47
*General Quality
Assessment for
biological river
quality by region,
1995*

Grade a   Grade b   Grade c   Grade d   Grade e   Grade f

SOURCE: Environment Agency

113

Figure 4.48
*Change in General
Quality Assessment
biological river
quality in regions,
1990 to 1995*

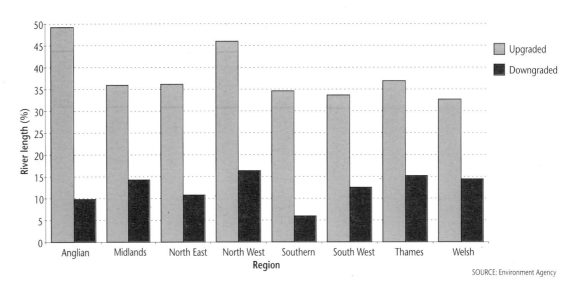

SOURCE: Environment Agency

Figure 4.49
*Significant changes
in biological river
quality between
1990 and 1995*

SOURCE: Environment Agency

The 'windows' are different measures of quality, each with their own value.

Where chemical quality is worse than biological quality this could be biased by the biology being monitored only in 1995 whereas chemistry was assessed over the period 1993 to 1995. In the south and east many GQA chemical classes are lower than expected because biochemical oxygen demand results are influenced by algae. These algae consume oxygen during the laboratory test resulting in a lower biochemical oxygen demand grade (due to higher biochemical oxygen demand readings) than probably exists in the river. In cases such as these, less damage is probably being done to the environment than the chemistry indicates. The chemical GQA largely measures the impact of sewage pollution whilst in some parts of the country other factors such as industrial effluent, acidification or intermittent storm sewer overflows influence biological quality more strongly. This may help, in part, to explain the better chemical than biological GQA classes in the north and west.

The improvements in both chemical and biological classifications from 1990 to 1995 reflect investment by the water industry in improving sewage-treatment work facilities as well as a reduction in the number of significant pollution incidents by pollution prevention activities, and higher river flows during 1993 to 1995 compared with 1988 to 1990. The

Biological grade better than chemical grade
Chemical grade better than biological grade
No significant difference

Figure 4.50
Differences between river chemical and biological General Quality Assessment, 1995

SOURCE: Environment Agency

Figure 4.51
Concentrations of total ammonia, un-ionised ammonia and dissolved oxygen during the operation of a storm overflow in Yorkshire

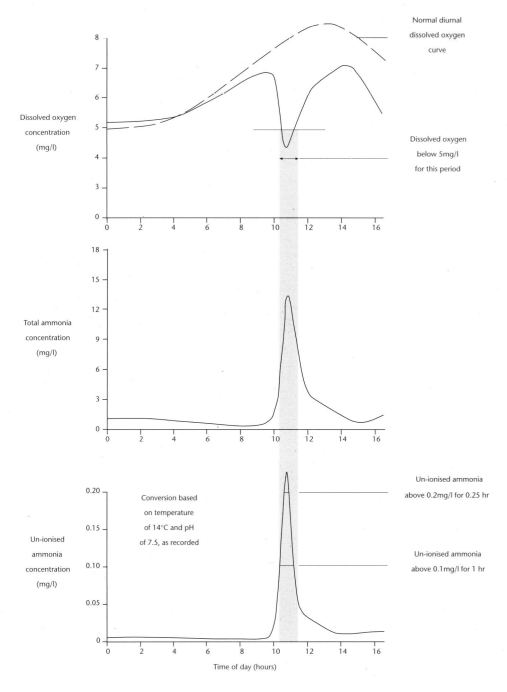

SOURCE: Foundation for Water Research

remaining areas of poor quality correlate well with areas of dense populations where urban runoff, overloaded sewerage systems, and a large volume of point discharges contribute to the poor quality. Better quality rivers exist where sewage-treatment works are few. However, the impact of recent droughts on water quality is also becoming evident. Sampling at the GQA chemical sites continues every year even though a full Survey, with biology, only takes place every five years. The results for the chemical GQA sites for 1996 show a slight reduction in the improvements seen in the 1995 results, particularly in the North East Region and other regions where droughts and low flows have occurred in 1995 and 1996 (Figure 4.7, Section 4.1). Other regions, e.g the South West and Welsh, where

drought conditions have not existed, show continued improvement (Appendix 5). As drought conditions continue in parts of the country, the deterioration on water quality is expected to continue, especially in headwaters suffering reduced flow which compromise dissolved oxygen concentrations.

Many urban areas with poor water quality are also affected by storm overflows from the sewerage system. The effects of storm overflows on river quality cannot be measured easily because of their transient nature and they require special surveys or automatic monitors. Furthermore, the loads of contaminants discharged from storm overflows vary in a complex way because of variations in the weather. Problems may occur during one type of storm but not during another. The GQA chemistry assessment is unlikely to reflect localised time-limited problems from overflows. The biology class may be affected but the twice-annual sampling may still not reveal the full extent of the problem. The aesthetic classification scheme should be more helpful in this and testing in the Midlands has shown that sites below storm overflows record low aesthetic scores (Section 4.6).

Automatic monitors have been used to measure river quality during the operation of storm overflows. Figure 4.51 shows the impact of an overflow on dissolved oxygen, total ammonia and un-ionised ammonia concentrations in the River Aire in Yorkshire. Un-ionised ammonia is toxic to fish and the length of time it remains at certain concentrations is critical to its toxicity. Automatic monitors can also be used to give more complete information about water quality. Figure 4.52 shows daily variability in dissolved oxygen for the River Mole, a lowland river in Surrey. Such variability is not usually taken into account in routine sampling programmes, although the biology may respond to such variability.

The relationship between biological GQA grade and habitat modification, as defined by the River Habitat Survey (Appendix 2) has been explored (Figure 4.53). The only clear pattern is that areas with poor water quality (grades e and f) also tend to have extensive habitat modifications. These are mainly in the urban and industrial areas where habitat modification is just one of the many factors which affect biological water quality. Other areas, for example the south west, show a consistency of biologically high class rivers despite much habitat modification, suggesting that this factor is not important in determining biological water quality in these situations.

The proposed GQA assessment of phosphate concentrations classifies 25 per cent of reaches as grades 1 and 2 (low concentrations of phosphate),

23.4 per cent as grades 3 and 4, 28 per cent as grade 5 and 22.9 per cent as grade 6 (highest concentrations) (Appendix 5). Rivers with the lowest concentrations are mainly in the north and west. In the south and east, many rivers are in the grades with the highest concentrations of phosphate (Figure 4.54). This broad picture reflects the higher population and hence higher sewage inputs of phosphate in the south and east and around major conurbations in the Midlands and Northern England. There is an apparent correlation between the density of channel vegetation (Figure 4.13) and phosphate concentrations. Vegetation choked channels occur where nutrient concentrations are high. From 1990 to 1995, 36 per cent of monitored river length moved into a grade of lower concentrations of phosphate. Seven per cent of river length moved the other way, giving a net change to lower concentrations of 29 per cent. (There is a risk of 15 per cent that a stretch of river is given the wrong grade and a similar risk that a river may be declared wrongly to have changed grade from one survey to the next. Allowing for this modifies the net improvement to 28 ±0.3 per cent at 95 per cent confidence.) These figures cover 22,000km of rivers and omit any rivers not assessed in 1990.

The survey results show that phosphorus concentrations in England and Wales are similar to those found in France and Germany where there are also dense populations. The highest phosphorus levels in Europe are found in a band stretching from southern England, across the central part of Europe through Romania to the Ukraine. In these countries, more than 80 per cent of the rivers usually have a concentration exceeding 0.125mg/l. In Poland and in the Belgian Flanders more than 50 per cent of the rivers have phosphorus concentrations exceeding 0.5mg/l (European Environment Agency, 1994) compared with about 20 to 30 per cent of English and Welsh rivers exceeding this value.

Trends in the Anglian and Thames Regions over the past 15 years show a reduction in phosphate since 1990,

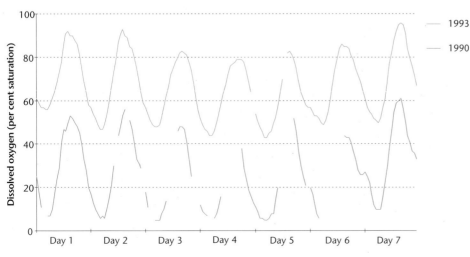

Figure 4.52
Daily variability of dissolved oxygen in the River Mole, for one week in 1990 and one week in 1993

SOURCE: Environment Agency

although concentrations in 1990 were particularly high due to the dry weather and low dilution flows (Figure 4.55). Most of the orthophosphate load comes from treated sewage effluents, and there is a strong negative correlation between orthophosphate concentrations and river flow (Figure 4.56). Even if effluent loads remain constant, river concentration will change depending on dilution (Kinniburgh *et al.*, 1997). Recent values are the lowest since 1981. Improvements measured in 1995 are related to 30 to 50 per cent reductions in the load of phosphate discharged in sewage effluents in the early 1990s. In most cases this observed reduction is a consequence of improved treatment of effluents to remove organic load (biochemical oxygen demand and ammonia), but it is also coupled with reductions in the amount of phosphorus used in detergents, which used to account for about 40 per cent of the phosphorus load from domestic sources to sewer. The quantity of phosphorus used in detergents in 1993 was about half of the quantity used in the early 1980s (Technical Committee on Detergents and the Environment, 1993).

The monitoring results for the Paris Commission and the North Sea Task Force also suggest that there has been a slight reduction in the orthophosphate load

Figure 4.53
River water quality and habitat modification, 1995

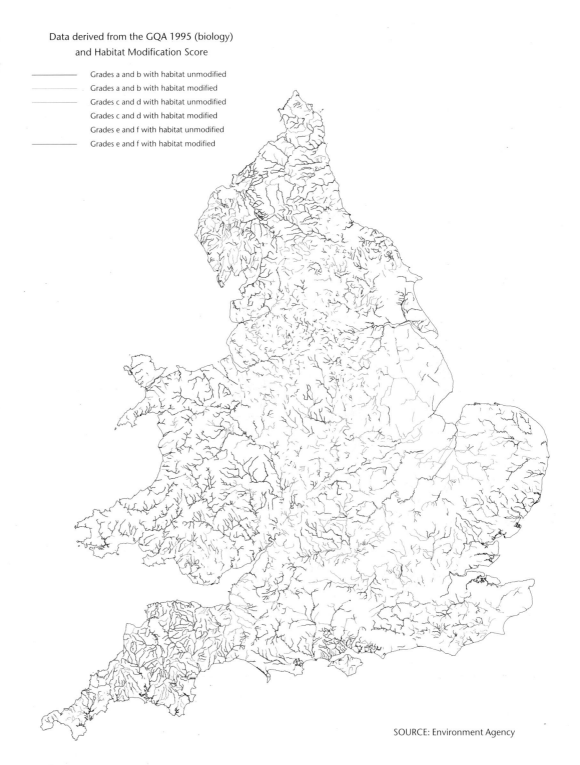

Data derived from the GQA 1995 (biology) and Habitat Modification Score

——————— Grades a and b with habitat unmodified
· · · · · · · · · Grades a and b with habitat modified
——————— Grades c and d with habitat unmodified
Grades c and d with habitat modified
Grades e and f with habitat unmodified
——————— Grades e and f with habitat modified

SOURCE: Environment Agency

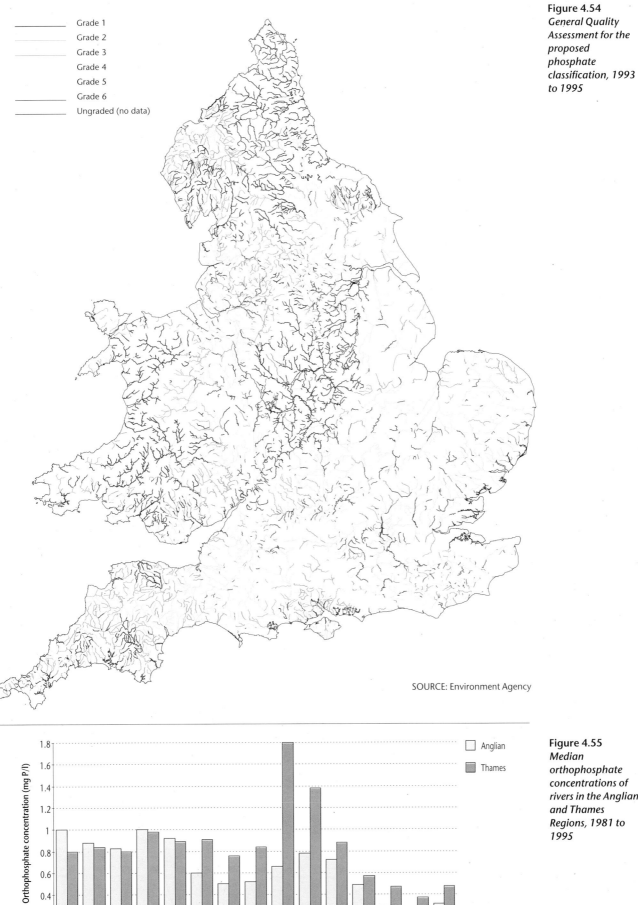

Grade 1
Grade 2
Grade 3
Grade 4
Grade 5
Grade 6
Ungraded (no data)

SOURCE: Environment Agency

Figure 4.54
General Quality Assessment for the proposed phosphate classification, 1993 to 1995

Figure 4.55
Median orthophosphate concentrations of rivers in the Anglian and Thames Regions, 1981 to 1995

SOURCE: Environment Agency

Figure 4.56
Relationship between orthophosphate concentrations and streamflow on the River Stour at Langham, Essex

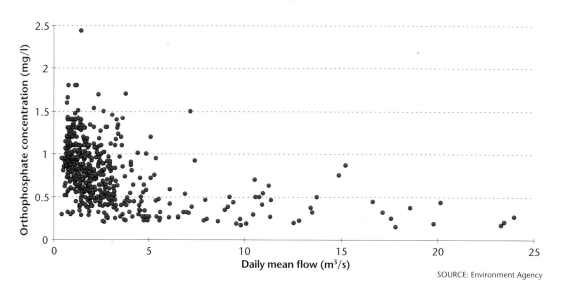

SOURCE: Environment Agency

Figure 4.57
Average river nitrate concentrations, 1993 to 1995

Nitrate concentration
mg/l

——————	>40.0
——————	20.0 to 40.0
——————	10.0 to 20.0
——————	5.0 to 10.0
——————	0.1 to 5.0
——————	0.0 to 0.1

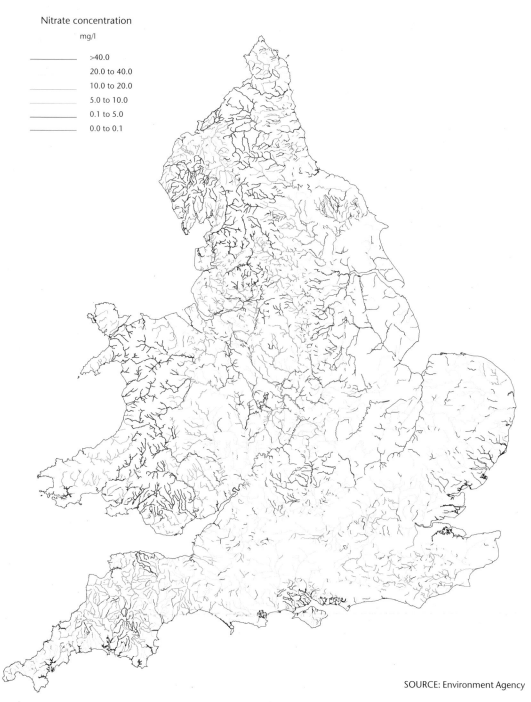

SOURCE: Environment Agency

discharged to the sea. A load of 31,600 tonnes estimated in 1990 had reduced to 26,889 tonnes in 1995. Rivers draining to the Thames and the Humber estuaries contribute 23 per cent and 17 per cent of the total load respectively but these have also shown the greatest reduction (NRA, 1995b). These estuaries drain large urban catchments with high populations, reflecting the reduction in phosphorus loads from lower concentrations in detergent and improved sewage treatment.

Nitrate data collected during the Quinquennial Survey (1993 to 1995) has also been mapped in advance of the development of a nutrient GQA. The regional pattern of average nitrate concentrations is similar to phosphate, with lower values (less than 5mg NO_3/l) in the north and west and higher concentrations (over 20mg NO_3/l) in the south and east (Figure 4.57). Background geographical influences account for some of the variation but inputs from agriculture, in particular, and from sewage effluent raise concentrations in the arable areas of south and east England. These are reflected in the distribution of Nitrate Vulnerable Zones (Figure 4.35).

The Quality of Lakes

The Agency has responsibility for lake quality, and is currently developing a monitoring scheme for lake water quality in order to provide an effective management framework. It is also considering a

better unified way of assessing the quality of standing waters as a whole. As a starting point, 63 lakes were surveyed in 1995/96 with about 12 water samples being taken at the outlet of each lake. These were analysed for phosphorus, chlorophyll 'a' and pH. The survey was not designed as a national assessment and therefore provides a selective view, with clear gaps in the north east and south east rather than a comprehensive picture of lake quality. There are also gaps in the knowledge of the quality of other standing waters such as ponds.

The pilot survey shows that lakes with relatively high concentrations of phosphorus and chlorophyll 'a' occur throughout the Midlands and East England (40 and 43 respectively out of 63 lakes) (Figure 4.58). There were no lakes with concentrations of total phosphorus less than 10µg/l although seven lakes in the Lake District and Wales have chlorophyll 'a' concentrations typical of low nutrient lakes. Like rivers, these differences reflect the natural concentrations of phosphorus, the distribution of sewage works and agricultural activity which are the major sources of phosphorus. Not all lakes with high phosphorus concentrations have high concentrations of chlorophyll 'a' (and hence algae); two lakes in Northamptonshire are examples. Other factors also limit algal growth, such as temperature, light and the residence time of water, but in general, there is a good relationship between high phosphorus and chlorophyll 'a'.

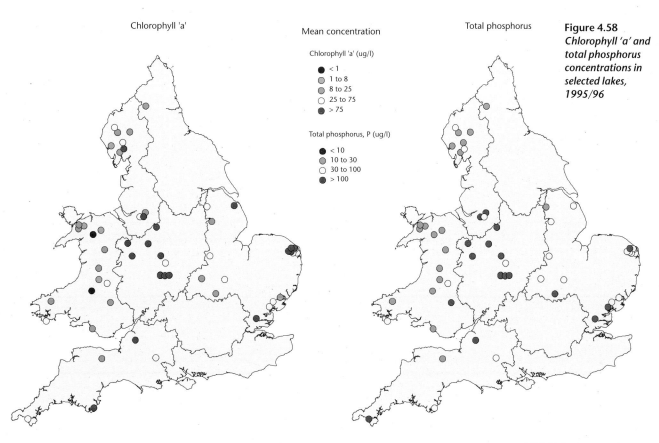

Chlorophyll 'a'

Total phosphorus

Mean concentration

Chlorophyll 'a' (ug/l)

● < 1
● 1 to 8
● 8 to 25
○ 25 to 75
● > 75

Total phosphorus, P (ug/l)

● < 10
● 10 to 30
○ 30 to 100
● > 100

Figure 4.58
Chlorophyll 'a' and total phosphorus concentrations in selected lakes, 1995/96

SOURCE: Environment Agency

Figure 4.59
The annual range of chlorophyll 'a' concentrations in Esthwaite Water and the North Basin of Windermere, 1984 to 1993

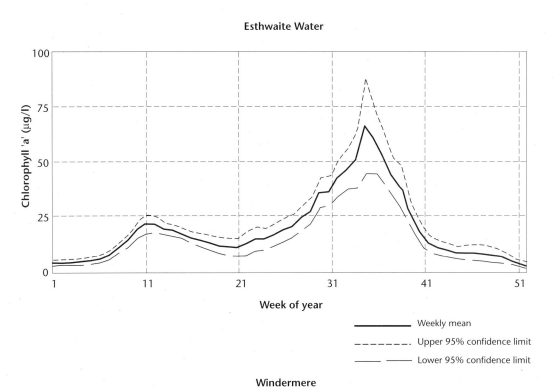

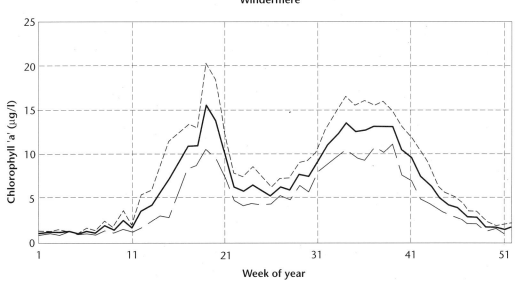

SOURCE: Environment Agency

Chlorophyll 'a' concentrations can vary significantly throughout the year so sampling needs to take account of this. Figure 4.59 shows the annual range for two lakes in the Lake District. The Agency has been exploring the use of aerial surveillance to obtain greater spatial coverage of the extent of algal blooms; this needs to take account of such variability and flights need to take place in calm weather to obtain maxima.

The Quality of Groundwater

Groundwater quality is monitored by the Agency at strategic locations around public and private supply sources and locally in relation to specific problems. It is more difficult to monitor than surface waters because it is not so easily accessible and can only be sampled through wells or boreholes. The water

companies also carry out monitoring of these sources because of their duty to supply wholesome drinking water which meets the standards of the EC Drinking Water Directive. About 1,500 sources are monitored routinely. By 1997, there had only been limited national collation and assessment of data. The Agency intends to extend this and to implement a groundwater monitoring strategy (Chilton and Milne, 1994). Unlike surface waters, there is currently no legal requirement to monitor for specific substances in groundwater, apart from nitrate. The range of parameters monitored has therefore varied amongst the regions, making national reports difficult to produce. However, some of the regions, particularly those where groundwater supplies a large proportion of potable needs, have collated information on various substances. For example, Figure 4.60 shows fluoride concentrations as medians for 1993 to 1996 measured in two aquifers in the Thames Region. Fluoride occurs naturally in groundwater. The data show that not only are fluoride concentrations well below drinking water standards (1,500µg/l as a maximum) but there are differences in concentrations between groundwater in the north west of the catchment (springs in oolitic limestone) and samples from the chalk boreholes. The lower concentrations in the oolite springs represent the effects of recent recharge.

A recent study looked at sources of groundwater pollution and found that a total of 251 abstractions were identified as being affected by 210 sources of pollution. Of these abstractions, 114 were public and 137 private boreholes. A further 368 public and private abstractions were considered to be at risk from existing point sources of groundwater pollution (Environment Agency, 1996b).

For the purposes of data analysis, the various land uses causing pollution and the contaminants identified were grouped into categories. A subjective assessment of the point source severity was applied on a scale of 1 to 5, where code 1 represented likely gross contamination of a major aquifer and code 5 represented slight contamination of a minor or non-aquifer. Some eight per cent of identified sites were subjectively placed in severity code 1 and nearly half (47 per cent) of the point sources were in the low severity classes 4 and 5. Further details are given in Appendix 6.

Twenty four per cent of all point sources identified nationally are causing contamination in the chalk, the most important aquifer in terms of potable supply; 19 per cent on Permo-Triassic sandstone and 16 per cent on the Carboniferous coal measures, only a minor aquifer, though the study specifically addressed major aquifers, and some areas without aquifers were not covered which will bias these results. Of the 1,205 sources considered, 777 (64 per cent) are known to have caused some groundwater contamination. The remaining 428 point sources are suspected to be causing contamination. The relationship between point sources of pollution and contamination of groundwater by region is shown in Figure 4.61.

The findings of this survey compare favourably with a Strategic Study on Groundwater in the UK which identified 14 major issues and 17 other issues of significance to sustainable development of groundwater resources (Grey et al., 1995). Many of these relate to issues addressed previously, e.g. low flows, sustainable yields, and nitrate pollution. Those relating to groundwater quality included acid mine drainage, contaminated land, landfill sites, solvents and pesticides. Solvents are a major concern around contaminated land areas, beneath industrial sites and airfields. They are suspected to lead to widespread aquifer contamination beneath major cities. Table 4.9 summarises the principal issues (Foster and Grey, 1997).

Groundwater pollution is particularly serious because of its long-term nature. Naturally it can take decades for pollutants to move through the ground, and effective clean-up of groundwater pollution is difficult and costly. Prevention is better than cure. The Groundwater Protection Policy was formulated to protect groundwaters from pollution and over-abstraction, not only for supply but also to protect the

Figure 4.60
Median fluoride concentrations in groundwaters of the chalk and Jurassic limestone aquifers in the Thames Region, 1993 to 1996

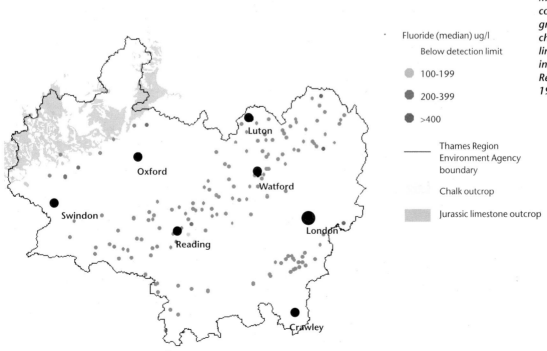

SOURCE: Environment Agency

Table 4.9
*Summary of
principal
groundwater
pollution issues*

Issue	Status	Trend	Learning curve
Nitrate	There is extensive pollution of the unconfined parts of the major UK aquifers. In many boreholes concentrations are at, or approaching, the maximum permissible concentration for drinking water. Treatment or blending is often required. In extreme cases, boreholes have been closed down completely.	Nitrate may take five to 50 years to reach the water table. Nitrate concentrations in groundwater have been rising steadily in many areas. This trend is likely to continue in the short term, although locally there is some levelling off.	A large amount of research and monitoring has been undertaken, and the key processes have all been identified. Improved understanding of natural in-situ denitrification, the effectiveness of land-use change in reducing nitrate leaching and the significance of preferential flows in the unsaturated zone are still required.
Pesticides	Pesticides are widely used by agriculture, industry and public authorities. There is a danger that some residual pesticide may find its way into groundwater. The maximum admissible concentration of any pesticide in drinking water is currently set at the very low level of 0.1µg/l. Groundwaters are well protected compared with surface waters but some pesticides, especially the triazine herbicides, mainly of non-agricultural origin, have already been detected in groundwaters.	Increasingly sensitive analytical methods mean that confirmed detections of pesticides in groundwaters are increasing. There is no systematic national survey to detect trends. The use of less persistent pesticides and lower concentrations means that the problem should eventually diminish.	Limited research on the occurrence of pesticides in UK groundwaters. Preferential flow, including through soakaways, may be important for rapid transmission to water table. Rate of degradation in aquifers likely to be slow but parameters unknown.
Non-aqueous phase liquids (solvents)	Non-aqueous phase liquids, both those denser than water and those lighter than water have been, and remain, in very widespread industrial use and are insidious groundwater pollutants. Small amounts of solvent can contaminate large volumes of groundwater.	Those denser than water give rise to greater concern. Groundwater beneath industrial sites and airfields is especially likely to be contaminated but dense-solvent contamination also appears to be widespread in aquifers situated beneath major cities.	The behaviour of light solvents is reasonably well understood, although more closely monitored experience of the evolution of pollution/remediation incidents is needed. It is still difficult to predict the fate and migration of solvents denser than water in UK aquifers, and further detailed research and monitoring is required.
Microbiological contamination	Contamination of groundwater with pathogenic organisms (e.g. Cryptosporidium) is rare but not unknown in British aquifers. Cryptosporidium does not respond to the normal chlorination process, but can be removed by slow sand filtration.	Recent work has been stimulated by the occasional detection of groundwater contaminated with pathogenic organisms.	Subsurface microbiology is a new discipline. There is interest in the transport and survival time of micro-organisms in aquifers.

Source: Foster and Grey, 1997

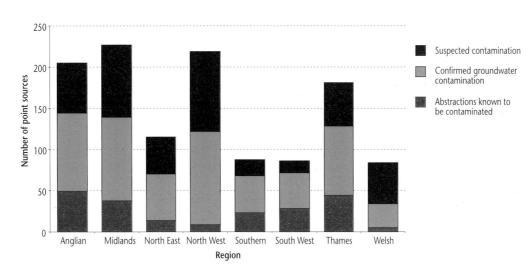

Figure 4.61
Number of point sources of groundwater contamination by region

SOURCE: Environment Agency

streams and rivers that rely on groundwaters (NRA, 1992a). The policy is based on the geology, soil, hydrogeology, geochemistry and ecology of the aquifer concerned and its associated springs, and gives greater protection to, and focuses resources on those areas where groundwater is both strategically more important and at greater risk of pollution. Public water supply boreholes are being computer modelled to define the areas from which they draw water. From these, maps of zones are being drawn up based on the water's travel time to the borehole. These zones are key factors in the Agency's approach to whether or not waste disposal or new abstraction will be allowed at a site. For a more general picture, there is also a series of groundwater vulnerability maps based on geology and soils (Environment Agency, 1997d). The Groundwater Protection Policy has been well received by industry and has stood up to rigorous scrutiny in several planning inquiries.

4.4   The Health of Freshwater Resources

Whereas standards are usually based on physical or chemical criteria – although not exclusively – it is also useful to look at their effects as an indication of environmental quality. In other words, how 'healthy' is our environment. There are not yet many ways of measuring 'health' so this section concentrates on specific issues of concern in relation to health, such as eutrophication and acidification. The evidence for bacterial contamination is also considered because this is of concern to human health if certain uses of fresh water are to be promoted.

Eutrophication

Eutrophication is a sign of poor 'health' in rivers and lakes and is defined as:

"The enrichment of waters, by inorganic plant nutrients, which results in the stimulation of an array of symptomatic changes. These include the increased production of algae and / or macrophytes, decreased biological diversity and the deterioration of water quality.

Such changes may be undesirable and interfere with water uses" (OECD, 1982 (modified)).

In lakes, eutrophication related problems include the production of excessive blooms of planktonic (floating) and benthic (bottom dwelling) algae, and changes in plant communities. The most well known are the potentially toxic blue-green algae (cyanobacteria) which pose a risk to recreational users of water as well as to livestock and domestic animals. Other problems associated with planktonic algae in lakes include the reduction in clarity of the water which can result in the disappearance of rooted plants and a consequent reduction in biodiversity. Algae photosynthesise during daylight hours, adding oxygen to the water, but continue to respire at night, consuming oxygen. Too many algae can lead to low oxygen concentrations at night which affect fish life. Furthermore, the decay of algal blooms and other plants can deoxygenate the water, killing fish and other wildlife. The high concentration of algae can also interfere with water treatment for public water supply by blocking filters and affecting taste and odour. Some 33 out of 41 lakes, designated as Sites of Special Scientific Interest, are affected by eutrophication (English Nature, 1997).

In rivers, eutrophication problems include most of those described for lakes, including potentially toxic blooms of benthic and planktonic toxic blue-green algae, deoxygenation and a reduction in biodiversity. Figure 4.52 in the previous section, has already shown a typical weekly cycle of dissolved oxygen measured in a lowland river which clearly shows the diurnal effect of phytoplankton. In addition, excessive growth of rooted plants in rivers and other drainage channels can cause a reduction in their flow capacity and increase the chance of flooding, unless they are cut. They also create a nuisance to anglers, particularly growths of *Cladophora*. In fast flowing salmonid rivers excessive growth of benthic algae also poses a threat to spawning success by reducing water flow through the gravels. Eutrophication can thus affect the biota,

Figure 4.62
The regional incidence of waters affected by blooms or scum of blue-green algae, or both, 1991 to 1996

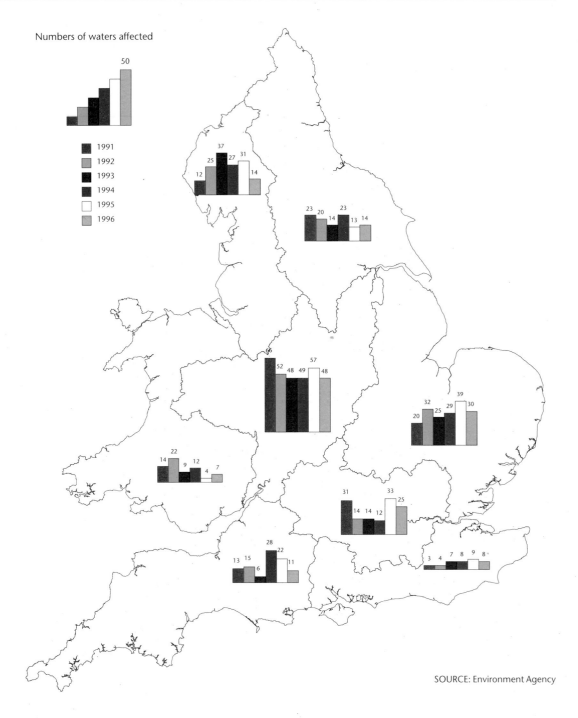

Figure 4.63
The number of problems due to blue-green algal blooms found out of all lakes visited, 1991 to 1995

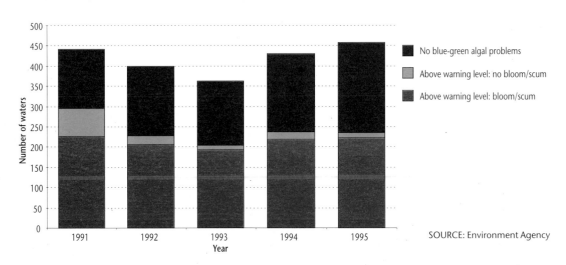

fishing, water sports and the general amenity of rivers, as well as interfering with water treatment as outlined above.

Nutrient enrichment, in certain circumstances, can lead to excessive growth of toxic blue-green algae. The Agency monitors algal blooms during the summer months and the results for 1991 to 1995 show that growths occur throughout England and Wales although the Midlands have the greatest number of affected waters (Figure 4.62). The number of lakes visited and found to have problems has remained at about the same level since 1991 (Figure 4.63). The extent of blooms in any particular year is largely weather dependent, with warm, sunny and calm conditions favouring blue-green algal growth,

although other factors, such as nutrients, light and temperature are important too. The reservoirs with the densest blooms of toxic algae were all in central England (the Midland Region) in an area of below average windspeed.

Eutrophic Sensitive Areas, as specified in the Urban Waste Water Treatment Directive, have been designated on 33 rivers, lakes or reservoirs (Figure 4.64). A further 48 waters are being assessed as to whether they are eutrophic or not as part of the 1997 review required by the Directive. These may be designated by DETR if sufficient evidence is available. Where an area has been designated as an Eutrophic Sensitive Area, there is a requirement for nutrient (usually phosphorus) reduction in discharges from

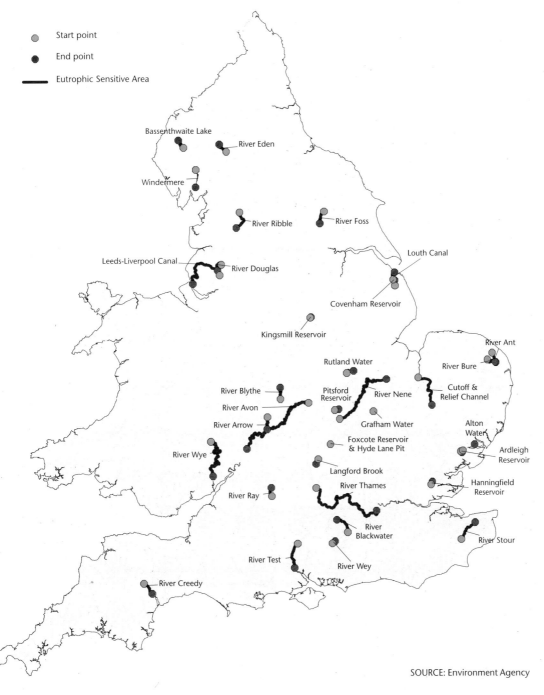

Figure 4.64
Eutrophic Sensitive Areas designated under the Urban Waste Water Treatment Directive, 1994

SOURCE: Environment Agency

sewage works exceeding a size of 10,000 population equivalence, unless it can be shown that this will have no impact.

In order to assess the impact of eutrophication, the Agency is developing a scheme for describing the trophic status of rivers. This will also be used to help identify candidates for designation as Eutrophic Sensitive Areas under the Urban Waste Water Treatment Directive. The scheme will be based on the analyses of macrophyte and diatom (microscopic algae) populations. The principle of developing biologically-based schemes as management tools for eutrophication control is important as they can give a direct measure of the eutrophication response. A

preliminary version of a Mean Trophic Rank for macrophytes has been developed through Environment Agency sponsored research. The Mean Trophic Rank uses a scoring system to describe the trophic status of rivers based on the species and their abundance at river sites. Each species has been allocated a score dependent on its tolerance to eutrophication, though the score can also reflect physical conditions. Tolerant species have a low score, so a low Mean Trophic Index tends to indicate a lowland, nutrient-rich river. This is illustrated in Figure 4.65 (the final methodology employed will differ in detail from these provisional results). There appears to be a broad correlation between this map and Figure 4.54, the map of orthophosphate grades.

Figure 4.65
Mean Trophic Rank scores based on aquatic plants, 1978 to 1997

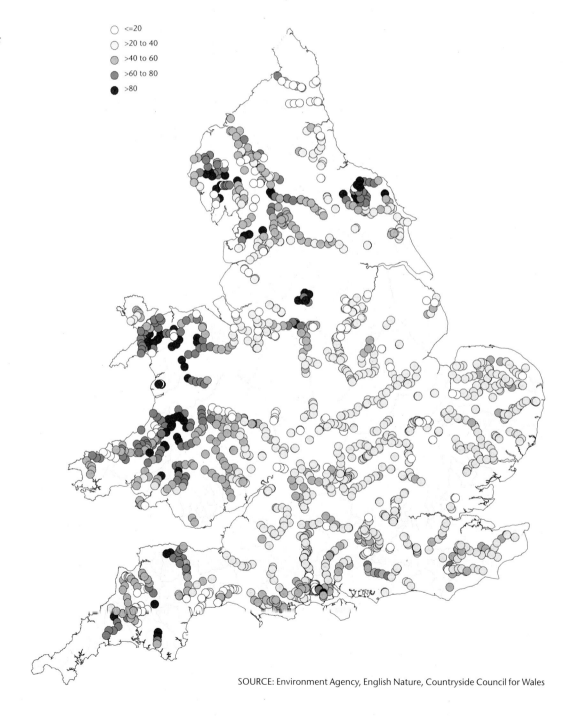

○ <=20
○ >20 to 40
◔ >40 to 60
● >60 to 80
● >80

SOURCE: Environment Agency, English Nature, Countryside Council for Wales

Acidification

Acid deposition is also affecting the 'health' of freshwater resources, particularly in Wales, the Pennines, South West England, and the Lake District. Whilst some waters are naturally acidic, the deposition of sulphur and nitrogen from the burning of fossil fuels has led to increased acidification in areas where the pH tends to be naturally low. An estimated 12,000km of Welsh streams are affected by acidification. A survey of the most sensitive fresh waters in 1990 to 1992 in each 10km grid square showed the general distribution of areas with low pH (Figure 4.66) (Critical Loads Advisory Group, Freshwaters Sub-Group, 1995). The Agency also monitors pH at its GQA sites, though these are located on main rivers and were not intended to survey

acidification. Thus only 0.05 per cent of GQA sites have a mean pH below 6.0 and 4.3 per cent of sites have a mean pH between 6 and 7. These sites occur almost exclusively in the north and west.

Acidified water releases aluminium from soils. High concentrations of aluminium are toxic to aquatic organisms including many species of insects and fish. Acidification has eliminated aluminium sensitive species from many upland waters. It is estimated that 5.4 per cent of Sites of Special Scientific Interest in Wales are affected by acidification and 1.3 per cent of sites in England. The impact on young salmon and trout in small nursery streams has affected the fisheries of several large rivers. Rare populations of natterjack toads in south east England may have been

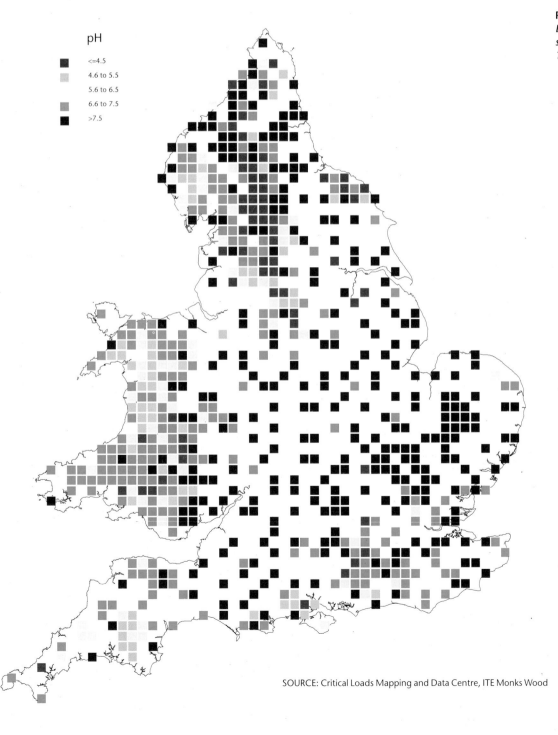

pH

- <=4.5
- 4.6 to 5.5
- 5.6 to 6.5
- 6.6 to 7.5
- >7.5

Figure 4.66
Distribution of pH in surface waters, 1990 to 1992

SOURCE: Critical Loads Mapping and Data Centre, ITE Monks Wood

lost due to the acidification of spawning ponds (Beebee *et al.*, 1990) but their decline is also linked to the drying out of shallow pools in heathlands. Other species, for example dippers (a riverine bird), are reduced in abundance by the reduction in their aquatic food supply (Ormerod *et al.*, 1991). Acidity and the resultant high aluminium concentrations also increase water treatment costs for water companies and may affect the quality of a number of private supplies which are common in rural areas.

Acidification has been tackled by reducing sulphur emissions from power stations and the costs of this are outlined in Section 5. However, nitrogen oxides also cause acid deposition and the increased use of cars and emissions from this source suggest future prospects are still not good. There has also been concern over increased nitrate runoff in headwater streams from atmospheric deposition. This could cause changes in stream biota of significance to conservation. Research is underway to determine the possible extent of such effects which are complicated by the interactions of nitrate with catchment vegetation.

An alternative to allowing slow recovery by reducing acid depositions is the rapid neutralisation of acid waters by the addition of limestone (calcium carbonate) to catchments or water bodies. There has been substantial research by the Agency and others into techniques and their effects. For example, Llyn Brianne Reservoir has been limed by the Agency and

its predecessors since 1991, to treat the River Tywi which flows from it. Water quality has improved sharply and numbers of young trout and salmon have increased (Figure 4.67). This has clear fisheries benefits, but liming can only be a partial and local solution as it is costly, success can be variable, and in itself, it may have adverse impacts on biodiversity and so may be inappropriate in areas of conservation importance.

Bioaccumulation

Many organochlorines such as polychlorinated biphenyls (PCBs) and certain pesticides are persistent in the environment and accumulate in biological tissues where they may exert toxic effects. For these reasons, DDT was banned from use in the UK in a phased approach over the period 1964 to 1984, and dieldrin was banned in 1989. With respect to PCBs, UK manufacture ceased in 1976 but production continued in many other countries until the late 1980s and these could be sold for use in electrical transformers until 1986. Some of these are still in use although there is a move for a phased removal of these. Significant effects on fish have not been found but concern has focused on their predators, notably humans, birds of prey and otters, which bioaccumulate contaminants in their food. These substances are now widely dispersed and are found in aquatic sediments and animals including fish, birds and otters.

Figure 4.67
pH in the River Tywi downstream of Llyn Brianne Reservoir and changes in the number of juvenile salmon before and after liming, 1990 to 1995

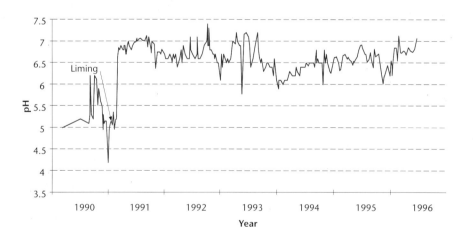

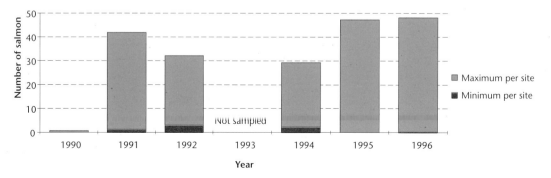

SOURCE: Environment Agency

In 1986/87, a survey of 23 sites in England and Wales found that concentrations of gamma-HCH and dieldrin in freshwater eels exceeded recommended limits for human consumption in a number of cases. In 1992, a survey of eight commercial eel fisheries led to limits being set for the human consumption of eels from the Humber, Yorkshire Ouse and inshore Thames fisheries. The results from a further national survey in 1995 to 1996 should help to establish trends in concentrations of these substances in eels (MAFF, 1989).

PCB levels remain relatively high in eels in some industrialised catchments in Wales (Weatherley et al., 1997). Concentrations of DDT residues (over 100μg/kg at 17 per cent of sites) and dieldrin (widespread at up to 100μg/kg) also demonstrate the legacy of past agricultural use. Concentrations of PCBs in the eggs of dippers, which feed on aquatic invertebrates, have been related to slight eggshell thinning, but no other ecological effects have been noted. Analyses of organochlorines in otter spraints for Wales, the River Severn and in East Anglia show that concentrations of PCBs, dieldrin and DDT residues were generally higher in East Anglia and in lowland stretches of western rivers. It is possible that organochlorines, mainly PCBs, are limiting the recolonisation of otters in these catchments (Mason and Macdonald, 1993a, 1993b, 1994). The effects of PCBs remain unclear. Healthy populations of otters occur in some areas with relatively high concentrations of PCBs in eels, a large part of the otter diet. Postmortem examinations have been undertaken on a total of 131 otters killed on roads between 1988 and 1996, mostly collected in Wales and south west England. The otters were generally in good health with no indication of pathological effects related to organochlorine contamination, although chemical analyses are not yet complete (Bradshaw, 1996; Simpson, 1997).

New uses of PCBs, dieldrin and DDT are now banned and the government has set a target to phase out all identifiable uses of PCBs by 1999 in line with the 3rd North Sea Conference agreement. Other chemicals implicated are still used, for example lindane, and other pesticides may bioaccumulate or cause effects not yet identified. Discharges of lindane and other substances are controlled by the Agency to ensure the achievement of EQSs (as shown in Section 4.3). New pesticides require approval from various government departments based on recommendations from the Advisory Committee on Pesticides. This process is intended to ensure the safe use of the pesticide, including the avoidance of harm to the freshwater environment. An important requirement is the provision of analytical methods to ensure that environmental monitoring can be carried out. The Agency works with pesticide manufacturers on practical analytical methods which are not yet available for over half of the approved substances. Pesticide distributors and agronomists must also

continue to promote best practice and develop farming systems which require lower pesticide inputs.

Endocrine Disruption

Endocrine disruptors are substances which interfere with the hormonal systems of animals, causing physiological effects such as impairment of reproduction. Invertebrates, fish, birds and mammals, including humans, may all be affected.

Laboratory tests indicate that many substances have hormone disrupting properties. These include naturally occurring substances such as phyto-oestrogens from plants and steroids excreted by animals and man-made substances. Synthetic substances which are thought to be endocrine disruptors include pesticides such as DDT and tributyl tin; alkylphenol ethoxylates (APEs) used as industrial detergents; alkylphenols which are plasticisers; polychlorinated biphenyls (PCBs) found in old electrical components; bisphenol A used in lining tin cans and dental fillings; and ethinyl oestradiol, the synthetic steroid used in the oral contraceptive pill. The most widely reported effect from endocrine disruption is a feminising (oestrogenic) response to these substances although other effects have also been identified, for example masculinising.

The first reported case of an oestrogenic effect detected in a natural freshwater population in this country has been that of roach in the River Lee. A histological study showed that up to 30 per cent of the males were intersex, with oocytes (egg-producing cells) in the testes. Sewage effluent was identified as the possible cause. Laboratory tests have shown that male rainbow trout and carp exposed to sewage effluent produce the egg yolk protein vitellogenin. In 1988, rainbow trout in cages were placed in the effluent channel of 15 sewage-treatment works across England. At each site male fish showed large increases in vitellogenin (Purdom et al., 1994). A further study between 1992 and 1995 used caged fish to look for oestrogenic effects in rivers and waters used for drinking water supply. Fish placed in 15 raw water storage reservoirs showed no vitellogenic response suggesting there was no apparent risk to drinking water supplies. However, fish downstream of sewage-treatment works on six rivers exhibited a vitellogenic response which was confined to undiluted effluent in some cases and up to 5km downstream in others (Figure 4.68) (Harries et al., 1995). The identity of the oestrogenic substances was not determined.

On the River Aire in Yorkshire, a high vitellogenic response has been observed in fish throughout the river and this has been associated with high levels of nonylphenol discharged from a wool scouring company. Concentrations of nonylphenol in the Aire have subsequently declined as most wool scouring

Figure 4.68
Mean plasma vitellogenin of male rainbow trout held at various sites in the River Lee for three weeks, July-August 1992

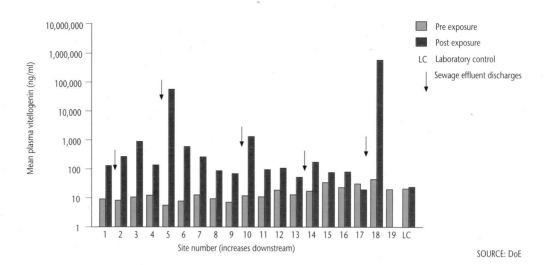

SOURCE: DoE

companies have complied with a voluntary ban on alkylphenol ethoxylate surfactants and switched to alternative detergents. The Agency is seeking further reductions by identifying other significant industrial sources including textile manufacturers.

Further studies have taken place on seven sewage effluents to identify the substances responsible for oestrogenic activity. This analysis found the natural steroids 17ß-oestradiol and oestrone, and the synthetic ethinyl oestradiol present at concentrations capable of inducing production of vitellogenin in male rainbow trout and roach. It suggested that these substances were likely to be widespread in sewage effluents, probably arising from the human population (Environment Agency, 1997f).

Vitellogenesis is only an indicator of oestrogenic activity in fish and subsequent stages in the development of the intersex condition have not yet been demonstrated in the wild. The full spatial extent of the exposure and response to these chemicals is also not clear. The implications for fish populations are unknown because some degree of intersex may not significantly affect the reproductive capacity of a population. The Agency is currently investigating these questions and has developed a strategic response. One aspect of this is the development of EQSs needed to guide the control of the highest risk chemicals. Some progress has been made, e.g. nonylphenol now has an operational EQS of $1\mu g/l$ as an annual average and $10\mu g/l$ as a maximum allowable concentration. However, development of EQSs for all substances is only one approach and many EQSs for pesticides did not consider long-term reproductive effects in their development. The Agency also wants to minimise exposure to these substances, to reduce inputs, and to seek minimal use of the substances. Such an approach has been taken with nonylphenol in advance of EQS development. As far as steroids are concerned, removal at source is not possible and therefore better sewage treatment processes are needed. Toxicity-based consents are also being developed to control complex discharges to the environment, where EQSs cannot control interactions between substances (Environment Agency, 1998b).

Ecotoxicological Studies

The Agency has commissioned a series of research and development projects to investigate the suitability of ecotoxicology tests for both effluent control and for monitoring receiving water quality. Eight sampling stations on the River Aire were selected on the basis of their proximity to known sources of inputs and to previously selected biological sampling points. The project included the assessment of established and more novel ecotoxicology methods with both laboratory tests and river deployments. A battery of tests were evaluated together with benthic macroinvertebrate survey data (taken, for this project, as the baseline for environmental quality). Tests selected included chronic and acute methods, sediment and water column tests, and lethal and sub-lethal endpoints. Species considered were water fleas (*Daphnia magna*), freshwater shrimps (*Gammarus pulex*) and non-biting midges (*Chironomus riparius*).

Figure 4.69 shows the results from the *Daphnia magna* river tests undertaken during September 1996 and offspring mortality increasing at downstream sites. The River Aire becomes increasingly industrialised from site 1 to site 8 and biological quality decreases from Very Good upstream to Bad beyond site 6. This research is at an early stage, with initial results indicating that the tests may be used as indicators of general water quality and to help determine the toxic impact of both point source and diffuse inputs. The programme is associated with the initiative to introduce toxicity based criteria for improved control of toxic waste discharges and the need to demonstrate environmental benefit. More extensive testing and detailed method development are required in future projects before the tests can be adopted as part of the Agency's routine investigation and assessment tools. Rigorous trailing at a wide range of freshwater sites and impacted areas is necessary.

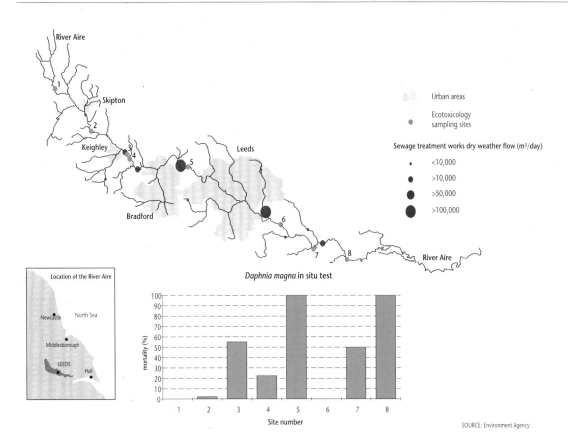

Figure 4.69
Ecotoxicity in the River Aire. Mortality of the water flea, Daphnia magna, held in the river for six days, September 1996

SOURCE: Environment Agency

Microbiological Pollution

Another aspect of organic pollution is that of contamination of water with micro-organisms. These are not usually pathogenic (disease causing) but they can serve as useful indicators of faecal pollution from human and other animal sources and hence possible contamination with pathogens. River water abstracted for drinking water must be treated to standards that ensure coliform numbers are below prescribed values before water enters the distribution system, a responsibility that lies with the water companies. There are no statutory requirements for the Agency to monitor microbiological contamination in fresh water, but because most rivers carry effluents, it is inevitably widespread. Land-use also has a significant impact on the bacterial quality of waters, and contamination also arises from livestock and wildlife. Monitoring has been carried out at various Harmonised Monitoring sites since the 1970s to give background information; the data for six sites are shown in Figure 4.70. These show that the number of faecal coliforms present vary substantially throughout the year but at no site is there any clear pattern of change over the last 20 years. They do provide some indication of the range of numbers. The South Tyne at Warden Bridge is upstream of the River Derwent and the River Stour at Langham is upstream of the River Stour at Wixoe. In both cases, there appears to be an increase in contamination at the downstream sites. Data collected for the Thames Region (Figure 4.71) show more clearly the spatial variability across a catchment, with less contamination in the headwaters, and particularly high concentrations directly below sewage works, for example rivers below Oxford and Crawley.

To put the values into some perspective, three limits are also shown on Figure 4.70:

i. the guideline value for water to be abstracted for potable supply with a minimum amount of treatment (20 coliforms/100ml expressed as 95 per cent of samples) under Directive 75/440/EEC;

ii. the guideline value for water to be abstracted for potable supply with treatment (2,000 coliforms/100ml expressed as 95 per cent of samples) which is also the mandatory limit for bathing water quality in designated waters under Directive 78/160/EEC;

iii. the guideline value for water to be abstracted for potable supply with enhanced treatment (20,000 coliforms/100ml expressed as 95 per cent of samples).

The River Stour at Langham is a designated surface water abstraction site and has to meet the standard of 2,000 coliforms/100ml expressed as 95 per cent of samples. The River Exe is also abstracted for potable supply but not at the site for which the data are plotted. Bathing water standards only apply at sites designated by the government and there are currently no designated freshwater sites; the limits are shown only to put the numbers into context. There is concern

Figure 4.70
Faecal coliform concentrations in selected rivers, 1978 to 1995

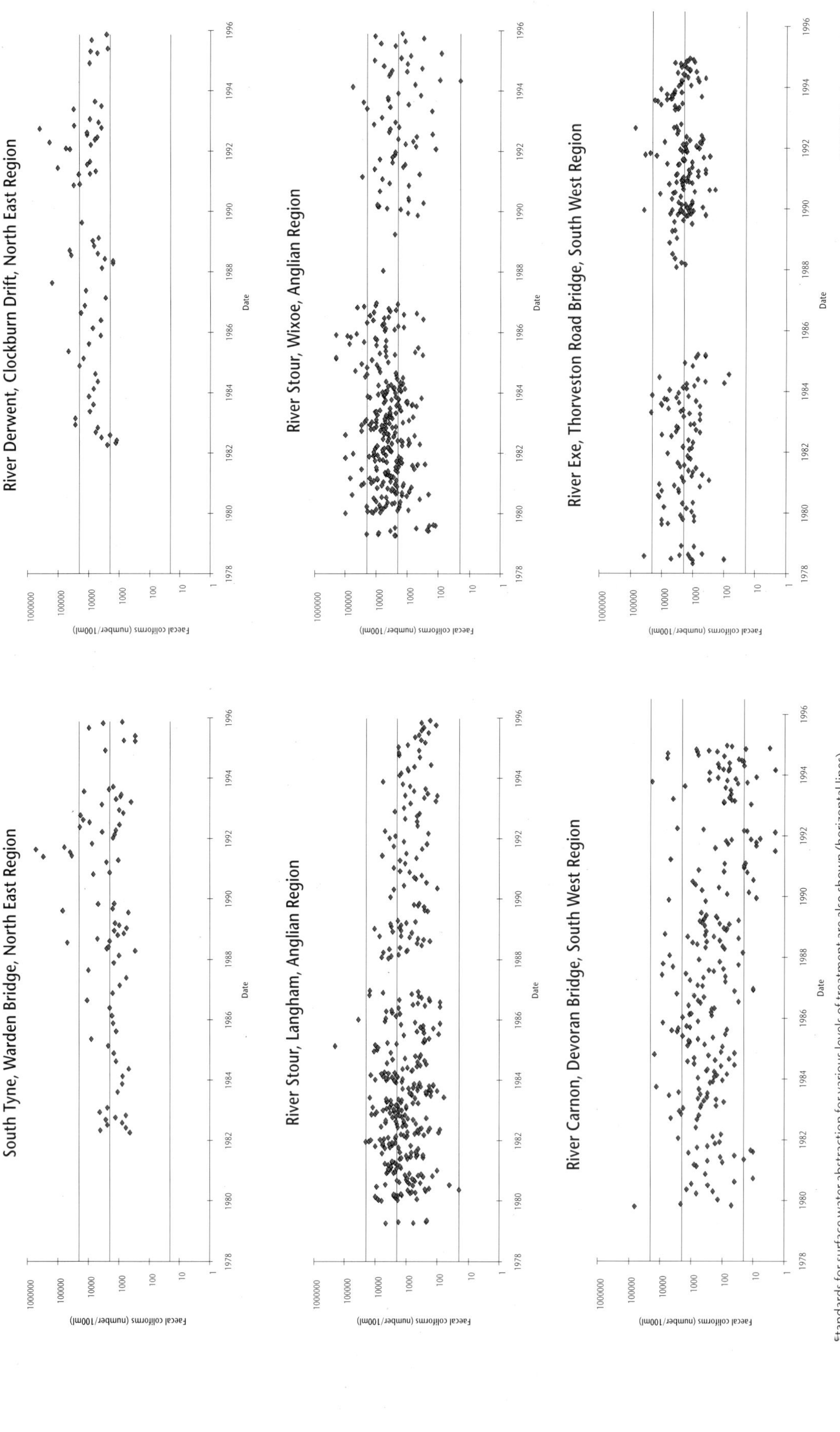
South Tyne, Warden Bridge, North East Region
River Derwent, Clockburn Drift, North East Region
River Stour, Langham, Anglian Region
River Stour, Wixoe, Anglian Region
River Carnon, Devoran Bridge, South West Region
River Exe, Thorveston Road Bridge, South West Region
Faecal coliforms (number/100ml)
Date
1
10
100
1000
10000
100000
1000000
1978
1980
1982
1984
1986
1988
1990
1992
1994
1996

Standards for surface water abstraction for various levels of treatment are also shown (horizontal lines)

SOURCE: Environment Agency

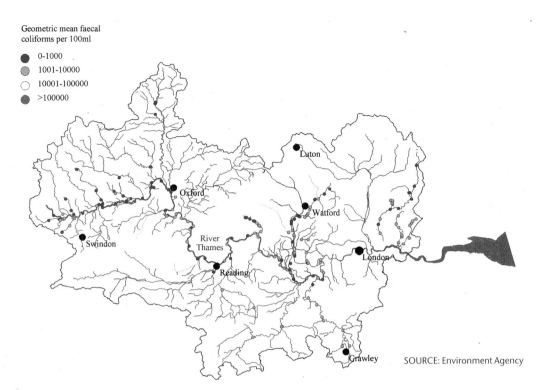

Geometric mean faecal
coliforms per 100ml

● 0-1000
● 1001-10000
○ 10001-100000
● >100000

Figure 4.71
*Faecal coliform
concentrations in
the Thames
catchment, 1995*

SOURCE: Environment Agency

however among people who use rivers, reservoirs, and lakes for other activities such as canoeing and windsurfing, about possible adverse effects from pathogenic contamination. These uses conflict with the role of rivers as effluent carriers, but there is a demand for more recreational use of waters. If bathing water standards were to be applied on a non-statutory basis at such sites, a full cost benefit appraisal would need to be done, as well as a technical feasibility study to determine how the standards could be met. Extra treatment at sewage works would be necessary and likely to be a substantial cost.

Cryptosporidium is a parasite that causes severe diarrhoeal illness; the source of Cryptosporidium oocysts is usually contamination from livestock by one route or another. The organism can contaminate water supplies because it is resistant to chlorination and outbreaks have occurred in various locations, for example, Torbay and Swindon, in the last few years. Catchment protection and efficient water treatment are the only ways of limiting their entry into drinking water supplies. Leptospirosis, also known as Weil's Disease, is spread by the urine of animals, particularly rats on riverbanks. This poses some risk to those who expose themselves to infected waters, and typically about eight people per year contract the infection in the UK due to contact with water. River users can minimise their risk of exposure by taking precautions.

4.5 Changes at Long-term Reference Sites

Environmental processes often act over very long time periods and the effect of human activities may not be noticed for several years or decades. Furthermore, natural changes may evolve over hundreds of years.

There is a need to take a long-term perspective if sustainable development is to be achieved, and if long-term changes are to be detected. This section looks at monitoring which addresses this aspect.

Harmonised Monitoring Scheme

The Department of the Environment, Transport and the Regions (DETR) and its predecessors have run a Harmonised Monitoring Scheme (HMS) since 1974 to provide a network of sites at which river quality is monitored in a consistent manner across Great Britain. The concentrations and loads at the HMS sites tend to reflect conditions in the lower reaches of the rivers and are not necessarily representative of conditions found further upstream or further inland. Problems associated with smaller rivers, e.g. acidification may be largely diluted or not present at all. Hence, the General Quality Assessment Scheme meets the needs on providing information for all rivers, but the record is much shorter than the HMS. Most HMS sites are also used as sites in the GQA. Most HMS sites are at, or just above the tidal limit or the confluence of major tributaries and can therefore be used to provide information on chemical loadings to the sea as well as long-term trends. The determinands reported have varied between sites over the years, but data are available for a number of core determinands.

Trend analyses, using the statistical seasonal Kendal Test (Hirsch and Slack, 1984) for sanitary determinands and nutrients have been carried out by the Agency to reveal statistically significant changes over the period 1976 to 1995 and to add information to the GQA results. Results were excluded for sites where more than 10 years data in total were missing or where continuous periods of more than five years had not been sampled. Some areas where the programme was changed during this period are therefore under-represented. The analysis allows for seasonal changes in concentrations of a determinand because it compares values in the same calendar month over all the years sampled. It combines results for each of the 12 months to give the average annual change in concentration of a determinand. It therefore indicates the broad pattern of change which may differ when trends over shorter sections within that period are assessed.

The analysis of trends in biochemical oxygen demand shows that water quality over the period 1976 to 1995 has improved, although changes are small in relation to the analytical error in measuring this determinand (Figure 4.72). These figures show the size and direction (improvements or deterioration) of the trend at each Harmonised Monitoring Site. They also give time series plots for four example sites. There is generally an improving trend in dissolved oxygen concentrations (Figure 4.73) with large improvements in the London area, South Wales and the north east. However, this assumes that the time of sampling during the day has remained constant which may not necessarily be true. Figure 4.52 has already shown the wide diurnal variation in dissolved oxygen in some rivers. Changes in sampling times could lead to erroneous conclusions about trends. Ammonia concentrations show less of a trend overall although some sites in the north east and north west show improvements (Figure 4.74), reflecting improvements in sewage effluent quality.

In terms of nutrients, there are few significant trends in phosphate concentrations apparent in the HMS data set because these increased initially, before a general downward trend from the early 1980s to 1995

(Figure 4.75). There are sites however, in the north west and north east where concentrations are increasing. Nitrate concentrations show slight increases at some Harmonised Monitoring Sites and more marked decreases at some sites in the Anglian and the Thames Regions (Figure 4.76). It is likely that sites with increasing inputs are arising from agricultural runoff and reflect the increasing concentrations of nitrate in the baseflow component of some rivers (arising from groundwater). Sites with reductions in nitrate may reflect changing agricultural practices with a move away from spring barley to winter wheat. Changes in nitrate concentrations in sewage effluents are also likely to be significant in some places. The River Lee in the Thames Region, for example, showed nitrate reductions. This river comprises 50 to 70 per cent sewage effluent in dry weather. Denitrification at a large sewage works in this catchment explains this change. Sewage treatment improvements are also likely to account for the long-term reductions in nitrite concentrations shown in Figure 4.77, although these may also relate to better oxygen levels in rivers.

Long-term Groundwater Data

Groundwater quality has been monitored in a few locations for over 40 years but records tend to be incomplete due to changes in institutional arrangements over the years, and there are no nationally recognised reference sites established yet. Nitrate concentrations in the Cotebrook source, in a sandstone aquifer in the North West Region, are plotted from 1950 to 1996 in Figure 4.78 as an example. This shows an increasing trend in nitrate concentrations in this area. Such increases contribute to the increase in river nitrate concentrations as measured by the HMS. Aquifers in other parts of the

Figure 4.72
Trends in biochemical oxygen demand in rivers, 1976 to 1995 for Harmonised Monitoring sites, and time series plots for four selected sites

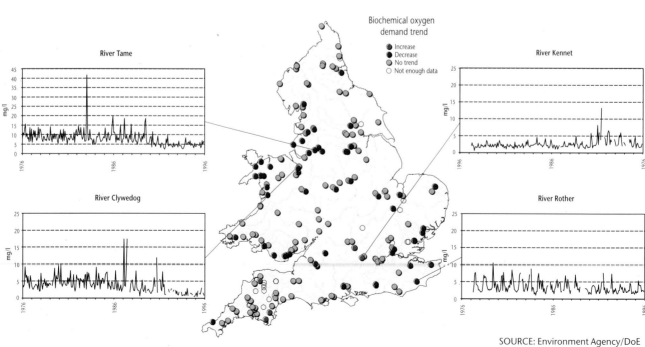

SOURCE: Environment Agency/DoE

Figure 4.73
Trends in dissolved oxygen concentrations in rivers, 1976 to 1995 for Harmonised Monitoring sites, and time series plots for four selected sites

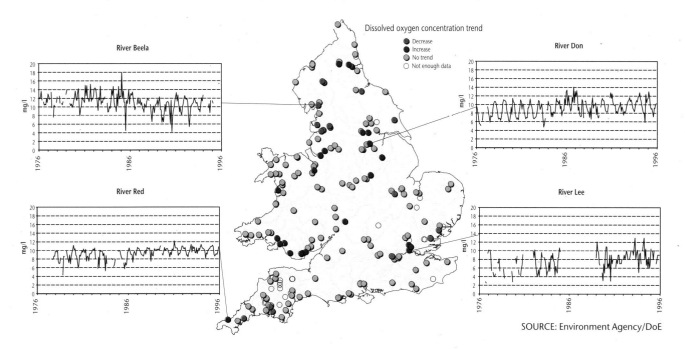

SOURCE: Environment Agency/DoE

Figure 4.74
Trends in ammoniacal nitrogen concentrations in rivers, 1976 to 1995 for Harmonised Monitoring sites, and time series plots for four selected sites

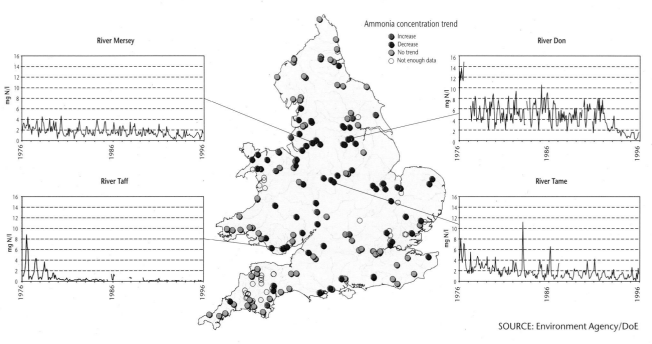

SOURCE: Environment Agency/DoE

Figure 4.75
Trends in orthophosphate concentrations in rivers, 1976 to 1995 for Harmonised Monitoring sites, and time series plots for four selected sites

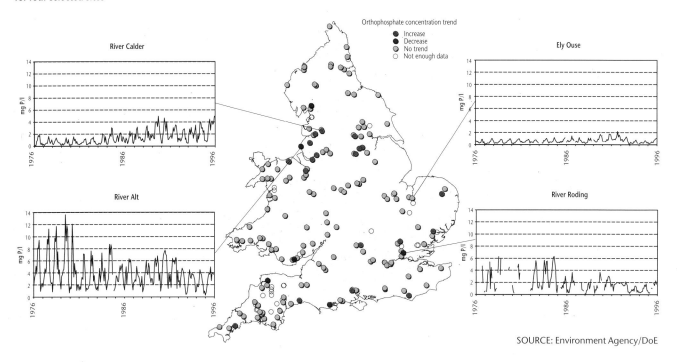

SOURCE: Environment Agency/DoE

Figure 4.76
Trends in nitrate concentrations in rivers, 1976 to 1995 for Harmonised Monitoring sites, and time series plots for four selected sites

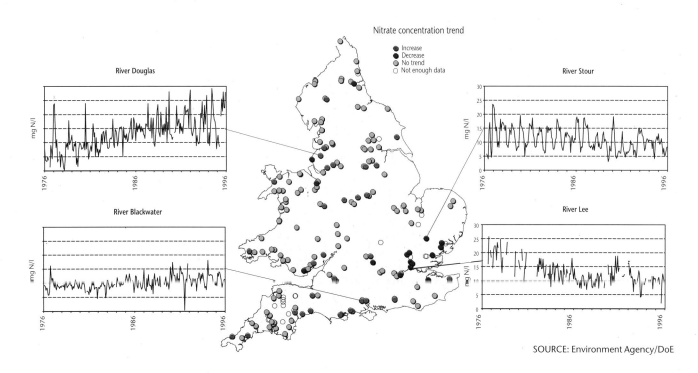

SOURCE: Environment Agency/DoE

Figure 4.77
Trends in nitrite concentrations in rivers, 1976 to 1995 for Harmonised Monitoring sites, and time series plots for four selected sites

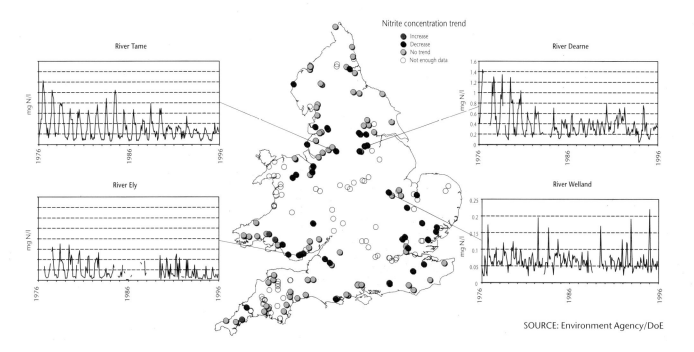

SOURCE: Environment Agency/DoE

country show stable nitrate concentrations over the past 16 years, for example, in the Jurassic limestone in the Anglian Region (see Figure 4.36). In areas where this is the case, river concentrations also tend to be fairly stable (see Figures 4.37 and 4.39) although these do show increases in nitrate concentrations in the 1940 to 1970 time period.

Long-term Lake Data

Long-term data sets are available from research organisations working on lakes in the English Lake District. These show some patterns of interest. The thermocline in Windermere and the biomass of zooplankton for a series of data from 1966 to 1992, corresponds well with the position of the Gulf Stream (Figure 4.79) (George and Taylor, 1995). Year to year variations in the quantities of *Aphanizomenon* (a type of algae) from 1955 to the mid 1970s relate more to summer wind speeds than other factors such as nutrient availability. Figure 4.80 shows data from Esthwaite Water, an eutrophic lake in the Lake District. Blooms of *Aphanizomenon* developed in the late 1950s when the nutrient loading was much lower, and in the late 1960s when the nutrient loading had increased considerably. Climatic records show that these

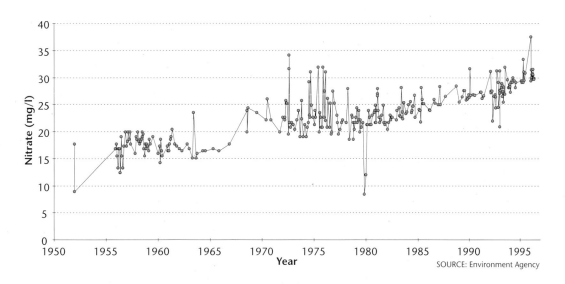

SOURCE: Environment Agency

Figure 4.78
Long-term groundwater nitrate concentrations in the Cotebrook Aquifer, the North West Region

Figure 4.79
Summer biomass of zooplankton in the North Basin of Windermere compared with the latitude of the north wall of the Gulf Stream

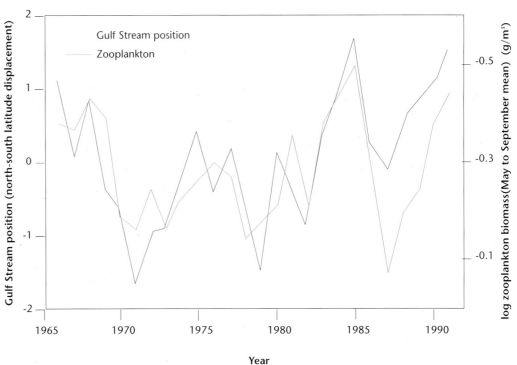

SOURCE: Institute of Freshwater Ecology

summers had been less windy than average, depicted in the stability of the seasonal thermocline in Figure 4.80. The figure shows that there is a cyclical relationship between the inter-annual fluctuations in the numbers of *Daphnia*, the abundance of *Aphanizomenon*, and the stability of the seasonal thermocline. (The *Daphnia* and *Aphanizomenon* time series have been detrended with a simple linear model.) Low *Daphnia* numbers in the late 1950s and the late 1960s coincided with high algae numbers and high thermocline stability. The '10-year' cycle of thermocline stability matches the cycle in Windermere and the Irish Sea suggesting that these cycles are produced by variations in some large-scale feature of the atmospheric circulation (George *et al.*, 1990).

There has also been work to evaluate the current condition of lakes relative to their historic, semi-natural status. This was done using mathematical models to estimate the input of nutrients that would be generated from a lake's catchment knowing the soil type, geology and agricultural activity before modern intensification post 1930s. Ninety lakes were selected and of these, 44 per cent showed a more than doubling of lake phosphorus over time (Figure 4.81) (Moss *et al.*, 1996).

Barton Broad, a shallow lake which forms part of the Norfolk Broads, provides an example of trends in lake quality. By the late 1970s the lake was badly affected by nutrient enrichment. It had large algal blooms, turbid water and the diverse plant and animal communities had disappeared. To restore the lake, the input of phosphorus was substantially reduced in

1980 by the installation of tertiary treatment at the sewage-treatment works discharging to the catchment. Over the next five years there were reductions in the amounts of phosphorus and algae in the lake (Figure 4.82), but the amount of change was less than had been expected. This was caused by the release of phosphorus stored in the lake sediment and it is now recognised that this reservoir of phosphorus can introduce substantial delays in the recovery of lakes. Barton Broad also shows the importance of river flow. During the drought of 1991 to 1992, phosphorus concentrations and algal biomass increased due to the release of phosphorus from the sediments combined with the lack of flushing of the lake. This case study illustrates the difficulty of reversing the effects of phosphorus enrichment, particularly in shallow lakes, and thus the need to prevent such changes from occurring rather than relying on subsequent restoration.

The historical development of acidification has been reconstructed from the remains of different types of diatoms (microscopic algae) in lake sediments (Figure 4.83) (Patrick *et al.*, 1995). The Institute of Hydrology's 'MAGIC' model has simulated similar increases in surface water acidity since the mid-nineteenth century. This trend corresponds with sulphur emissions which rose steadily following the industrial revolution. The model has been used to predict the change that could occur as sulphur emissions are reduced. The figure shows that pH may stabilise slightly above 1990 levels based on these predictions.

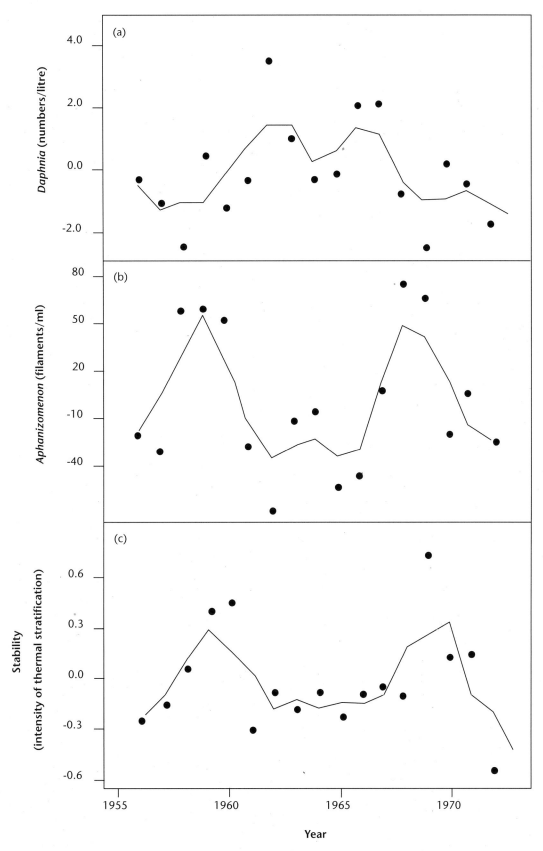

SOURCE: Institute of Freshwater Ecology

Figure 4.80
Relationship between the year to year changes in the number of water fleas (Daphnia), algae (Aphanizomenon), and the thermal stratification (stability) in Esthwaite Water, 1955 to 1974

Figure 4.81
Modelled change in eutrophication status of 90 lakes from the 1930s to 1992/93, based on total phosphorus, total nitrogen and chlorophyll 'a'

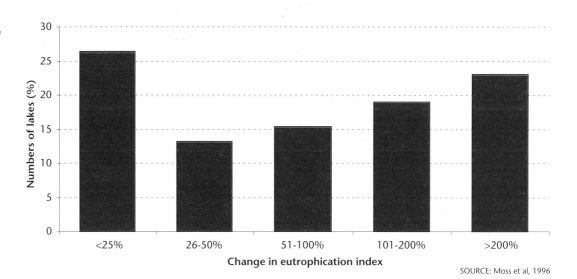

SOURCE: Moss et al, 1996

Figure 4.82
Phosphorus and chlorophyll 'a' concentrations in Barton Broad, the Anglian Region, 1978 to 1995

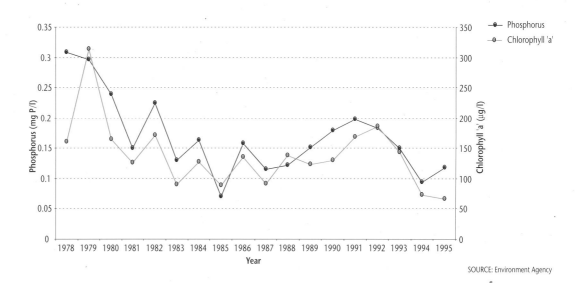

SOURCE: Environment Agency

Figure 4.83
pH reconstructed from diatoms for 1850 to 1990 for Scoat Tarn, North West England and pH simulated by the MAGIC model for 1850 to 2030.

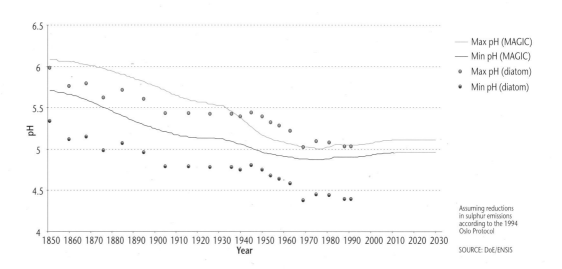

Assuming reductions in sulphur emissions according to the 1994 Oslo Protocol

SOURCE: DoE/ENSIS

Environmental Change Network

The detection of long-term environmental changes caused by natural and man-induced changes in climate and other factors requires careful monitoring. The Environmental Change Network (ECN) was launched in January 1992 as the UK's integrated network for monitoring environmental change. It is coordinated by the Natural Environmental Research Council and there are currently 14 sponsoring agencies, including the Environment Agency. The objectives of the network are:

    to maintain a set of sites within the UK to obtain comparable long term data sets of variables identified as being of major environmental importance;

    to provide for the integration and analysis of these data sets, to identify changes, and to understand the causes of change;

    to make these data sets available as a basis for research and prediction;

    to provide, for research purposes, a range of representative sites where there is good and reliable environmental information.

The network comprises 11 terrestrial and 38 freshwater sites spread across the UK. It is intended to expand the network in the next few years to ensure a more complete coverage. A set of standard protocols are being developed for monitoring to ensure consistency in data gathering, collection and interpretation. Protocols for measurements relevant to the freshwater sites will include meteorological data, water chemistry, physical variables, flow, macroinvertebrates, macrophytes, diatoms and plankton species.

Consistent data collection, with good quality control, is essential to meet the long-term aims of the programme. These are to be able to interpret future changes in the environment and to provide early indication of potential changes, not yet identified. The network has not been running for sufficient years yet to provide useful results.

Acid Waters Monitoring Network

In the light of the uncertainties and long-term nature of changes in acidification, monitoring is needed to show the response to investment in emission controls. The UK Acid Water Monitoring Network of the government, started in 1988, provides long-term data from 22 sites, nine in England and Wales, for this purpose. So far, an analysis of trends to 1993 has revealed few significant changes in water quality, any gradual change being likely to be masked by annual variability over this short period (Patrick et al., 1995). A Welsh regional survey of 77 streams, which were sampled in the winters of 1984 and 1995, indicated an average improvement in chemistry over this period of about 0.2 pH units (Figure 4.84). Of four streams for which data were available over the whole 12 years, three showed significant declines in non-marine sulphate concentrations (the main driver of acidification), though only one showed a significant increase in pH (Figure 4.85). Despite the evidence of a slight improvement in stream chemistry there was no recovery across the region in populations of macroinvertebrates, juvenile salmon and trout, or dippers.

Overall Perspective

The long-term information shows that significant progress has been made in reducing anthropogenic sources of pollution in rivers for the substances considered, suggesting that regulation has been effective in many cases, although it is too early to

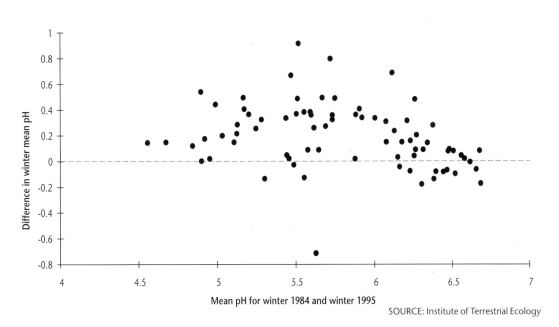

SOURCE: Institute of Terrestrial Ecology

Figure 4.84
Change in winter mean pH for 77 streams sampled in 1984 and 1995, plotted against the mean pH for each site for two years

Figure 4.85
Sulphate concentrations and pH from acidic deposition in a stream near Beddgelert Forest, North Wales, 1983 to 1996

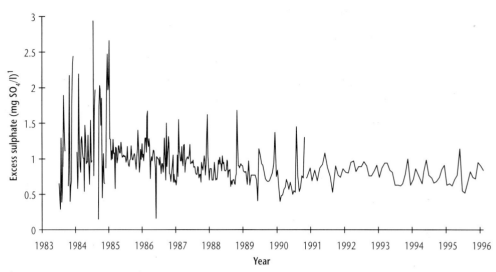

[1]Calculated from measured streamwater concentrations by subtracting the seawater derived fraction

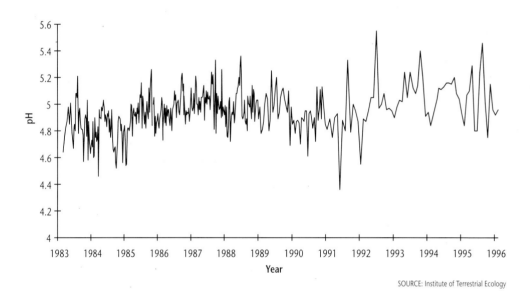

SOURCE: Institute of Terrestrial Ecology

show the impact of some measures, for example, emission controls to reduce acidification. There is not much information presented here on groundwaters due to the lack of national databases, and the impact of regulation will take longer to take effect in these waters due to longer residence times. The information for lakes shows clearly the impact of both climatic variability and anthropogenic activities. Many substances are not monitored by these schemes and many of the networks have only been put in place in the last decade. These networks should provide valuable information to assess changes in the environment, and to dissociate natural from anthropogenic effects in the future.

4.6   Aesthetic Quality

Aesthetic quality ranks high in public perception of the environment because it is what is readily seen, heard or smelt. Issues such as landscape, litter and

odour are of great importance to river users and until 1995, had not generally been monitored nationally. Some developments in tackling this issue have been made in recent years and these are reported here, but this is very much a starting point. Tastes differ; what one person considers aesthetically pleasant may not be what pleases others, so methods need to be developed. The Agency will be increasing its awareness of public tastes for the environment but in the meantime, we are working on the problems of gross litter.

General Quality Assessment

In 1995 some river sites across the country were sampled to test the aesthetics GQA classification system, which considers the amount of litter, colour, odour, stagnation and the presence of oil and foam on river banks (Appendix 5). More extensive testing was undertaken in the Midlands Region which illustrates

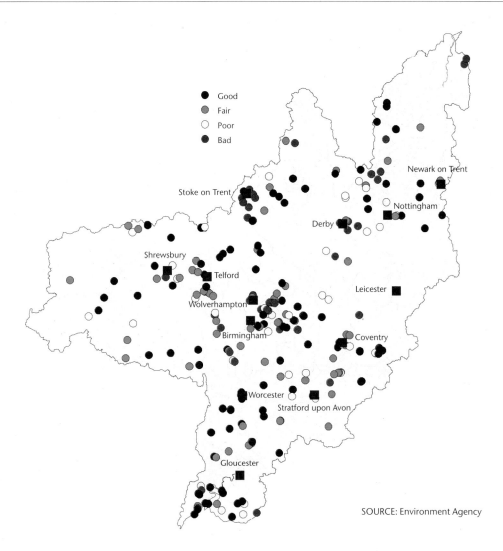

Figure 4.86
Aesthetic General Quality Assessment of rivers in the Midlands Region, spring 1995

SOURCE: Environment Agency

the results that can be obtained (Figure 4.86). The picture of aesthetic quality is biased towards sites with public access and with known problems from intermittent sewerage system discharges, although some 'clean' sites were included for reference purposes.

Results have demonstrated the poor aesthetic quality of some rivers. Many rivers draining urbanised catchments, particularly in Wales and the west of England, have poor aesthetic quality even though the chemical quality is Very Good or Good. Often this is the result of general litter, oil and sewage derived litter emanating from the discharge of combined sewer overflows. It may also relate to the number of pollution incidents which can be high in urbanised areas where the sources are waste oil, transport and roads. Fuels and oils accounted for 26 per cent of incidents in 1996 and these tend to arise more frequently in urban areas, affecting the aesthetic quality. As a result of these incidents, the Oil Care Campaign was launched by the NRA in 1995 with help from industry in an attempt to alleviate this problem. This is being continued by the Agency.

A further source of litter in urban areas is fly tipping. It is illegal to dispose of any solid matter into rivers without consent. The Agency has powers to control

illegal dumping and to recharge for clean-up and works with local authorities to achieve this. A further cause of aesthetic problems are misconnections of foul drains to surface water sewers, requiring difficult tracing exercises to identify. The education of 'Do It Yourself' enthusiasts is necessary and the enforcement of building regulations. The water industry, government agencies, sanitary products manufacturers and various charities had a 'Bag It and Bin It' campaign recently to reduce the number of sanitary products in waste waters.

The Agency plans to use the aesthetic aspect of the GQA to check progress in improving sewerage systems and reducing spills from sewer overflows and tackling other aesthetic problems. About £850 million has been allocated to resolving these issues by the water companies nationally between 1995 and 2005.

Landscape Studies

In order to protect and enhance the water environment, there is a need to understand what elements of the landscape we want to protect, and what elements are degraded and need restoring. Landscape assessment allows this to be done. This is a process which aims to:

communicate a clear understanding of how the river landscape has developed and to describe the main formative influences on its character;

provide base-line information on the character and quality of the existing river landscape and its sensitivity to change;

identify major issues affecting it and how these may be addressed;

identify the scope, need and opportunity for enhancement of the river landscape.

The term 'landscape' refers primarily to the appearance of the land, including its shape, form, colour and elements. It also reflects the way in which these various components combine to create specific patterns and pictures that are distinctive to particular localities. The landscape is not purely a visual phenomenon because its characterisation relies closely on its physiography and history. Hence, in addition to the scenic or visual dimension of landscape, a whole range of other factors, including geology, topography, soils, archeology, landscape history, land-use, ecology, architecture and cultural associations, influence the way in which landscape is experienced and valued. The landscape is an important part of our natural resource base and provides a reservoir of archaeological and historical evidence as well as an environment for plant and animal communities. As a human habitat, the landscape holds special meaning for many people as the source of numerous experiences and memories. Many of these are visual, but at times the landscape may evoke other emotional, cultural and even spiritual responses.

Recent approaches to landscape assessment have tended to avoid the issue of evaluating relative quality between different types of landscape. Quantitative approaches which involve scoring different attributes of landscape have been dismissed as over-simplistic and misleading while other more qualitative methods are fraught with problems of subjectivity. Instead, the emphasis is now on understanding the character of individual landscapes and assessing their intrinsic quality using a combination of objectivity and subjectivity. Thus it is possible to assess whether a landscape is intrinsically of a high or low quality, in good or poor condition, or in need of conservation or enhancement without the need for comparisons with other dissimilar types. The methodology for river landscape assessment developed by the NRA follows this approach. It requires an appropriate value class (1 to 4) to be attributed to each individual landscape type depending upon its intrinsic quality and condition. The main purpose of this evaluation is to help determine where conservation or enhancement measures should be targeted. In addition to the value classes, the most appropriate management strategy (conservation, restoration or enhancement) is also attributed to each landscape type to indicate what

degree and type of intervention is required to maintain or improve the quality of the landscape. Details on evaluation matrices are given in Appendix 7.

Landscape assessment is a tool that is used on a local basis when development plans or other proposals are being assessed. As such, there is no national view on how many river landscapes would benefit from restoration or enhancement.

Other Aspects

The colour of rivers, lakes and reservoirs can be affected by land-use and discharges and this can lead to costs incurred by water companies for treatment as well as a loss of aesthetic quality. Peat coloured water from the upland areas in England and Wales is an example and whilst this is largely natural, peat erosion due to overgrazing and trampling may have exacerbated the effects. The cost of resurfacing and revegetating to overcome this is estimated to be £12,000 per hectare. Abandoned mines have also led to discolouration of water, and the stark example of the Carrick Roads and Falmouth Creek in Cornwall turning orange in January 1992, due to the closure of the Wheal Jane mine, hit the national headlines. Dealing with abandoned mines is an enormous task. Through a programme of prioritisation, taking into account environmental and socio-economic factors, and in partnership with others, it is hoped that the aesthetic problems caused by abandoned mines can be reduced.

Point discharges may also lead to discolouration of rivers. The River Cherwell below Banbury sewage works can be coffee coloured due to a food processing company in the catchment. In the East Midlands, textile dyeing and finishing is very much a part of the regional industry but rivers like the Soar/Sence and the Erewash, in the Lower Trent catchment, have at times been turned pink, purple and inky black. The Agency has developed a method of setting standards for colour on discharge consents as a means of controlling the aesthetic problem and applied colour standards to sewage works effluents discharging into the Soar and Erewash in January 1996. Ozone treatment is part of the process at Leek STW to remove colour from the effluent. Continued pressure by the Agency on the water utility company and the textile industry is starting to show results. It is also behind the industry's efforts in considering alternative and innovative treatment systems, some of which also help to reduce waste.

A survey to measure the extent of participation in leisure day visits to canals and rivers as part of a wider survey, and to estimate the scale and value of these visits showed that people were generally well satisfied with the standard of upkeep of the freshwater environment, and where provided, with any waterside facilities and information (Figure 4.87) (Social and Community Planning Research, 1997).

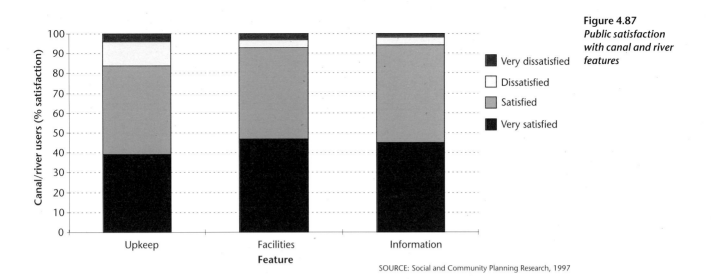

Figure 4.87
Public satisfaction with canal and river features

SOURCE: Social and Community Planning Research, 1997

4.7 Summary of the State of Fresh Waters

Table 4.10 *Summary of the state of fresh waters*

Viewpoint	State	Trend	Comments
Land use and environmental resources	**Renewable water resources:** 77,000Mm³/yr reduced to 39,000Mm³/yr in drought years. Distinct regional and temporal variations. Low per person availability.	Less resources available in recent summers due to lower summer rainfall and higher temperatures. NW/SE gradient in rainfall amounts. Greater variability and volatility in recent years.	Peak demands also increasing in summer. Climate change is an issue.
	Storage of water resources: usable reservoir capacity = 1,560Mm³ Estimated chalk aquifer capacity = 21,000Mm³	Greater drawdown of storage in summer droughts. Droughts reduce recharge by 50 per cent.	Reflects peak demands, related to high summer temperatures and increasing demand for irrigation.
	Low flow sites: Over 30 recognised and more being investigated. Greatest problems in south and east but low flows occurred in many rivers in the north and west in 1995 and 1996.	Increased awareness due to frequency of droughts in recent years. A number of problems have been solved and others are scheduled.	A joint review with English Nature of the extent of Sites of Special Scientific Interest affected currently being done.
	Flood risk: 10,683km² at risk of 1 in 100 year flood, of which 611km² is built up, in the absence of flood defences. Total of 34,000km flood defences.	1,100km of flood defences improved or built in last four years.	Planning controls essential.
	Riverine habitats: 20 per cent unmodified; 38 per cent semi-natural; 42 per cent extensively changed. Headwaters show signs of degradation.	First survey of this type.	
	Wetlands: 15 thought to be affected by over-abstraction, 100 thought to be at risk of drying out. Only about 10 sq km of Fenland remaining.	Since the 1930s, 64 per cent loss of wet grasslands in the Thames Valley, 37 per cent loss in the Broads. Rate of up to 4.4 per cent loss per year in Humberside, and 0.2 per cent in Cumbria. Loss of reedbeds 0.2 to 0.6km² per year.	
	Lakes and ponds: about 180,000 standing water bodies; only 1,700 greater than 4ha and 12,500 greater than 2ha.	78 per cent loss of ponds since 1880. Creation of gravel pits, garden ponds, reservoirs and other still waters increasing stock.	
Key biological populations and communities, and biodiversity	**Aquatic plants:** relatively rich. Distribution reflects natural climatic and geographic variability.	Decline in some species especially on wetlands. 20 to 33 per cent of flora species became locally extinct in last 150 years, 50 per cent declined. Increase in exotic species.	Attributed to changes in farming, drainage, nutrient enrichment, but some longer term changes too.
	Macroinvertebrates: 76 families found in England and Wales in 1995. Extensive occurrence of freshwater white-clawed crayfish in North England and Wales, sparse elsewhere.	Insufficient information available from previous years. Decline of white-clawed crayfish due to predation and disease.	

Viewpoint	State	Trend	Comments
	Fisheries: salmon and sea trout catches fairly constant over the 1990s. Fish kills can be caused by pollution incidents causing oxygen depletion and high concentrations of toxic ammonia.	Salmonid decline since 1990 due to effects of low flows and siltation. Decline in spring salmon over 25 years. The loss of wild brown trout continues. Vast improvements in some rivers, e.g. Tees, since 1970s. Coarse fish appear to have stable populations in last few years. Creation of still water coarse and game fisheries increased since the 1970s.	Not much nationally consistent data: Implementation of Fisheries Classification System planned. Catch, especially spring salmon could be affected by conditions in the North Atlantic too. Siltation linked to changing land use.
	Non-native and exotic fish: cause local problems.	Increasing number of non-native species.	Fish introduced for recreational purposes; difficult to control.
	Birds: exotic species, e.g. Canada goose widespread. Six primary bird habitats dependent on fresh waters.	Decline in yellow wagtail, kingfisher, grey wagtail. Spatial distribution of yellow wagtail declining. Increase in mallards, coots and whitethroats. Swans restored after ban on lead weights.	Some species' decline linked to severity of winters and African rainfall. Causes not generally well understood.
	Water voles:	67 per cent decline since 1977.	Probably due to habitat loss and mink predation. A target in the Biodiversity Action Plan.
	Otters: 23 per cent of surveyed sites occupied in England, 53 per cent sites in Wales.	Improved from six per cent sites in England in 1977; need further habitat improvements.	Thought due to ban on organochlorine pesticides and improved habitat restoration.
	Amphibians: common frogs and toads widespread.	Some evidence of decline due to loss of breeding habitat.	Toads vulnerable to traffic; this increasing pressure needs monitoring.
	Natterjack toad confined to a few sites.	Serious decline due to habitat loss; drying out of shallow water in early summer and/or acidification.	
	Rare, threatened and vulnerable species: 47 dependent on fresh waters.		Action plans being developed by various organisations.
Quality. Compliance with standards, targets, classification schemes	**EC Dangerous Substances Directives:** List I, 1.3 per cent sites non-compliant; failures include HCH (10 sites), and cadmium (5 sites). List II, 4.6 per cent sites non-compliant; failures for copper, zinc and pH in the south west, north east, north west and Midlands.	Reduction of loads since 1985 due to need to meet commitment to North Sea agreements.	Wool processing/ pesticide uses of HCH continue to be an issue. Minewaters cause local problems (metals). Consent reviews needed in some cases.
	Pesticides: problems associated with PCSD, cyfluthrin, and permethrin clustered around Aire catchment in the north east. Sheep dips, isoproturon, diuron cause problems, largest number in the north east and Midlands. Atrazine a problem in groundwater.	Spate of pollution incidents from sheep dips. New synthetic pyrethroids more toxic to aquatic life than organophosphates. Decline in atrazine and simazine since withdrawal from non-agricultural use in 1993.	Some problems linked to textile industry. Main use of atrazine now on maize.

Viewpoint	State	Trend	Comments
	Freshwater Fish Directive: 6.5 per cent of reaches non-compliant.	Compliance improved since 1980s due to investment by water industry and agriculture. 22 per cent of failures in 1996 due to low flows.	31 per cent of failures due to point source discharges; investment planned by 1999 to improve these.
	Nitrate limits: 68 catchments designated as Nitrate Vulnerable zones, covering 600,000ha	Stable in some surface waters, increasing in others. Long-term groundwater sites show either stable or increasing nitrate concentrations.	Linked to farming practices. Groundwater takes a long time to respond to change.
	Classified rivers: >90 per cent Very Good to Fair by chemistry and biology; 8 to 9 per cent Poor; 1 to 2 per cent Bad. South West, Welsh and Southern Regions have highest proportion of good quality rivers. Poorest rivers in urban areas of the north west and north east. High nutrient concentrations in east and south east, lowest in north and west.	Significant improvement from 1990 to 1995. Expected further improvement to 2005, although the drought of 1995 and 1996 has caused reduced quality in some areas. Phosphorus decreasing in some places due to load reductions from change in detergents and treatment processes	Reflect investment by water industry and pollution prevention activities. Short-term problems due to storm overflows which affect urban quality. Distribution of nutrient concentrations linked to sewage and agricultural inputs.
	Selective lakes: show high concentrations of phosphorus and chlorophyll 'a' in Midlands, and East England.	First year of survey.	The lack of monitoring and lack of unified classification scheme is now being addressed.
	Groundwater quality: not monitored consistently, but contamination thought to be widespread, particularly from solvents, nitrate, pesticides and waste disposal.	Not known, except for nitrate where it is either stable or increasing	Key issue - a monitoring strategy and programme still being developed.
Health of environmental resources	**Eutrophication:** 33 waters designated as eutrophic, currently 48 other sites being considered. Algal blooms greatest in the Midlands. Eutrophic rivers greatest in south and east.	Little change in incidence of toxic blue-green algal blooms over past five years.	Algal blooms and scum in lakes and reservoirs associated with calm weather.
	Acidification: widespread in uplands of north and west, affecting fisheries and some Sites of Special Scientific Interest.	Some improvements expected up to 2010 with emission reductions. Some rapid improvements occurred where liming has taken place.	Nitrogen oxides from transport emissions cause increasing concern.
	Bioaccumulation: toxic substances widely dispersed. Many freshwater eels exceed HCH, dieldrin and PCB limits.	Increased awareness. Improved testing of chemicals before use.	PCBs, dieldrin and DDT now banned.
	Endocrine disruption: some rivers with high incidence of intersex in fish, linked to sewage effluents and/or industrial discharges.	Awareness increasing as surveys done, but not known how long the phenomenon has been in existence.	Precautionary action needed.
	Microbiological contamination: high below sewage inputs, but can be highly variable.	Stable over 20 years.	Possible implications for recreational users.

Viewpoint	State	Trend	Comments
Long-term reference sites	**Harmonised Monitoring Scheme (HMS):** good data sets for some determinands. Regional variation reflects inputs.	HMS from 1976 to 1995 show general reductions in copper, zinc, lead, lindane, biochemical oxygen demand and ammonia. Current nitrate load to sea not as high as late 1970s. Orthophosphate load declined slightly recently.	General reductions in loads, but nitrate increasing at some sites in the north west and north east.
	Long-term groundwater data: limited number of collated data sets and no recognised reference sites established yet.	Some aquifers show increasing nitrate concentrations, e.g. sandstone in north-west, others more stable, e.g. Jurassic limestone.	See previous comments on nitrate.
	Long-term lake data: sets from Windermere link thermocline to Gulf Stream; algae related to windspeeds.	Lake phosphorus estimated to have doubled since 1930 in 44 per cent of selected lakes.	Relevant to climate change issue. Link to inputs from human activities. Restoration can be slow.
	Environmental Change Network:	Insufficient records yet.	
	Acid Waters Monitoring Network:	Insufficient records yet.	
Aesthetic quality	**General aesthetic assessment:** not much consistent data, but some sites are aesthetically poor.	Insufficient records yet.	Key issue linked to storm overflows, pollution incidents, fly tipping.
	Landscape studies:	Recent expenditure to restore and enhance habitats, particularly in some urban areas.	Public awareness and expectations increasing.
	Colour: Local problems occur due to discharges from textile and other industries and abandoned mines.	Natural variations but some increase in peatiness thought to be due to overgrazing. Threat of mine closures large.	Land-use important.

5 Responding to the State of Fresh Waters

This section looks at what has been done by various economic sectors to reduce the pressure of human activities on the state of fresh waters. Most efforts to reduce pressures involve investment, so the section is based on how much has been spent on taking action rather than a detailed description of all the actions taken. In this sense, investment has been taken as a proxy for economic activity directed towards protecting the environment. Some actions, of course, are not readily quantifiable in terms of monetary cost but can help to reduce pressures, for example voluntary efforts towards the efficient use of water, and waste minimisation. Education and information create a greater awareness of the issues that threaten sustainable development and should also elicit a response from society. However, such a response is hard to measure and so the benefits of better access to information are hard to quantify.

Much of the emphasis in this section is on the water industry because most abstractions and discharges relate to the services that this sector supplies. Investment information from the water industry has been collated by OFWAT since privatisation and so is readily available. Later in this section, the expenditure by farming, industry and others on the freshwater environment is considered, but information has been less easy to collate from these sectors and may be incomplete. The final part of the section looks at studies that have investigated how much society is willing to pay for improvements to the freshwater environment.

5.1 Sectoral Overview of Impact of Investment to Date

Water Industry: Sewerage and Sewage Treatment

Improvements in river quality between 1990 and 1995 are largely attributable to improvements in the treatment of sewage effluents by the water industry immediately prior to and post privatisation in 1989. The impact of sewage effluents on river quality has been known for decades and is the reason for much pollution control legislation. Altogether, there are about 6,500 sewage-treatment facilities in the UK where about 95 per cent of the polluting load is removed by treatment before being discharged. Of these, there are 125 sewage-treatment works (STWs) serving populations of 100,000 or more, and a further 564 serving populations of 10,000 or more. This level of treatment is amongst the highest level in OECD countries, probably reflecting the density of population, and is only exceeded by Germany (OECD, 1994).

Investment in treatment processes has varied through time. Figure 5.1 relates total capital investment to water quality classifications in England and Wales over the past 25 years and shows some relationship between investment and the percentage of reaches classified as good or fair. The historic data for capital investment relate to the total invested, not only that spent on discharges to fresh waters, so the link to water quality is tentative; it is assumed that the pattern of investment on these is similar to the overall picture. The figure shows good correlation between expenditure and river quality improvements in the 1990s (with a few years delay), but also shows how investment in the mid 1970s did not appear to bring about significant improvements in water quality; some investment has been for asset renewal over the years rather than to bring about environmental improvements. With the privatisation of the water industry in 1989, the water utilities were required, amongst other things, to improve their sewage-treatment works to ensure that the quality of their effluents complied with the conditions of their discharge consents because many were failing to do so. Investment valued in excess of £1,100 million (at 1996/97 price base) for sewage works discharging to fresh waters took place over the period 1990/91 to 1994/95, which was reflected in the improvement in the number of sewage works complying with their consent conditions. This investment was equivalent to about £20 per person in 1991/92 compared with an investment of £5 to £6 per person per year during most of the 1980s and an investment of about £13 to £14 in the last two years.

The capital investment on fresh waters of £1,100 million has been broken down to water company level (Figure 5.2). There is no straightforward relationship between the amount of investment and reduction in organic concentrations from STWs (Table 3.4) because capital expenditure to effect improvements will vary depending on the size of the works and the process changes required. As increasingly tighter standards are required (that is further levels of sewage treatment) the capital costs are significantly greater but the relationship is not linear. Figure 5.2 also indicates the amount of investment per person in each company region on sewage treatment improvements. This shows how costs have varied substantially between £11 per person in the area served by Thames Water Utilities and £40 per person in South West Waters' area. The amount spent reflects many factors. Some companies have had to spend substantial amounts on improving discharges to coastal waters which are excluded from this report; other areas have relatively low resident populations compared with those served by STWs during the tourist season, both of which can cause apparent anomalies.

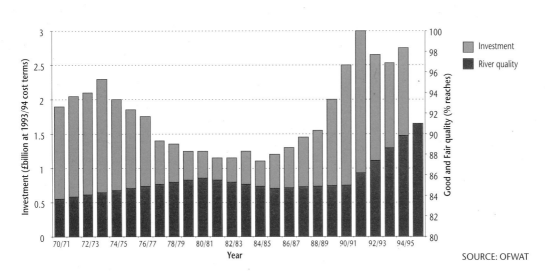

SOURCE: OFWAT

Figure 5.1
Water quality investment and river quality, 1970 to 1995

This investment, which has brought about a reduction in pollution loads and improvements in consent compliance, together with investment in the sewerage network to reduce the impact of storm overflows valued at £2,270 million, giving a total of £3,370 million, has resulted in the significant improvements in river water quality stated in Section 4.3. To put this into some perspective, £40 billion was invested in the rail and trunk road infrastructure in the 15 year period after 1979 (Department of Transport, 1996). On a national basis, river improvements have cost about £0.25 million per kilometre. It is worth noting that the driver for the investment at the time of privatisation was compliance with consents, rather than river quality improvement, and there are cases where investment has not necessarily led to improvements in river quality grades. This is particularly true where the cost driver for investment was a suspended solid condition in a consent. A further feature that needs to be recognised is that the cost of STW improvements will depend on the process changes required and this is not linearly related to reductions in load or river quality improvements.

Whilst the initial investment programme (1990 to 1995) of the water companies was taking place, the Urban Waste Water Treatment Directive (UWWTD) (91/271/EEC) was agreed. This Directive specifies levels of sewage treatment according to the size of the STW and the sensitivity of the receiving water and specifies effluent standards that must be met. Secondary treatment is the norm but tertiary treatment is required, where necessary, to protect the environment. Many STWs across England and Wales already meet the requirements of the UWWTD but others do not, so that over the period 1995 to 2005, water companies will need to invest more capital to ensure that these standards are met. A total of £6 billion has been allocated to this programme, of which £1.6 billion is for works discharging to the freshwater environment (the rest is for discharges to estuaries or coastal waters). Where rivers have been designated as Eutrophic Sensitive Areas under the UWWTD, sewage-treatment works exceeding a size of 10,000 population equivalence, are required to reduce their nutrient loading. About 50 works across the country are required to reduce their phosphorus loads by 1998 at an estimated cost of £20 million.

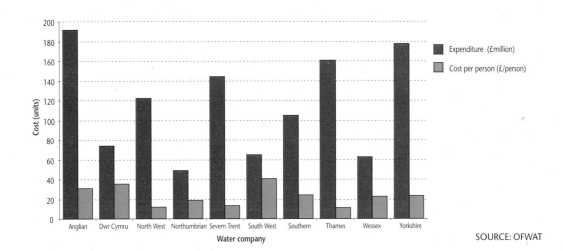

SOURCE: OFWAT

Figure 5.2
Water companies' capital expenditure on sewage treatment works with related costs per person of population served, for the five year period 1990/91 to 1994/95

It is not clear whether this investment will lead to improvements that can be measured by the chemical GQA scheme because the investment to meet BOD and suspended solid standards has been planned to meet the requirements of the Directive which relate to levels of treatment and effluent quality rather than the needs of rivers. Furthermore, some of the investment is to deal with unsatisfactory sewerage systems including the frequency with which storm overflows operate. Reducing such operations and more effective screening of these discharges will improve the aesthetic GQA class. The removal of phosphorus in relevant Eutrophic Sensitive Areas identified under UWWTD may be detected by the nutrient GQA in future and should also lead to reductions in the eutrophic state.

While the requirements of the UWWTD were being programmed into the water company investment programmes for the time period 1995 to 2005, the former NRA identified rivers where there was a need for improvements to sewage works discharges, based on environmental needs. These needs were driven through the failure of a non-statutory river quality objective, poor river quality, or a restriction in river-uses due to water quality. There was no 'statutory' need for these improvements and because the investment programme for the UWWTD was already large, only a limited number of these schemes received financial approval over the five year period, 1995 to 1999 at an estimated cost of £522 million. The amount of investment allocated to these discretionary environmental schemes per region is given in Table 5.1. In some regions, most of the money is being allocated to one or two major ongoing schemes, e.g. the Mersey Basin programme in the North West Region and the River Trent in the Severn Trent Region. People living and working in the Mersey Basin will see the effects of a long-term programme that started in 1985 and is still being funded to the tune of £130 million. Its objectives are to improve water quality so that by 2010 all rivers are clean enough to support fish, and to stimulate waterside development for business, recreation, housing and tourism. These improvement schemes were targeted by the NRA to ensure that river quality is improved or maintained at existing levels where there is a threat of deterioration and focuses expenditure where environmental benefit can be maximised. In rural areas, these schemes are helping to restore the flow to many dried up rivers and wetlands. The Norfolk Broads, a national nature reserve, will also benefit from improvements to sewage works that will help maintain biodiversity. The Agency is monitoring progress with these schemes to ensure that the environmental benefits are realised.

Table 5.1 *Water company investment allocated to specific environmental schemes over the period 1995 to 1999 at the discretion of the Secretary of State*

Water company	£ million
Severn Trent	194
North West	130
Yorkshire	60
Anglian	42
Thames	41
Wales	27
Wessex	18
Southern	10
Northumbrian	0
South West	0

The Agency is also monitoring sewage works which have traditionally met high standards even though their legal consents have not specified this need. For example, many works in the Midlands and the north west do not have standards specified for ammonia in their consents. The water quality downstream of these works reflects this traditional treatment to high standards and could deteriorate if the water companies change management practices. Provided that water companies continue to run these works well, and invest in maintaining works, water quality downstream should not deteriorate. The operating expenditure by water companies is falling but it is not clear how much of this is due to efficiency and how much is 'eating into' the reserves necessary to protect the environment.

The UWWTD recognises a need for sewers and STW to be sized so that overflows do not cause a flooding problem to properties or an environmental problem. Areas where investment is required have been identified and included in the water companies investment plans for the period 1995 to 2005. The cost of this programme is estimated to be £850 million nationally. In the Greater Manchester area, £450 million is to be spent on sewerage schemes and resolving unsatisfactory storm overflows which should improve some of the worst quality rivers in the country.

To resolve the problems caused by storm sewers and to ensure that the finance allocated is spent effectively, it is important to understand the interaction between the various components of urban drainage systems (sewers, various treatment works and receiving waters). To do this, the former NRA in collaboration with the water industry developed a methodology for assessing the problems and designing solutions. This methodology, including planning tools, is described in detail in the Urban Pollution Management (UPM) Manual (Foundation for Water Research, 1994). The methodology requires understanding the processes which contribute to the pollution problems on an individual basis and selecting a level of planning which is commensurate with the complexity of the problem and the likely cost of the solution.

Overall, the Agency is concerned that the water companies do not appear to have generally espoused excellence in their delivery of the sewerage and sewage treatment function. Given the tremendous developments in design, sensor and information technology that have taken place since privatisation, it is sad that, with some notable exceptions, the industry has no real-time awareness or understanding of how its sewerage and sewage treatment systems are operating or responding to changing conditions, whether minute to minute, hour to hour, day to day, month to month, or year to year. Solutions to environmental problems and challenges seem to be almost entirely dominated by static, conservative, civil engineering techniques rather than by adopting a more dynamic, risk management, chemical engineering approach based on awareness of the operating environment and responding to it. We do not think it unreasonable to expect that the sewerage and sewage treatment business (which is at least as complex in terms of variability of inputs as any major chemical manufacturing plant) should be fully aware of the inputs to its sewerage system, how the sewerage system is responding to those inputs, and how the treatment system is responding to the quality and quantity of sewage arriving at the works.

The Agency is actively encouraging and participating in research and development into real-time control systems for sewerage management and treatment works operation. We believe that, for major urban areas at least, such systems offer an opportunity for the water companies to make optimal use of the capacity of their sewers and treatment plants, thereby avoiding some significant capital investment and potentially reducing costs to customers, whilst minimising the risk of pollution to receiving waters.

Water Industry: Supply

Some of the investment in sewage treatment has pay-backs for the water industry itself where water is reused further down river. Annual operational costs of water resource provision and treatment is about seven pence/m³. Capital expenditure on treatment of drinking water cost about 10 pence/m³ in 1992 to 1994 and eight pence/m³ in 1994/95. The average cost to customers of water delivered to the tap is 59 pence/m³, so treatment costs represent about 25 per cent of the total (OFWAT, 1996b). The water supply industry spent a total of £43 million on environmental protection in 1994; this figure was based on a pilot survey of postal questionnaires and is only a crude indicator of activity undertaken for environmental purposes (DoE, 1996b).

If rivers do not meet required standards, then the costs of additional treatment are high. For example, on the rare occasions that nitrate concentrations are high in the River Thames, Three Valleys Water Company, who abstract directly from the Thames and have limited sources with which to blend the water, obtains bulk supplies from one of the reservoirs of Thames Water Utilities. Nitrate contamination of fresh waters has required water companies to invest £151 million in capital works (1990 to 1995) to treat or blend to meet standards required. By the year 2000, 30 nitrate removal plants will have been constructed. Pesticides in surface and groundwaters have exceeded the requirements of the EC Drinking Water Directive in places in the south and east so that a high level treatment process using granulated activated carbon is being added to treatment facilities at a total cost of £1 billion nationally over the period 1990/91 to 2004/05. The greatest investment has been required in the Thames and the Anglian Regions reflecting the greater agricultural use of pesticides, lower flows and lower dilution rates together with the greatest abstraction rates in the south and east. The investment equates to £5 per kilogramme of pesticide used. Based on capital expenditure from 1992/93 to 1995/96, the cost in Anglian Region has been about one pence per 100 litres (10 pence/m³) supplied, about 2.4 pence per person per day.

Whether this approach is more cost effective than restricting the use of pesticides is debatable; a study into alternative ways of dealing with pesticide pollution did not provide a definitive answer, with water treatment being more cost effective than restricting usage in one catchment, but the opposite was true in another case (Table 5.2). The study also

Table 5.2
Costs of alternative approaches to pesticide pollution

Catchment	No restrictions - water treatment costs (£million)	Water protection zone scenario (£million)	Restricted usage by farmers (£million)
Leam	2.4	0.9	3.1
Colne	3.4	1.1	1.0

Source: DoE/WRc

suggested that the water protection zone scenario was a favourable option in both catchments (Crathorne et al., 1995). The Agency has applied for a water protection zone in the River Dee and will continue to pursue this approach where relevant.

Dŵr Cymru (Welsh Water) has had to improve treatment in some areas where water sources have become more acidic due to acid deposition. The cost was estimated at £100,000 per year (1988 prices) equating to 0.1 to 0.8 pence/m^3, depending on the actual process used.

Water companies can also protect their intakes from pollution incidents by providing bankside storage as buffers in some circumstances. Such storage can be expensive and gaining planning permission can be difficult, especially if floodplains are affected, so this option is not always possible. A case of solvent pollution in the River Severn in 1994 affected the water supply of 140,000 people in the Worcester area, cost the water supply company £1.5 million in compensation to domestic customers as well as a £45,000 fine and £67,000 in legal costs, and unknown costs to industry. Another case involving phenol on the River Dee in 1984 affected the taste of the water supply of two million people in Cheshire and Merseyside. This is said to have cost Dŵr Cymru £10 million in remedial measures and £400,000 in compensation. Hence, preventing incidents is very cost beneficial. Ironically, the greatest proportion of pollution incidents in 1995 was from the water industry (30 per cent), such incidents having increased by 13 per cent since 1991. Some of these are considered to be due to the increased reliance on automatic equipment and alarms, which sometimes fail. Others are due to overloaded sewerage systems, a problem being addressed by ensuring compliance with the UWWTD.

Investment in leakage control should also have pay-backs for water companies by delaying the development of new resources such as reservoirs, and have pay-backs for the environment by ensuring that no more water is abstracted than is absolutely necessary. The Agency demands reductions in leakage by the water companies before considering any case for investment in new reservoirs. Nevertheless, leakage detection requires intensive manpower and can be expensive. Traditionally it has been accepted that expenditure on leakage control should be increased to the point where the incremental costs involved are in balance with the incremental costs of alternatives for balancing supply and demand; for example, resource development or demand management, including environmental costs or benefits or both (OFWAT, 1996a). The Director General of OFWAT continues to say he has "yet to see the costs of leakage control analysed on a convincing basis". Water companies assume incremental operating costs between 2.4 pence/m^3 where no additional resources

are likely to be required in the foreseeable future (Dŵr Cymru) and 50 pence/m^3 where additional resources are likely to be needed (Thames Water). OFWAT considers that these estimates seriously undervalue leakage control and demand management. The Periodic Review in 1994 allowed for over 20 pence/m^3 delivered, plus an additional 10 pence/m^3 for incremental operating costs. Despite allowances in the past, only three of the Water Supply Companies reported significant progress in reducing leakage over the period 1992/1993 to 1994/1995, and three companies reported increased leakage (OFWAT 1996a). As outlined in Section 3 of this report, short-term targets to reduce leakage were set by the Director General of Water Services in October 1997, recognizing that water is a valuable resource not to be wasted.

In 1994, the Strategic Business Plans of the water companies allocated capital resources to resolving 'low flow' rivers where these are due to abstractions. A total capital expenditure of £5.35 million was allocated over the period 1995 to 1999 to deal with eight schemes which were selected on the basis of cost effectiveness. Further schemes are being evaluated for inclusion in the next planning round of the water companies.

Farming

Farming practices have been shown to have many impacts on fresh water, including:

> surface runoff and groundwater pollution by excess fertilizers, pesticides, slurry (includes application to crops, sheep dips etc.);

> emissions of ammonia from livestock which contributes to acidification and global warming;

> drainage of wetlands and extending field margins right up to river banks to increase the area of productive land with consequent loss of habitats and biodiversity;

> overgrazing and change in land use leading to soil and bank erosion and siltation of rivers with consequences for biota and fisheries;

> increasing demands for water for spray irrigation in the east of England.

Some of these impacts have been known for decades (e.g. nitrate pollution) whereas others are only just becoming apparent (overgrazing). The pressures are being tackled with some significant benefits to fresh waters.

Farm Waste Management Plans and grants for slurry pits have led to a 68 per cent reduction in serious pollution incidents from farms. This has contributed to improvements in GQA river quality grades in regions where these incidents caused particular problems. The River Torridge catchment in the South West Region is a good example. This catchment is dominated by livestock farming and, over the past 40 years, changes in farming practices have led to fewer, larger farms supporting increased livestock densities. A campaign to reduce pollution from farms commenced in 1984 resulting in a net improvement in water quality of 39 per cent between 1985 and 1995. The number of farm pollution incidents decreased from a high of 93 in 1991 to 39 in 1996, and many of these later incidents were category three (minor). The salmon rod catch also increased by 300 per cent between 1990 and 1995 but the catches in 1990 were at an all time low, and stock levels are still considered to be well below target levels, due to other problems such as siltation. It is not clear how much of this improvement is attributable to water quality and how much to other factors (NRA, 1996c). Farm waste facilities have cost the farming industry £150 million directly with an additional £150 million provided in grants by MAFF over the period 1989 to 1994.

Nitrate in surface and groundwaters largely comes from agricultural sources, so farming practices have been looked at over the last 10 to 15 years with a view to reducing the quantities of nitrate that runoff into rivers or leach into groundwaters. Changes from growing spring barley to winter wheat has reduced nitrate runoff in some areas. Farmers in Nitrate Sensitive Areas are compensated for restrictions on their use of fertilizers and farming practices in these areas. The cost of this was £3.6 million in 1995/96. The implementation of Best Farming Practices in recently established Nitrate Vulnerable Zones is likely to cost the farming industry £10 million in terms of improved farm waste facilities, with grants from MAFF contributing £0.8 million per year.

MAFF pays incentives to farmers, totalling £7.5 million per year, to preserve grazing marshes in 33 Environmentally Sensitive Areas which cover over 2.7 million hectares. The use of sensitive agricultural practices, such as the maintenance of water levels, has stopped the decline in these areas which include the Somerset Levels, the Broads and North Kent Marshes. A habitat scheme, water fringe option aims to create waterside buffer strips for wildlife. In 1995/96 this option had been taken up on 5,100 hectares at a cost of nearly £1 million per year. The six pilot areas include the Shropshire Meres, Yorkshire Derwent and the Upper Hampshire Avon.

Higher stocking ratios may be causing overgrazing which is leading to increased soil erosion in parts of the country. The shift towards maize, oilseed rape and linseed crops in other parts of the country may also be leading to greater soil erosion. A study in Yorkshire has suggested that sedimentation has reduced the original capacity of water supply reservoirs by 7.5 per cent,

valued at £0.65 million per year (or £74 million capital cost) by Yorkshire Water Services (White et al., 1996). Sedimentation of reservoirs will occur naturally and it is not known how much changing farming practices have contributed to this. Sensitive catchment management should lead to cost savings by both the water industry and farming but, with the current subsidy on the head of sheep in hill farming areas, it is expected that this problem could become more serious unless alternative action is taken. High levels of support under the Common Agricultural Policy have stimulated intensification of production, sometimes with consequent adverse effects on the environment. The 1992 Common Agricultural Policy reform package marked an important change of emphasis with a reduction in EC support prices and a new requirement on all member states to introduce measures to encourage environmentally sensitive farming. The Agency believes that while financial support mechanisms and incentives are retained as agricultural policy instruments they should also have a key role in achieving environmental goals. This is particularly so in the current period of change when agriculture is being asked to realign its fundamental objective of maximising production to a more sustainable balance of both food production and environmental management, and to encourage farmers to go beyond currently accepted good practice.

Furthermore, the Agency sees agri-environmental instruments as an important vehicle for delivery of environmental benefits. Some of the benefits include:

the preservation, maintenance and restoration of river corridor and wetland habitats and associated species;

the maintenance and improvement of fish stocks;

the protection and improvement of water quality by the implementation of codes of good agricultural practice and extensification of agriculture that goes beyond the requirements of these codes;

the protection of river banks from erosion so as to reduce the need for 'hard engineering' and from the illegal dumping of waste materials in order to protect river banks;

a reduction in flooding through runoff attenuation, reduction in channel siltation and damage to flood defences.

Power Generation

The effects of acid deposition have been recognised since the 1970s and have arisen due to emissions from the burning of fossil fuels and releases of ammonia from livestock. The Agency's principal means of controlling acid emissions is by the authorisation of Part A processes under the Environmental Protection Act 1990. The Agency reviewed power station emissions in 1996 and varied authorisations, lowering the limits applicable in a phased manner between 1996 and 2005. The limits will then remain at the 2005 level beyond that date. These reduce sulphur emissions from this sector by 85 per cent of the 1991 levels by employing technological and efficiency improvements within cost constraints agreed with the electricity generators. This is a major part of the UK commitment under the 1994 Oslo sulphur protocol to reduce emissions of sulphur to 80 per cent of 1980 levels by 2010 and will meet the interim 2005 target. Overall, this is estimated to reduce by 39 per cent the area in which exceedance of freshwater critical loads for sulphur occurred in 1989 to 1992 in England and Wales. Substantial areas will continue to receive acidic deposition above their critical load.

The EC Large Combustion Plant Directive (88/609/EEC) requires companies that generate electricity in England and Wales to reduce emissions of nitrogen oxides by 30 per cent from a 1980 baseline by 1998. Current emissions are already below those required by the National Plan which implements the Directive. It is anticipated that as a result of recent reauthorisation of power stations, releases will fall by a further 35 to 47 per cent from 1991 levels. These changes include emissions from gas fired stations whose introduction has increased. The key to further controls will be the new nitrogen protocol due to be negotiated in 1997. The cost to industry of these improvements over the period 1990 to 1995 has been £900 million on emission abatement, in addition to investment in new technologies and new plant which have also reduced emissions.

Other Industries

In 1994 about £1 billion was spent by industry (excluding the water industry) on the treatment of effluents to water, of which £330 million was capital and £680 million operating costs. The largest proportion of this expenditure was spent by the chemical industry (DoE, 1996b). Some 12 per cent of capital spending in the chemical industry was related to environmental protection, although it is not known what proportion of this relates to fresh waters and what proportion to other media (Chemical Industries Association, 1996).

The textile industry has had to look at its disposal of effluent following problems with certain pesticides in rivers. Many of these pesticides arrive on imported fleeces. The scouring of a batch of imported wool containing lindane in the north east led to exceedances of the EQS for total HCH (a List I substance) in 1994. Similarly, moth-proofing

chemicals (List II substances) are also associated with this industry. A programme for improvement was agreed with the textile industry in 1991 but further development and investment in treatment processes is being sought by the Agency working with the DETR, MAFF and the industry. Costs are unknown at this stage.

Dealing with the effects of abandoned mines has also required investment, though the burden has rested on the Agency rather than the polluter up to now. Due to a change in legislation in the Environment Act 1995, this situation will change at the turn of the century. The issue of discharges from abandoned coal and metal mines has always been a difficult one for the Agency because of the lack of effective legislation. There is an exemption under Section 89(3) of the Water Resources Act 1991 which permits water pollution to occur. Because of this, and because of commitments given during the passage of the Coal Industries Act through parliament, the Agency has been working closely with the Coal Authority to put in place a programme of environmental improvement. The Agency has developed and applied a protocol for assessing the environmental impact of minewater discharges which has resulted in a priority listing of 35 discharges for England and Wales. Of these 35 sites, the top 10 were selected to proceed to detailed technical feasibility studies. This in turn has resulted in two sites being earmarked for construction in 1997/98. The sites where construction of remediation schemes will take place are Old Meadows (North West Region) and Gwynfi (Welsh Region). The rolling programme of remediation schemes has meant that a further 10 sites have been identified to proceed to the detailed feasibility stage. Groundwater rebound in the Midlands and North East Regions, from pits closed in recent times, is probably the major minewater problem facing the Agency at the moment as this could lead to further outbreaks of polluting discharges. Where and when such discharges will breakout is difficult, if not impossible to predict. The Agency is also concerned about pricing negotiations between the power generators and the coal producers which could lead to further mine closures.

Following the Wheal Jane contamination, the then NRA set up a treatment plant to remediate the minewater discharge. The water, which has a pH of 3.6 and a total metals loading of 400ppm, has been treated with lime to balance the pH and precipitate the metals out of solution thus reducing the impact on the receiving watercourse and estuary. There is also a passive wetland system that treats one per cent of the flow. At present the indications are that the wetland will not provide a long-term solution because the concentration and volume of flow are too great to be treated. The scheme has provided useful information on the limits to which a wetland system can be used to remediate minewater discharges. The active treatment plant generates huge volumes of heavy-metal contaminated sludge which is currently disposed of in a tailings dam. Future disposal of this sludge and indeed the sediment in the tailings dam pose long-term environmental challenges. The treatment costs from 1992 to 1999 will amount to some £11 million, with a further £2 million being spent on the development of a long-term treatment plant.

The Oil Care Campaign launched in 1995 has cost industry a minimal amount but it is hoped that this will substantially reduce the number of incidents involving petroleum products which exceeds 6,000 per year. New regulations on the storage of oil are currently being consulted upon and may also contribute to a reduction of incidents. It is anticipated that this may cost industry £1.35 million. It will also make savings on lost oil, fines and clean-up operations.

The River Dee in North Wales is an important source of drinking water for two million people, and in its catchment there are many industries ranging from small manufacturers to major industrial processes. In order to protect the drinking water intake, intensive monitoring currently costs £660,000 per year, shared by the water companies and the Agency (about eight per cent) which form the Dee Steering Committee. It is hoped that this area may be designated as a Water Protection Zone shortly at a capital cost of £4.6 million to industry in the area. This is less than the £10 million cost of the phenol pollution incident in 1984 and will reduce the costs of intensive monitoring and the risk of expensive pollution clean-up.

The costs associated with the clean up of groundwater pollution are also high. There are no national figures but two case studies provide examples of the costs involved. Pollution of a drinking water source in Cambridge by solvents from a tannery will cost an estimated £5 million over 25 years to clean up. Another case of pollution of a drinking water source at Elton, north of Peterborough, by old landfill sites is likely to cost £9.5 million over the next 25 years. The remediation plans include additional treatment of the drinking water, intensive monitoring, pumping at the landfill sites to reduce groundwater levels and the construction of barriers around the landfills. It is not known how many such cases occur across England and Wales, but the figures are likely to run into hundreds.

The National Rivers Authority

From 1989 to 1996, the National Rivers Authority acted as 'Guardians of the Water Environment'. During 1994/95 the Authority spent a total of £460 million, which was split between its various functions in the following way; water quality £81 million; water resources £86 million; flood defence £241 million; fisheries £24 million; recreation and conservation £8

million; and navigation £6 million. About £107 million came from government grants and the rest was raised through charging schemes, licence fees, precepts, levies and interest. Local authority levies for flood defence works was the largest single income at £142 million (NRA, 1995f). Not all of this effort was on the freshwater environment and the funds were split between fresh water and coastal needs. Over the five year period from 1990/91 to 1994/95, the Authority spent about £2,193 million, of which it is estimated that about £960 million was on fresh waters. About £230 million of this was on capital expenditure.

The Environment Agency

The Environment Agency had a total budget of £581 million in 1997/98 to facilitate the whole range of its activities. Expenditure on flood defence is about £260 million although this includes coastal flood defences. The estimated amount to be spent on fresh waters is £80 million. The planned expenditure on water resources of £81 million will mainly relate to the freshwater environment as does the planned £21 million for fisheries functions. About £8 million is allocated to navigation and recreational functions and £6 million is allocated to conservation which will largely be spent on the freshwater environment. The allocation to pollution prevention and control is £177 million, of which there is an estimated allocation of £58 million to the freshwater environment. This suggests that broadly, the amount likely to be spent on the freshwater environment by the Environment Agency in 1997/98 is £254 million, of which about £62 million is for capital investment (two-thirds on flood defence) and the rest for operational expenditure.

On a local level, habitat and landscape enhancement schemes have been undertaken by the Environment Agency to improve and restore areas which have been adversely affected by human activities. The cost of two such schemes in London ranged from £45,000 for the enhancement of 650m of the River Pool in Lewisham to £37,000 for 180m of channel rehabilitation in Bromley. These schemes have provided significant improvements in the diversity and extent of flora and fauna and transformed the appearance and wildlife interest of the streams, as well as increased appreciation of them by residents. They represent good value for money when these costs are compared with those that industry is spending.

In 1995/96, the Agency completed 200 schemes to improve fisheries ranging from the construction of fish passes, the cleaning of gravels of spawning areas, the creation of riffles and pools and the restoration of bankside vegetation. These schemes cost the Agency about £1.3 million; a similar amount is expected to be spent routinely on improving habitats for fisheries.

Table 5.3
Summary of investment on the freshwater environment

Sector	Estimated five year, 1990/91 to 1994/95, capital investment (£million)	Planned investment (£million)	Comments (figures are £ million)
Sewerage and Sewage Treatment	£3,370	£1,600 (1995 to 2005)	Planned investment is to meet new Directive requirements, but latter five years will be reviewed in current round of asset management planning.
		£522 (1995 to 1999)	Planned investment is to meet specific Environmental Schemes
Water Treatment	£215	£1,005 (1990 to 2005)	Planned investment is allocated for new treatment facilities for pesticide removal, and £5.4 million for alleviating low flows. Estimated five year figure includes £151 for nitrate removal, £0.5 due to acidification, £10 for pollution incidents and other costs.
Farming	£344	£10	Estimated five year figure includes £300 spent on waste management plans, £3.6 on nitrate sensitive areas, and £7.5 per year on environmental sensitive areas. The planned investment relates to nitrate vulnerable zones.
Power generation	£900		Reducing emissions to reduce acidification
Industry	£1,650	£4.6	Estimated figure based on 1994 expenditure multiplied by five. Planned investment for Dee Water Protection Zone
Non-departmental public bodies	£230	£13 (1992 to 1999)	Planned investment based on level of capital expenditure of the Agency in 1997/98 and includes alleviating Wheal Jane mine discharge at £13 million from 1992 to 1999

Summary

What has been the total investment made on fresh waters? From the figures given above, the capital investment over the five years, 1990/91 to 1994/95, is estimated to have been £6,700 million (about £1,300 million per year) of which about half has been spent by the water industry (Table 5.3). This figure excludes operating costs but includes grants made to farmers in environmentally sensitive areas. It also makes broad assumptions where figures are only available for part of the period or for a different time period, and assumes that rates of investment were similar for the whole of the period. This enables an estimate to be made, where the figures are very much indicative, not actual, and it gives some idea of the relative investment by different economic sectors. The estimates have been based on information readily available. The Agency needs to get a better handle on investment on the environment and is developing a database of economic figures.

5.2 The Value of the Freshwater Environment

The expenditure on protecting the freshwater environment can be justified by reference to the value people attach to a clean environment. There are many indications that people do value fresh waters. Many people enjoy pursuits that involve water, such as angling, boating and walking by rivers and canals. The value of the riverside developments in cities like Birmingham and Leeds has risen substantially in recent years. Rivers play an important part in the cultural and social life of the country.

These general impressions are borne out by opinion surveys, like the one carried out by OFWAT in 1993. Table 5.4, based on the OFWAT survey, summarises the priority attached by customers to environmental aspects linked to the provision of water and sewerage services. This suggests that customers attach a higher priority to tackling some of the issues raised by this report, such as low flow rivers and water quality, than

Table 5.4
Priority attached to investment needs by customers

Investment need	Per cent of customers attaching high priority
Ensuring no rivers run dry	56
Reducing risk of sewage flooding houses	54
Replacing lead pipes	51
Cleaner water in rivers and estuaries	46
Reducing smell from STWs	40
Reducing holes in roads by water companies	32
Improving taste in tap water	31
Reducing restrictions, e.g. hosepipe bans	15

to increasing water stocks which would reduce the need for hosepipe bans.

In 1997, the Agency commissioned a survey to establish the importance to water company customers of protecting and improving the environment. This was precipitated by the review of water company prices, due in 1999. Telephone interviews were held with 2,500 water bill payers across England and Wales. The main findings were:

environmental improvements and an adequate supply of water are key issues to customers. Some 69 per cent said they would be willing to pay more, an average of £36 per year, to achieve these objectives;

the quality of water in rivers and seas was regarded as very important by 86 per cent of customers;

customers want to see water company profits spent on ensuring a reliable water supply (96 per cent), cleaning rivers and coastal waters (96 per cent), preserving water resources in the environment (94 per cent), and ensuring high quality drinking water in the future (94 per cent);

Ninety-five per cent of customers would prefer to have the same water bill in the year 2000 as now and have environmental improvements, than receive a lower bill and have no environmental improvements;

customers believe that water companies are working towards improving the environment, but 59 per cent think that they should do more (NOP Social and Political, 1997).

A major issue for environmental management is how to put these values in perspective, compared to alternative issues that the public value, such as health and education. One possible framework is cost-benefit analysis, where one attempts to determine how much the public is willing to pay as a measure of relative value. Studies have been conducted to determine such measures using a variety of techniques, including contingent valuation (a questionnaire based approach) and hedonic pricing (which estimates how much value a good environment adds to an asset such as property).

A contingent valuation study done by the NRA regarding alleviating low flows in the River Darent found that households were willing to pay about £3 to £6 per year to resolve these issues and to restore flows to ecologically acceptable levels (NRA, 1994b). This amounts to £2.2 million per year. A study for the former DoE suggested that households were willing to pay £25 per year (£600 million nationally) to reduce acid deposition affecting aquatic ecosystems (Ecotec, 1993).

A study to investigate the cultural, heritage and environmental value of canals in terms of both their use and passive-use values assessed the maximum amount of money people were willing to pay to preserve the canal system. The economic benefits provided by canals are both use related (recreational) and non-use related (cultural, heritage and environmental). The study found that the recreational value of canals ranged between £2.50 and £16 per trip, depending on the assumptions made about travel costs. Using a contingent valuation survey, a mean willingness to pay figure of £6.78 per household per year was derived; this incorporates both use and passive-use values, which if multiplied by the number of households in England and Wales gives a total annual preservation value of over £100 million (Adamowicz *et al.*, 1995).

None of these techniques are without their problems, theoretical and practical. Nevertheless they can add some value to the process of environmental

Table 5.5
The value of water quality improvements

Improvement	Value
Existence value of improved water quality[1]	0.2 to 0.5 pence per km per year per household
Aesthetic improvement	£1.20 per person per visit
Improved fish populations (benefit to informal recreation users)	8 to 11 pence per person per visit
Improved canoeing possibilities	10 pence per person per visit
Improved angling	£3.86 to £25.66 per visit

[1] The existence value is the amount people would be willing to pay simply to know that the environment was being protected, without necessarily wanting to use it.

protection. The Agency has been developing techniques to assess the value of water quality improvements to put cost into perspective. A methodology has been developed. Table 5.5 shows the values for benefits achieved (Foundation for Water Research, 1996).

These figures can be compared with the cost of water quality improvements realised over the period 1990 to 1995, previously stated as £0.25 million/km. On existence values alone, the national figure assuming 20 million households is £0.2 to £0.5 million/km over the five year period. The costs of improvements are in the same order of magnitude as these values without considering the benefits to recreational activities, or the benefits of protecting rivers to provide water resources essential for our society.

The Agency is also looking at other techniques to help put a value on the environment including consensus building approaches, which attempt to build a community perspective on value. These will inform the way in which the Agency reports on and prioritises the protection of the freshwater environment.

5.3 Responding to Potential Threats and Opportunities

There is a need to think ahead about how society is changing or likely to change, and to predict the impact of these changes on fresh waters so that timely action can be made. Prevention is better than cure. This report has already given some indication of the likely increase in some pressures but the future picture is drawn together here.

There is an expected 4.4 million increase in the number of households, above the 1991 number, by the year 2016, with the greatest demand being in the east, south east and south west. All these households will need a water and sewerage service which can pose a potential threat to the freshwater environment if the provision of other services are not adequately planned. Previous sections have shown how water stocks are low compared with the demand placed on

them and this will need sensitive consideration in development proposals. In some areas, particularly in the south east, towns have developed near headwaters where the dilution available for the increased sewage effluent is becoming insufficient to maintain river quality. In these cases, the carrying capacity of the river is being reached. Any further development will mean that a deterioration in river quality is unavoidable. The Agency liaises closely with planning authorities to highlight areas where this problem could arise, so the development can be planned with minimal detriment to the freshwater environment, and the needs of society met.

Development areas, both for residential and commercial properties, add significant increases to the load of sewage arriving at a treatment works. Some works have been designed to accommodate extra flow in advance of the development and consents to discharge have been set for the final expected load. In the interim, before development is complete, the quality of effluent will tend to be higher than that required by the consent because the works is operating below capacity. Consequently river quality benefits in this interim period. When the works becomes fully loaded and the quality of effluent equals that specified in the consent, then river quality will return to that planned for in the consent. This may appear as a deterioration in future years. Campaigns to promote the wise use of water could have a benefit here; reduced water demand would lead to reduced sewer flows and hydraulic loading on sewage works. Urbanisation changes the natural way in which rain runs off the land surface and the way in which it can infiltrate. Hard surfaces stop infiltration so urban development will reduce the amount of water recharging aquifers reducing water resource availability in these areas. This is a particular concern in the Southern Region where over 70 per cent of potable supply arises from groundwaters. Hard surfaces also cause rain to run off more rapidly than is the case if it passes through soil surfaces. This changes the flow characteristics of rivers and can lead to increased peak (flood) flows. The Agency works with planners and developers to ensure that increased flooding does not occur by designing urban drainage systems appropriately, but does not have powers to insist on its recommendations being adopted.

Industrial development areas can cause higher than average risks of pollution incidents, which can be critical if drinking water supplies are nearby. Planning is the first step in minimising pollution risks. The Dee catchment in North Wales, where 307 pollution incidents (eight of which were major) occurred in 1995, exemplifies the need for more proactive pollution management. An application for designation of the River Dee as a Water Protection Zone under the provisions of Section 93 of the Water Resources Act 1991 went to Public Enquiry in March 1995. If the Secretaries of State are minded to grant this designation, it will considerably strengthen the Environment Agency's powers to prevent pollution.

Changes in agricultural production to meet the different and essential demands of society and lifestyles, reflected to a certain extent in the EC Common Agricultural Policy, are also a potential threat. Crops have differing requirements for irrigation, fertilizers, pesticides and land management and all these can impact on fresh waters unless well managed. Sometimes the impact is not realised until after changes in crop type or land management have occurred; the extent of siltation of rivers due to soil erosion is only just being evaluated on a national basis, but could have serious effects on fisheries. Better forethought is required and making environmental awareness part of agricultural practice should turn this threat into an opportunity. An increase in livestock numbers has created problems in the past but pollution due to waste is now well under control. The potential for overgrazing and outdoor pig rearing leading to soil erosion still needs to be evaluated to determine the full extent of any problems.

The number of cars and lorries has been increasing over the last 20 years and is set to increase further. Burning of petrol and diesel contributes carbon dioxide – a greenhouse gas – and also releases nitrogen dioxides, threatening further acidification. Pollution incidents due to transport were reported for the first time in 1993 and by 1995, the number of incidents due to this sector had increased by 19 per cent. The incidents include spillages of petrol and diesel, as well as products being carried, for example chemicals, and milk. Transport accounts for a growing number of major incidents. Runoff from roads also carries pollutants into fresh waters including silt, toxic substances, oil, pesticides and salt. With the volume of traffic forecast to be 29 to 63 per cent above the 1988 level by 2021, the pollutant load from these sources is expected to increase unless suitable road maintenance activities are promoted. The Agency is discussing ways to identify changes in operations and vehicle design which could reduce the risk of pollution with representatives of the transport

industry. The emergency response is critical, and improved liaison with the fire and rescue services has, in some cases, prevented pollution. However, the impact of burning fossil fuels on climate change also needs to be considered because climate change has potentially serious consequences for the freshwater environment. Reducing the pressure from transport's use of petrol and diesel is needed if the freshwater environment is to be protected.

The standard of living is also rising. Over the last 20 years, the economy has grown in real terms by around a half, and broadly similar growth rates are projected for the future. We have more leisure time compared to people 50 years ago, and with increased mobility and disposable income, many people are able to spend more time on diverse recreational activities. With increased technology, it is expected that people will have shorter working lives, giving more time for leisure which is now a major contributor to the economy. However, boating, angling and other watersports conflict with each other and sometimes with the natural aquatic ecosystem. These conflicts are set to increase locally unless adequate plans are made to avoid them.

Massive investment in sewerage and sewage treatment is ongoing and will continue in fulfilment of European Union obligations, particularly the Urban Waste Water Treatment Directive. There will as a consequence be substantial environmental improvements. Nevertheless we are concerned that delivery of the improvements will not be in environmental priority order, as the driver for investment is the statutory obligation to provide a level of treatment rather than the environmental need for that level of treatment. The basis for investment in water quality has hitherto been driven by environmental need, through the adoption of the river quality objective approach, and debated locally through Local Environment Agency Plans. The advantage of this approach is that it focuses expenditure where environmental benefit can be maximised. The proposed EU Water Framework Directive may create a regulatory platform providing a balance between the river quality objective and process control approaches, requiring a high level of environmental understanding for successful implementation. The Agency is confident that such understanding is well developed in England and Wales and wishes to maintain it as the basis for regulatory decision making, taking environmental and financial costs and benefits into account.

The requirements to set national water quality standards which endeavour to observe, or endeavour to respect, the guideline standards in Water Quality Directives causes some concern. This is an area where the statutory obligation on the Agency is tempered by the need to take environmental and financial costs and benefits into consideration in each consent decision.

The tools for shaping such decisions are still in development.

The Dangerous Substances Directive (76/464/EEC) also causes concern because all emissions of dangerous substances to the aquatic environment must be prior authorised, no matter how small. Reviews of trader and domestic inputs to sewers, and of discharges from sewage-treatment works are required in order to fulfill this obligation. Significant inputs will, of course, need to be effectively controlled through consents and monitoring. Minor inputs, for example copper and zinc from domestic plumbing, will require a less prescriptive method of control if we are to avoid a vast amount of environmentally unproductive effort. The Agency's Charging for Discharges Scheme assumes that if dangerous substances are identified on the consent then we monitor for them, and accordingly places such discharges in a higher charge band than for similar discharges without dangerous substances. This reflects the additional costs of monitoring. The Agency intends to review the Charging for Discharges Scheme in order to, amongst other things, ensure that dischargers of substances that we need to monitor for regulatory control purposes continue to pay for the work that we undertake, but that minor dischargers are not excessively penalised.

The Agency expects to explore further over the coming years the opportunities for introduction of incentive charging type schemes to drive environmental improvement. We are interested in investigating enhancements to the current cost recovery approach, as well as more radical targeting systems whereby dischargers can be 'rewarded' by lower charges for hitting stringent targets or 'penalised' financially for missing them. Such mechanisms would, of course, require primary legislation.

In some catchments a substantial proportion of the river flow is from sewage-treatment works. In some cases water companies are rationalising their assets, diverting sewage from several small works to a major treatment works, usually lower down the catchment. Whilst this may result in a net improvement in the level of treatment and a quality improvement in the catchment below the new works, the upstream catchment may be severely impacted by the loss of the water resource that the sewage effluent represents. The Agency has limited powers to ensure continuity of river flow in such circumstances and would like to have them strengthened to facilitate integrated management of water quality and resources.

6 Conclusions: The Agency's Opinion on the State of the Freshwater Environment

A reasonable question to ask now is, "What does all this information add up to?" Bearing in mind that measuring the state of the environment provides the basis for assessing priorities for action and charting progress with respect to environmental management plans and targets, an analysis needs to be done to decide which pressures and states cause the greatest concern and what the issues are to which strategies and actions need to be targeted. But concern will also depend on value judgements, and the value of the freshwater environment will depend on its ability to meet the needs of the human population, of other species, and on its ability to sustain itself with a minimum of human interference.

6.1 Pressures

The information on pressures on the freshwater environment shows that industrial demand for water is declining and the threat from pollution incidents has been reduced, especially from the agricultural and heavy industrial sectors, as preventative action is taking effect. The pressure from direct discharges has also reduced, due to better sewage treatment following investment by water companies, and the pressure from storm overflows is set to decrease with the investment planned by 2005. The pressure caused by atmospheric deposition of sulphur is set to reduce with large-scale investment by the power generating industry. The use of some pesticides has discontinued in certain applications, reducing the pressures from some, but not all, toxic substances.

On the other hand, many more pressures are growing. Against a background of climate change and social changes, domestic and agricultural demands for water are increasing and reached very high levels during the hot dry summers of 1995 and 1996. As well as increasing use within the home, the use of water in the garden is rising. Pressures from diffuse pollution are also giving cause for concern. These relate to the use of pesticides, soil erosion, the disposal of industrial solvents, and urban and road runoff as well as problems caused by abandoned mines. Waste disposal sites still cause pressures on groundwaters and traffic-related pollution incidents are on the increase. With a predicted continued increase in traffic, this pressure is a major concern. The pressures exerted by society and lifestyles are also increasing with the demands for services (water supply and sewage treatment) for a planned 4.4 million new households by 2016 being paramount. Many of these new households are expected to be in the south and east of England where the freshwater environment is already suffering stress, and where many rivers and groundwaters have reached their capacity in terms of resources available for abstraction and carrying capacity for discharges. It is in these parts of England too that the impact of climate change is likely to be greatest. There is an expected increase in hot dry summers, raising water demands and depleting river flows. Urbanisation is already intense, and the loss of aquatic habitats extreme. With even more houses, more land will become urbanised with the consequent risk of the loss of more freshwater habitats and hence of biodiversity. River channelisation and other flood defence works to protect commercial property and homes could also cause further habitat loss unless planning is sufficiently farsighted. Lifestyles are also changing rapidly with people having more leisure time and more disposable income to spend on recreational activities, including travel. The freshwater environment offers an opportunity for meeting the needs of these changing lifestyles but local problems can arise if conflicts amongst users, and between users and the environment, are not managed.

Climate change is a growing concern because climate naturally affects the weather and thus the state of the freshwater environment. The effects of climate change include the spatial and temporal availability of water resources, the demand for water resources, biodiversity, the river flows available for dilution of effluents, the frequency of algal blooms, the demand by recreational users of rivers, and the frequency of storms and flooding.

Overall, the pressures caused by the changing climate, changing lifestyles, and increasing urbanisation pose the greatest challenges to the future management of the freshwater environment.

6.2 State

Some very significant improvements have taken place in the state of the freshwater environment. Since the privatisation of the water industry and the establishment of independent regulation by the NRA (and now the Agency) and OFWAT in 1989, net improvements in both the chemical and biological quality of rivers have occurred in over a quarter of the total length of rivers that are routinely sampled. This is the combined result of investment in sewerage and sewage treatment by the water industry, improved farm management practices, and pollution prevention initiatives. But the recent droughts have halted further improvements. Significant reductions in the discharges of toxic substances have also been achieved as a result of tighter regulation, changing patterns in industry and agriculture, and the discontinued use of some chemicals. Populations of fish, otters and some bird species are recovering in some areas where they have been absent for many years. There has also been a reduction in the number of significant flooding events in the last 30 years; the result of good development control and flood defences.

The total capital expenditure by both industry and agricultural sectors on schemes to improve the freshwater environment over the period 1990 to 1995 is estimated to be around £7 thousand million. About half of this is accounted for by expenditure by the water industry, mainly to meet statutory obligations. There will, no doubt, be different views on the extent to which the environmental improvements that have occurred represent value for money for those that have had to bear the costs. The evidence, nevertheless, suggests that investment does produce real environmental results and the experience gained over this period should provide a firmer basis for the targeting of future investment to maximise environmental benefits.

Despite these improvements, there are certain aspects of the freshwater environment that show signs of degradation or stress. In particular, there has been a significant loss of freshwater habitats, including wetlands and ponds, which has affected the populations of water voles, amphibians and the rare white-clawed crayfish, as well as affecting the diversity of aquatic flora. Other habitats show signs of degradation, especially headwaters, due to the impact of diffuse pollution ranging from the impact of residues of sheep dip, and the legacy of abandoned mines, to the effects of acidification. Some lakes and rivers show signs of eutrophication due to nutrient enrichment and many rivers suffer from low flows due to over-abstraction, threatening biodiversity as well as recreational use and aesthetic quality. Fisheries show signs of deterioration in some areas due to the impact of low river flows and siltation. The evidence of widespread disruption to the reproductive systems in fish due to chemical substances is potentially a serious threat to biodiversity. All together, 47 species dependent on fresh waters are rare, vulnerable or threatened.

This may not be the complete picture because, despite the volume of information available, much of the monitoring of the environment to date has been driven by statutory needs, e.g. compliance with mandatory standards, rather than to form an opinion on the state of the freshwater environment generally. There has been relatively little monitoring of the 'health' and 'aesthetic quality' of the freshwater environment. There is a need for much more information on the extent of health effects, e.g. endocrine disruption in other forms of wildlife (besides fisheries) and measures of the value of the environment as perceived by the public. Similarly,

long-term data sets are limited. Information on groundwater quality and lake quality is patchy and there is a need for much more extensive information on fish and aquatic life, wetlands, and river corridor wildlife populations.

6.3   Response

This all adds up to the need to check the threats posed by the pressures that are increasing, and to reverse the trends of deterioration or decline in the state of fresh waters. Some of the pressures are interlinked; climate change exerts a pressure on water resources and several pressures may affect one measure of the state of fresh waters; biodiversity is affected by diffuse pollution and climate change. At the same time, we need to continue efforts to maintain fresh waters in their current state where these are good, for example, where there are high quality rivers. This is particularly important because of the need to protect public health, which is often taken for granted. The Agency has already developed an Environmental Strategy to deal with the major problems that need to be addressed across all media to protect and improve the environment for the millennium and beyond (Environment Agency, 1997e). Our principal and immediate concerns are being met by:

- addressing the causes of, and ameliorating the effects of, climate change;

- improving air quality and thus the specific causes of acidification of fresh waters;

- improving the biodiversity of our freshwater habitats;

- ensuring long-term and integrated approaches to our management of water resources;

- managing our freshwater fisheries in a sustainable way;

- delivering an integrated approach to the management of river basins generally, with respect to their multiple use by both industry and the public;

- reducing the impact of land use on diffuse sources of pollutants and soil erosion on surface waters and the long-term impact of pollution on groundwaters;

- managing wastes so that they do not add to the polluting pressures on fresh waters, particularly groundwaters;

- ensuring that the industrial impact on the freshwater environment is progressively reduced, both for the benefit of industry itself and for the enjoyment of fresh waters by everyone.

All of these encapsulate issues that have been brought out in this report. There are a number of specific issues relating to the freshwater environment that need to be addressed if a more sustainable balance between the needs of society and the health of freshwater ecosystems is to be achieved. These are as follows, with full details in Table 6.1.

i. *Current climatic variability and potential long-term climate change*

Over the past nine years the UK has experienced exceptional climatic extremes including the wettest winter period (December 1994 to February 1995) and the driest summer (June to August 1995) on record. The average temperatures over the period have been the highest on record since 1845. These extremes have already exerted significant pressures on the freshwater environment and presented real management challenges. Predicted long-term climate change scenarios have potentially serious implications for the state of the freshwater environment as a whole.

Climate change is a global issue. The Agency is approaching it by investing in research to predict the effects and, by using its regulatory powers, to reduce emissions of greenhouse gases from the major industrial processes. The proposed EC Water Framework Directive should provide a mechanism to integrate water resources and water quality issues, and should take account of the likely effects of climate change.

ii. *Pressures on water resources*

Although England and Wales are relatively well supplied with water resources, their distribution, both regionally and seasonally, is not well matched with patterns of demand. The average effective rainfall is low in the south and east of England and becomes critical during periods of drought. This is the part of the country that is likely to be under the greatest demand for new housing development and is predicted to experience the greatest impact of climate change, placing even greater pressures on water resources. Twenty-nine rivers have already been identified by the Agency as suffering from low flows because of high rates of abstraction, and many Sites of Special Scientific Interest are reported to be at risk from low water levels. The Agency is currently working with English Nature and the Countryside Council for Wales to identify critical sites, and to identify the changes needed to water company abstraction licences. It is already clear that the requirement for alleviation of low flows will affect water yields and there may be a need to renegotiate licences at some cost to the Agency.

The Agency is approaching this issue by encouraging and demanding more efficient use of water, implementing schemes to alleviate low flows, and ensuring that all environmental needs are fully taken into account in the next asset management plans of the water companies.

iii. *Habitat loss and modification*

England and Wales have a long history of destruction and modification of freshwater habitats. National surveys such as the Countryside Survey in 1990 suggest that there has been a significant recent decline in areas of wetlands, and in streamside habitats and ponds; many sites are reported to be at risk of further deterioration. The Agency's own River Habitat Surveys show that over 40 per cent of river habitat sites across England and Wales have been subject to modification. The UK Biodiversity Action Plan has identified seven freshwater habitat types (chalk rivers, mesotrophic lakes, eutrophic standing water, aquifer fed waterbodies, reedbeds, fens and grazing marsh) to be of particular concern because of their vulnerability. The Agency's Environmental Strategy recognises the need to enhance biodiversity and the resolving of this issue in fresh waters will contribute to this overall objective. Improving habitats will also have 'knock-on' effects for freshwater fisheries and integrated river-basin management. The Agency is already working with others to implement the EC Habitats Directive. Changes to abstraction licences and discharge consents may be needed, but the pay-off from this Directive will be to ensure the protection of some of Europe's most important sites of conservation. The Agency also has an important role to play in ensuring that habitats are protected and it will work with the Town and Country Planning Systems to ensure that the trend of habitat loss is reversed.

iv. *Changes in flora and fauna*

Despite the reported recent recovery of some species, others have been declining and some populations are still disappearing because of factors such as habitat loss, pollution, nutrient enrichment, and competition with 'alien' species. By recognizing biodiversity in its Environmental Strategy, the Agency has already shown that it intends to tackle this issue. By helping to improve air quality, the effects of acidification will be reduced, and by resolving these problems our role in managing freshwater fisheries will be enhanced. Furthermore, of the action plans that have been drawn up for rare, threatened or vulnerable species identified in the UK Biodiversity Action Plan, 47 are directly dependent upon fresh waters and the Agency has either a primary or contributory role or both for 15 of them. The Agency is also contributing to the review of fisheries legislation in England and Wales which is looking at the need to manage fisheries on a sustainable basis but within the context of maintaining biodiversity.

v. Groundwater pollution

The presence of contaminants such as nitrate, industrial solvents and pesticides in groundwater appears to be widespread. Problems are being discovered at an increasing rate where they are being looked for. Groundwater pollution is of particular concern because of its long-term nature and the difficulties and costs of remediation which are often intractable. Implementation of a nationally-consistent scheme for groundwater monitoring is a priority for the Agency if the nature and extent of groundwater pollution are to be properly assessed. Many parts of the Agency's Environmental Strategy address this issue. By managing waste and regulating major industries effectively, groundwater pollution should be reduced. Furthermore our contribution to conserving the land will tackle the issue of diffuse pollution. The Agency will continue vigorously to apply its Groundwater Protection Policy to ensure that the quality and uses of groundwaters are protected from pollution, to implement the EC Groundwater Directive to control discharges, and to monitor the impact of designated Nitrate Vulnerable Zones.

vi. Hazardous substances

Some categories of substances, such as pesticides, continue to be of concern because of their widespread occurrence in fresh waters. The effects of long-term, low-level, exposure to combinations of these chemicals in the environment is poorly understood. Endocrine disruption is one such effect that requires further investigation. There are many links between the Agency's Environmental Strategy and the need to reduce the risks from hazardous substances in the freshwater environment. Biodiversity and freshwater fisheries will benefit from progress on this issue, which we are approaching by regulating major industries effectively. This includes continuing the efficient and effective delivery of Integrated Pollution Control, ensuring the achievement of environmental quality standards, and promoting precautionary action where risks are high but scientific certainty low. The government is developing a chemical strategy; the Agency will provide information for this.

vii. Nutrient enrichment

The General Quality Assessment (GQA) 'window' for phosphate levels in rivers in 1995 placed over one-third of the river stretches monitored in the two grades indicative of high phosphate concentrations (5 and 6). About three-quarters of the lakes with Site of Special Scientific Interest status are reported to be affected by nutrient enrichment which also affects some riverine Sites of Special Scientific Interest. More than 200 blue-green algal bloom incidents, mainly on lakes and reservoirs, have been reported each year since national reporting started in 1991. There is a need to tackle nutrient enrichment so that the threats to freshwater fisheries and biodiversity are reduced. Integrated river-basin management and the regulation of major industries are strategic tools that will deliver improvements. The Agency is actively using its pollution control powers to tackle this issue and implementing the requirements of relevant EC Directives. Other bodies – MAFF, English Nature and DETR – have significant roles too. The Agency is developing an eutrophic control strategy which proposes to tackle problems on a case by case basis; this will be subject to public consultation in 1998.

viii. Poor river quality

Despite recent general improvements in river quality, there were significant deteriorations recorded by the chemical and biological General Quality Assessments in about 225km of rivers over the period 1990 to 1995. About 10 per cent of the total monitored length of rivers in the GQA network is still of Poor or Bad quality and in need of improvement. This issue has been addressed in the Agency's Environmental Strategy by recognising the need for effective regulation of major industries. Investment on storm overflows is currently underway and further needs will be identified to the water companies in the current round of asset management planning. The Agency will continue to use its pollution control strategy of minimisation, prevention and enforcement to effect improvements. It is also carrying out detailed work on benefit assessment of maintaining and improving water quality. This will be fed into the investment planning process of the water industry. By improving water quality, other parts of the Agency's strategy will be realised – enhancing freshwater fisheries and biodiversity.

ix. Aesthetic and recreational quality of fresh waters

Millions of people live or work in close contact with fresh waters or visit them as a source of recreation: the freshwater environment is closely connected with our quality of life. Although no freshwater sites have been designated under the EC Bathing Waters Directive, rivers, lakes and reservoirs are widely used for water sports involving varying degrees of water contact. The health risks associated with these activities need to be properly assessed. Furthermore, aesthetic pollution is an important issue in terms of public perception and the values people place on the environment and further effort needs to be put into determining what the priorities are perceived to be and how they can be assessed. Action to find or develop appropriate areas for watersports that are noisy, like water skiing and jet skiing, is needed; this is a growing area of recreation and plans need to be made to ensure that its growth does not conflict with other users. The Agency will approach this issue by delivering integrated river-basin management and working with local authorities and others to maximise the aesthetic and recreational use of fresh waters.

x. *Changing lifestyles and increasing urbanisation*

Society puts more and more demands on the freshwater environment to support economic activities, to provide the services needed by an increasing number of households, and to support higher standards of living. Urbanisation in the form of more houses, paved areas, roads and traffic is also taking place at an increasing rate with consequent impacts on fresh waters. Many

parts of the Agency's Environmental Strategy are based on an understanding of this pressure, specifically the need for effective management of water resources, conservation of the land, and integrated river-basin management. The Agency is also approaching this issue by working with others to provide information to increase awareness and has recognised the role of education to ensure that the needs of society are met in a manner which sustains and improves the freshwater environment.

6.4 Final Word

Freshwater quality has improved over the last 20 to 30 years in some respects but is under increasing pressure from the range of pollutants now found. In terms of freshwater resources, there is a growing pressure as society changes, environmental awareness increases, and as the impact of climate change is felt. Biodiversity likewise is under threat due to a range of human activities including its use of chemicals, leading to habitat loss and effects on species. Furthermore, as technology develops, monitoring techniques show up problems of which we were previously unaware. There is a need for continuing and increasing efforts at effective management and the implementation of the Agency's Environmental Strategy if the current position is to be improved, and if the threat of increasing pressures is to be checked.

Table 6.1 *Key issues, responses and links to the Agency's Environmental Strategy*

Freshwater issue	Human activities affecting	Response	Links to Environmental Strategy
Climate change	Emissions of greenhouse gases. Natural change may be occurring too.	Need to determine effect of climate change on water quantity, agriculture, water demand, water quality and biodiversity and prepare accordingly. Reduce emissions of greenhouse gases according to agreed government targets.	Climate change Air quality Biodiversity Integrated river-basin management Regulating major industry.
Pressures on water resources			
- low water stocks	Increasing water demand by households, and farming in east of England. Climate change, affected by society, affects resource availability.	Demand management including low water usage applications and reuse. Need sustainable water resources strategy. More efficient water use. Tackle leakage.	Climate change Managing water resources Integrated river-basin management Biodiversity Freshwater fisheries
- low flow rivers	Abstraction, climate change causing droughts and lower recharge. Has knock-on effect to habitats.	Develop specific local solutions and implement. Influence legislation over licences of right. Implement minimum acceptable flows and/or river flow objectives. Influence Asset Management Plans of water companies	
- flooding events	Urbanisation, changes in land-use, and climate change may affect severity of storms.	Provide effective flood warning systems. Implement Flood and Coastal Defence Policy. Report on the state of flood defences.	
Habitat loss and modification	Rural land-use change - ploughing to edge of streams, urban development, including roads, river management activities. More land in agricultural production through drainage. Abstraction may also deplete wetlands.	Implement restoration schemes, conservation projects. Common Agricultural Policy reform. Water level management plans for wetlands. Development control. Implement EC Habitats' Directive. Guidance to Planning Authorities, and promote use of *Policy and Practice for the Protection of Flood Plains.*	Air quality Biodiversity Freshwater fisheries Conserving land Integrated river-basin management Managing water resources
Changes in flora and fauna	Loss of habitat. Loss of fish in headwaters due to acidification and low or variable flows. Siltation of river beds from farming practices in some areas. Exotic species competing. Erosion and impact by recreational uses. Impact of hazardous substances, especially pesticides.	Reduce acidification by emission control. Tighter controls on use of toxic substances. Contribute to achieving UK's biodiversity action plan and link these with Local Environment Agency Plans. Introduce standard fisheries classification scheme and regular monitoring. Continue habitat assessments. Tackle pollution of headwaters. Develop long-term strategies for salmon, trout and coarse fisheries and introduce target based fisheries management. Locally, use Local Environment Agency Plans to balance conflict between recreation and loss. Manage angling pressure. Reduce overgrazing - best agricultural practices. Promote Agency guidance on control of exotic species. Contribute to review of fisheries legislation.	Air quality Biodiversity Freshwater fisheries Integrated river-basin management

Freshwater Issue	Human activities affecting	Response	Links to Environmental Strategy
Groundwater pollution	Farming - nitrate leaching. Pesticides from certain uses. Industrial solvents and other organic pollutants. Landfill leachates.	Best practice in use of fertilizers and pesticides. Pollution prevention to address solvents. Continue to implement Groundwater Protection Policy. Implement national monitoring scheme.	Water resources Conserving land Managing waste Regulating major industries
Hazardous substances	Wool processing industry, farming (use of pesticides including sheep dip chemicals), minewaters (close down of mines). Discharge of wastes to rivers - natural oestrogens and other chemicals (pesticides, plasticisers)	Agency working with MAFF and HSE on restricting use or changing formulations of certain pesticides. Local action plans for minewaters. Agency working with Coal Authority to reduce impact of mine workings. Continue delivery of Integrated Pollution Control, pollution prevention. Implement toxicity based consents. Establish extent of endocrine disruption and cause/effects. Target priority sectors and processes to minimise discharge of known endocrine-disrupting substances. Work with others to improve science base.	Biodiversity Freshwater fisheries Integrated river-basin management Regulating major industries
Nutrient enrichment	Use of fertilizers, animal wastes, human wastes (via sewage-treatment works).	Monitor benefits of Nitrate Vulnerable Zones and Eutrophic Sensitive Areas. Continue to work with farmers to promote best practice. Develop and implement the Agency's Eutrophication Strategy.	Biodiversity Freshwater fisheries Integrated river-basin management Regulating major industries
Poor water quality in 10 per cent of rivers.	Treated sewage effluents, storm overflows, urban drainage, minewaters, etc. Misconnections in urban areas. Pollution incidents.	Tighter consent standards. Influence developers regarding urbanisation. Work with industry regarding minewaters. Trace misconnections and stop illegal discharges. Upgrade sewerage network to reduce storm overflows (planned investment). Pollution prevention campaigns. Reduce risk of transport related pollution by working with others. Influence asset management plans of water companies. Explore greater use of water protection zones	Freshwater fisheries Integrated river-basin management Managing waste Regulating major industry
Aesthetic and recreational quality	Storm overflows from sewage system, recreational uses, inadequate disposal of litter. Rivers carry treated effluents, and input from other animals - livestock and birds which gives rise to microbiological contamination. Demands of recreational users.	Expenditure on storm overflows planned over next 10 years. Influence development by negotiating aesthetically pleasing riverside developments. Work with local authorities to control illegal dumping. Use Local Environment Agency Plans to agree actions. Cost/benefit appraisals to determine whether action warranted on microbiological contamination. Research into links between water quality and recreational activity. Encourage development of sites for 'noisy' recreational activities.	Freshwater fisheries Integrated river-basin management Managing waste Regulating major industries
Changing lifestyles and accelerating urbanisation	Growth of population, housing, demands for water and sewage, traffic movements, building in floodplains.	Work with planning authorities. Provide freshwater environment that meets demands of society and biodiversity.	Water resources Biodiversity Conserving land Integrated river-basin management

APPENDIX 1

National and International Standards and Targets

A1. 1 EC Directives

European policy and legislation place a responsibility on Member States to comply with environmental standards and controls. The UK government meets these requirements through Regulations issued as Statutory Instruments. The Directives are intended both to address important environmental problems and to establish uniform controls on competing companies in different Member States. Directives set emission standards and environmental quality objectives (or standards) for a number of substances and waters used for particular purposes. The Agency has direct responsibilities for 26 pieces of existing legislation which require specific actions to be taken and information to be reported back to government departments for formal reporting to the European Commission.

Directives of relevance to this report are given in Table A1.1

Table A1.1
EC Directives relevant to this report

Directive number	EC Directive title
75/440/EEC 79/869/EEC	Quality of surface water abstracted for drinking, and sampling requirements
76/464/EEC	Pollution caused by the discharge of certain dangerous substances into the aquatic environment
76/160/EEC	Quality of bathing water
78/176/EEC	Waste from the titanium dioxide industry
78/659/EEC	Quality of fresh waters needing protection or improvement in order to support fish life
79/409/EEC	Directive on the conservation of wild birds
80/68/EEC	Protection of groundwater against pollution caused by certain dangerous substances
80/778/EEC	Quality of water intended for human consumption
82/883/EEC	Procedures for the surveillance and monitoring of environments concerned by waste from the titanium dioxide industry
82/176/EEC	Limit values and quality objectives for mercury discharges by the chlor-alkali electrolysis industry
83/513/EEC	Limit values and quality objectives for cadmium discharges
84/491/EEC	Limit values and quality objectives for discharges of hexachlorocyclohexane
84/156/EEC	Limit values and quality objectives for mercury discharges by sectors other than the chlor-alkali electrolysis industry
86/280/EEC	Limit values and quality objectives for discharges of certain dangerous substances included in List I of the Annex to Directive 76/464/EEC (DDT and others)
88/347/EEC	Amending Annex II to Directive 86/280/EEC on limit values and quality objectives for discharges of certain dangerous substances included in List I of the Annex to Directive 76/464/EEC (aldrin, dieldrin, endrin, hexachlorobenzene, hexachlorobutadiene, chloroform)
88/609/EEC	Limitation of emissions of certain pollutants into the air from large combustion plants
90/415/EEC	Amending Annex II to Directive 86/280/EEC on limit values and quality objectives for discharges of certain dangerous substances included in List I of the Annex to Directive 76/464/EEC (dichloroethane, trichloroethane, perchloroethane, trichlorobenzene)
91/67/EEC	Fish health
91/676/EEC	Protection of waters against pollution caused by nitrates from agricultural sources
91/271/EEC	Urban waste water treatment
92/43/EEC	The conservation of natural habitats and of wild fauna and flora
96/61/EEC	Integrated pollution prevention and control

The key Directives are discussed in the relevant sections of this report. The new Directive on Integrated Pollution Prevention and Control (96/61/EEC) is significant as it will extend the approach introduced under the Environmental Protection Act 1990 to a wider range of industrial processes. Another important development expected is the introduction of a new Water Resources Framework Directive which will replace a number of existing Directives and integrate requirements for managing water flows with the protection of the ecological quality of the aquatic environment. The Agency is now contributing to research and discussions on how the Directive should be formulated.

A1.2   International Commitments

There are international commitments which require routine monitoring. These relate to the achievement of agreed targets and arise from the following:

The Paris Commission (PARCOM) which, in 1988, reached an agreement on surveys of the riverine inputs of certain substances into the sea;

The North Sea Conference Declarations, which have resulted in a similar need to make regular estimates of the loads of certain materials entering coastal waters from various land-based sources. These materials were listed in Annex 1A of the 3rd North Sea Conference. The UK has undertaken to apply the targets to the whole of its coastline. Inputs of 36 dangerous substances from direct discharges were to be reduced by 1995 to 50 per cent of the 1985 inputs. In addition to reducing inputs from point discharges by applying best available technology, diffuse inputs of dioxins, mercury, cadmium and lead from all sources, including atmospheric and land runoff, were to be reduced by 70 per cent;

The UN Convention on Biodiversity was signed at the UN Conference on Environment and Development at Rio de Janeiro in 1992. The Convention promotes the restoration of degraded ecosystems and the recovery of threatened species. It requires each contracting party to develop or adapt national strategies, plans or programmes for the conservation and sustainable use of biological diversity. The government's response to the Convention is the UK Biodiversity Action Plan.

A1.3   National Standards and Targets

The UK has maintained a long-held stance in Europe over its preference for the use of environmental quality objectives and standards as the basis for pollution control, related to the uses to which waters meet. The Surface Waters (River Ecosystem) (Classification) Regulations 1994 introduced a scheme whereby river stretches could be assigned one of five classes relating to the type of ecosystem that should be maintained in that stretch. These classes would become Statutory Water Quality Objectives set by the Secretary of State after consultation, in accordance with the Water Resources Act 1991. The classification scheme allows the Environment Agency to make plans so that water quality does not deteriorate and to determine where improvements may be desirable. The scheme is currently being tested in eight pilot catchments across the country to confirm that it does form a workable basis for water quality planning and to determine whether the scheme should be used to form the basis for statutory (legally binding) standards. Further schemes may, in time, be developed for other types of controlled waters, for example lakes, estuaries, groundwaters and for other uses, such as abstractions for industry and agriculture, watersports, and special ecosystems. The Agency continues to use non-statutory river quality objectives as a widespread basis for planning water quality improvements and to set discharge consents accordingly.

In 1989, the government issued non-statutory guidance on environmental quality standards (EQSs) related to List II dangerous substances (DoE circular, 7/89). Standards are specified for fresh waters and marine waters. Even though the requirement to establish standards for List II substances came from the Dangerous Substances Directive (76/464/EEC), the standards themselves have been derived and agreed nationally. The achievement of these EQSs requires discharge consent standards to be set appropriately.

The UK Biodiversity Action Plan is the government's response to its commitments under the Convention on Biodiversity, signed at the United Nations Conference on Environment and Development at Rio de Janeiro in 1992 (DoE, 1994). The goal is to conserve and enhance biological diversity within the UK. The Action Plan brings together existing and new programmes for the designation and management of sites and species. A Biodiversity Steering Group has been established to develop costed targets for key species and habitats, and to improve information coordination and public awareness (DoE, 1995a). The first tranche of plans for 116 species and 14 key habitats were published in 1995 and have been endorsed by the government. It is intended to publish plans for a further 286 species and 24 habitats by the end of 1998.

APPENDIX 2

River Habitat Survey

The River Habitat Survey assesses the physical structure of watercourses (NRA, 1996a). Along a 500m stretch of river, data relating to the channel, banks and riparian corridor are recorded, including features present at 10 equidistant spot-checks and a sweep-up check between the spot-checks. The national reference site network is based on three sites per 10km square in England and Wales, surveyed between 1994 and 1996. The network represents over 2,200km or 6.6 per cent of the river length classified for water quality.

The Habitat Modification Score indicates the extent of artificial modification of a site. The scoring and classification system is given in Table A2.1.

A scoring system for Habitat Quality Assessment has been developed. This is based on the diversity of features and the occurrence of certain natural features. The following variables are included:

flow types

channel substrates (e.g. bedrock, gravel)

channel features (e.g. mid-channel bars, islands)

bank features (e.g. cliffs, side bars, point bars)

bank vegetation structure

Table A2.1
The Habitat Modification Score of the River Habitat Survey

Spot-check feature	Score per entry
Reinforced bank[1]	2
Resectioned bank[1]	1
Embanked[1]	1
Berm (lower bank)[1]	1
Culvert[1]	8
Artificial substrate[1]	2
Ford[1]	2
Poaching (trampling)[1]	1 for 3 entries 2 for 6 entries
Sweep-up feature	
Culverts	8
Weirs	3
Groynes	1-6 depending on number
Roadbridge	1-6 depending on number
Realignment	1-6 depending on number

[1] *If these features are not recorded in spot-checks but are found in the sweep-up, score 1 for occurrence on one bank, 2 for both banks.*

Habitat Modification Score	Category
0-2	'semi-natural'
3-8	predominantly unmodified
9-20	obviously modified
21-44	extensively modified
>44	heavily and extensively modified

- channel vegetation (liverworts and mosses, emergent and submerged vegetation)

- land-use within 50m (broadleaf or native coniferous woodland, moorland/heath, wetland)

- trees and associated features (including overhanging boughs, underwater tree roots)

- special habitat features (waterfall>5m high, braided or side channel, debris dam, natural open water, fen, carr, flush, bog)

APPENDIX 3
Environmental Quality Standards

Table A3.1
List I substances covered by the EC Dangerous Substances Directive (76/464/EEC)

List I substances	Statutory EQS[1] (µg/l)	Number of discharges
mercury and compounds	1	752
cadmium and compounds	5	2,196
hexachlorocyclohexane (all isomers)	0.1	123
DDT (all isomers)	0.025	15
DDT (pp isomers)	0.01	1
pentachlorophenol	2	88
carbon tetrachloride	12	51
aldrin	0.01	35
dieldrin	0.01	58
endrin	0.005	37
isodrin	0.005	7
hexachlorobenzene	0.03	20
hexachlorobutadiene	0.1	14
chloroform	12	73
trichloroethylene	10	48
tetrachloroethylene	10	51
trichlorobenzene	0.4	31
1,2-dichloroethane	10	87

[1] *Standards are all annual mean concentrations.*

List II substances	Operational EQS[1] (µg/l)	Measured as
lead	10	AD
chromium	20	AD
zinc	75	AT
copper	10	AD
nickel	150	AD
arsenic[2]	50	AD
boron	2000	AT
iron	1000	AD
pH	6.0 to 9.0	P
vanadium	20	AT
tributyltin[2]	0.02	MT
triphenyltin[2]	0.02	MT
PCSD	0.05	PT
cyfluthrin	0.001	PT
sulcofuron	25	PT
flucofuron	1	PT
permethrin	0.01	PT
atrazine and simazine[2]	2	A
azinphos-methyl[2]	0.01	A
dichlorvos[2]	0.001	A
endosulphan[2]	0.003	A
fenitrothion[2]	0.01	A
malathion[2]	0.01	A
trifluralin[2]	0.1	A
diazinon	0.01	A
propetamphos	0.01	A
cypermethrin	0.0001	A
isoproturon	2.0	A

A = annual average, P = 95 per cent of samples, D = dissolved, T = total, M = maximum.

[1] *Standards quoted for metals are for the protection of sensitive aquatic life at hardness 100 to 150mg/l CaCO₃; alternative standards may be found in DoE circular 7/89.*

[2] *Standards for these substances are from the Surface Waters (Dangerous Substances) (Classification) Regulations, 1997, SI 2560 in which case these are now statutory.*

Table A3.2
Environmental Quality Standards applicable to List II substances

177

APPENDIX 4

Parameters Specified in the EC Freshwater Fish Directive (78/659/EEC)

The standards of the Freshwater Fish Directive are summarised below. Member states shall not set values less stringent than those in column I (Imperative) and shall endeavour to respect the values in column G (Guideline).

Table A4.1
Standards of the Freshwater Fish Directive

Parameter	Salmonid		Cyprinid	
	G	I	G	I
Temperature (°C) (where there is a thermal discharge)	Temperature at edge of mixing zone must not exceed the unaffected temperature by more than:			
		1.5		3
	The temperature must not exceed:			
		21.5		28
		10		10
	The 10°C limit applies to breeding periods when needed			
Dissolved oxygen (mg/l O_2)	50%>9 100%>7	50%>9 When <6, must prove not harmful to fish population	50%>8 100%>5	50%>7 When <4, must prove not harmful to fish population
pH		6 to 9		6 to 9
Suspended solids (mg/l)	<25		<25	
Biochemical oxygen demand (mg/l)	<3		<6	
Total phosphorus	No G or I standards applicable			
Nitrites (mg/l NO_2)	<0.01		<0.03	
Phenolic compounds (mg/l C_6H_5OH)	Must not adversely affect fish flavour			
Petroleum hydrocarbons	Must not be present visibly, detectable by taste of fish, harmful to fish			
Non-ionised ammonia (mg/l NH_3)	<0.005	<0.025	<0.005	<0.025
Total ammonium (mg/l NH_4)	<0.04	<1	<0.2	<1
Total residual chlorine (mg/l HOCl)		<0.005		<0.005
Total zinc (mg/l Zn)	At water hardness >100mg $CaCO_3$/l			
		<0.3		<1.0
	There are also limit values for hardness between 10 and 500mg/l			
Dissolved copper (mg/l Cu)	At water hardness >100mg $CaCO_3$/l			
	<0.04		<0.04	
	There are also limit values at hardness between 10 and 500mg/l			

APPENDIX 5
General Quality Assessment Classification Scheme

A5.1 Methods for Chemical Scheme

There are 8,000 sites sampled by the Agency across England and Wales, each site characterising a stretch of river or canal so that 40,000km of rivers are assessed. In the main, these sites and the monitoring are the same as those used to make decisions on developments that may affect water quality, discharges, abstractions and changes in the use of land. Sites are sampled a minimum of 12 times a year and the data collected over three years is used to obtain the required precision of results.

The GQA scheme requires an assessment against chemical standards expressed as percentiles. These are values which the chemical determinand should not exceed (or fall below in the case of dissolved oxygen) (Table A5.1). The percentiles are calculated from the samples taken, assuming a normal distribution for dissolved oxygen and lognormal for biochemical oxygen demand (BOD) and ammonia (NRA, 1994a). The estimates of the percentiles are compared with the standards set for six grades relating to biochemical oxygen demand (BOD), ammonia and dissolved oxygen (DO). Ammonia and BOD are indicators of pollution which apply to all rivers because of the ubiquitous nature of the risk of pollution from sewage or farms. Dissolved oxygen is essential to aquatic life. High BOD and ammonia concentrations can lead to low DO concentrations so these concentrations are also important in assessing water quality. Some forms of ammonia are also toxic to fish. A grade is assigned to each river length according to the lowest standard achieved. For example, if a site is grade A for BOD but grade B for ammonia and DO then it is assigned grade B overall. There is a degree of error in assigning grades which results from the limited number of samples taken. This gives an average risk of 19 per cent that a particular stretch of

river is placed in the wrong grade and a risk of 25 per cent that a river may be declared wrongly to have changed grade from one survey to the next. Further details of statistical errors are given in the Water Quality Series Report No. 19 (NRA, 1994a).

A5.2 The Biology General Quality Assessment

The biological scheme is based on groups of macroinvertebrates (small animals including mayfly nymphs, snails, shrimps and worms) that are found on the river bed. Macroinvertebrates are used because they:

do not move far;

have reasonably long life cycles;

respond to the physical and chemical characteristics of the river;

are affected by pollutants which occur infrequently and which are not measured by spot-sampling used in the GQA (chemical) scheme;

provide a picture of quality integrated over time.

Eighty-three groups of macroinvertebrates are considered in assessing biological quality. As different groups respond differently to pollution, they are given scores of 1 (pollution-tolerant group) to 10 (pollution-sensitive group). The presence of groups sensitive to pollution suggests better water quality than for sites where only pollution-tolerant groups are found.

Table A5.1
Standards for the chemical General Quality Assessment

GQA grade	Description	Dissolved oxygen (percentage saturation) 10-percentile	Biochemical oxygen demand (mg/l) 90-percentile	Ammonia (mgN/l) 90-percentile
A	Very good	80	2.5	0.25
B	Good	70	4	0.6
C	Fairly good	60	6	1.3
D	Fair	50	8	2.5
E	Poor	20	15	9.0
F	Bad	<20	>15	>9.0

Table A5.2
GQA Scheme for Biology

Grade	Outline description
a - Very good	Biology similar to (or better than) that expected for an average and unpolluted river of this size, type and location. High diversity of groups, usually with several species in each. Rare to find dominance of any one group.
b - Good	Biology falls a little short of that expected for an unpolluted river. Small reduction in the number of groups that are sensitive to pollution. Moderate increase in the number of individuals in the groups that tolerate pollution.
c - Fairly good	Biology worse than expected for an unpolluted river. Many sensitive groups absent, or number of individuals reduced. Marked rise in numbers of individuals in groups that tolerate pollution.
d - Fair	Sensitive groups scarce and contain only small numbers of individuals. A range of pollution tolerant groups present, some with high numbers of individuals.
e - Poor	Biology restricted to pollution tolerant species with some groups dominant in terms of the numbers of individuals. Sensitive groups rare or absent.
f - Bad	Biology limited to a small number of very tolerant groups such as worms, midge larvae, leeches and water hoglouse, present in very high numbers. In the worst case, there may be no life present.

By comparing groups found in the sample with those expected if the river were unpolluted, rivers can be classified into one of six grades (Table A5.2).

Each stretch of river has a representative biological and a chemical sampling site allocated to it. Although the biological and chemical sites are not always coincident, they are subject to the same water quality and, as far as possible, are not separated by tributaries, discharges, weirs or other potential influences on water quality. Two biological samples are collected in a year, one in spring (March to May) and one in autumn (September to November). The samples are collected using a nationally standard method incorporating three minutes active sampling with a pond net. At some deep sites this is not possible, so the samples are collected by doing three to five trawls with a Medium Naturalist's Dredge or by using an air-lift sampler, followed in both cases by a one minute sweep with a pond net. Every sample is supplemented by a one minute visual search for animals living on the water surface, or attached to rocks, logs or vegetation.

All the samples are analysed in laboratories. The methods used to wash and sort the samples vary, depending on what was most effective in different places (largely determined by the amount of silt or weed in the samples). In 1995 a scheme of quality control was established in every laboratory, to ensure that an average of no more than two taxa were missed. This involved re-inspecting 10 per cent of all samples. There was also a second audit in which 60 samples from each region were re-analysed by an independent assessor. This demonstrated that an average of 1.9 taxa were missed during analysis.

Other information collected at the site include the width and depth of the stream and the percentage cover on the river bed of boulders, gravel, sand and silt. For GQA, all these items are calculated as annual averages. Information supplied from maps include the grid reference, the slope of the river, its altitude above sea level and the distance of the site from the source of the river.

There are two values determined for each sample:

the number of different groups (known as taxa) present;

the average score per group (taxon). This is calculated by dividing the BMWP (Biological Monitoring Working Party) score by the number of taxa. The BMWP score is calculated by totalling the weighted score for each taxon. The score is weighted according to the taxon's sensitivity to pollution; the highest score (10) being given to the most sensitive taxa. Low values for the BMWP score generally indicate pollution.

Having calculated these two values, they are compared to those expected to occur at a site in a similar, but pristine river. As there is much natural variation due to geology and habitat a mathematical model, RIVPACS (the River Invertebrate Prediction and Classification System), is used to predict the fauna, from which the number of taxa and average score per taxon expected in the absence of pollution can be calculated. This model uses the physical data, measured both at the site and from maps, to calculate these expected values.

River biological quality is then expressed as ratios of the actual values from sampling compared with the

Grade	Ecological quality index	
	i) for taxa	ii) for average score per taxon
a	0.85	1.00
b	0.70	0.90
c	0.55	0.77
d	0.45	0.65
e	0.30	0.50
f	<0.3	<0.50

Table A5.3
Link between biological General Quality Assessment grades and ecological quality index

Biological measure	Value	Standard error	Number of samples	EQI	Confidence of biological Grade (%)					
					a	b	c	d	e	f
ASPT	4.50	0.18	2	0.94	4	81	15	-	-	-
No. of taxa	22	1.56		0.88	67	33	-	-	-	-
Combined					4	81	15	-	-	-

Table A5.4
Example of statistical confidence for the biological GQA

predicted values for both the number of taxa and the average score per taxon. Both ratios are known as Ecological Quality Indices (EQI). An EQI of 1.0 or more indicates that the taxa found in the sample were those expected under conditions of natural water quality. Each EQI is then compared with those set for the biological grades (Table A5.3) and the site assigned the lower of the two grades, if these differ for the two indices.

The divisions between grades are based on the need to detect changes in biological quality. The extremes (grades a and f) are set to reflect very good and bad quality with intermediate grades set pragmatically between these extremes.

The biological classification of waters is not precise and there is a risk that rivers may be classed wrongly, though it is unusual for this error to extend beyond the neighbouring grade. One source of error is that species may be missed during sample processing, introducing a small pessimistic bias into assessments of biology. The uncertainty produced by monitoring gives an average risk of 22 per cent that a particular stretch of river is placed in the wrong class. This produces a risk of bias. The risk of assigning a grade which is too low is about 12 per cent compared with the risk of an overestimate which is 10 per cent. An example of the statistical confidence of assigning a grade is given in Table A5.4.

The use of the biological classification will be a key part of the Agency's method of meeting its duties, particularly in describing the state of the environment and planning improvements in river quality. The BMWP Score can show whether or not a site is

affected by pollution but cannot be used alone, with any degree of confidence, to compare results at different times or in different locations. The introduction of the RIVPACS system has resulted in much greater potential for the use of biological data in river management.

A5.3 The Pilot Nutrient General Quality Assessment

Nutrients are important indicators of water quality because whilst they are essential for life, excessive amounts can lead to an imbalance in the ecosystem known as 'eutrophication'. This often results in blooms of algae which can be toxic. Nitrogen and phosphorus are the nutrients in rivers most likely to be affected by human activities. Naturally, phosphorus concentrations tend to be low and limit the amount of algae growth. There is uncertainty about the relationships between nutrient concentrations and their effects on the ecology of rivers. However, monitoring the concentrations of nitrogen and phosphorus is necessary to show differences and trends in the nutrient status of rivers.

The Environment Agency is testing a pilot scheme for phosphorus based on average concentrations of orthophosphate, measured as phosphorus. The classification proposes standards related to differing levels of phosphate concentrations, but which could be reworked in future in the light of developments in knowledge (Table A5.5). It includes the standard of 0.1mgP/l as a grade boundary between class 3 and 4. This was set as a guideline value by the former DoE as one of many criteria for selecting eutrophic rivers in implementing the EC Directive on Urban Waste Water

Treatment (91/271/EEC). However, they point out that this value is only indicative of possible present or future problems. The other boundaries have been set so that significant changes in orthophosphate inputs to rivers will be reflected in a change of grade.

Table A5.5
Boundaries for the phosphate classification

Grade	Grade limit (annual average concentration of orthophosphate – mgP/l)
1	0.02
2	0.06
3	0.1
4	0.2
5	1.0
6	>1.0

It is important to note that the phosphate classes reflect natural variations in phosphate concentrations due to differences in geology and soils across the country, as well as inputs from sewage and agriculture. The results will therefore reflect these differences and changes over time, but further analysis would be needed to compare present concentrations with the possible semi-natural state.

The procedure used for the phosphate classification is very similar to that for the chemical GQA. However, laboratory analyses for orthophosphate before 1994 were not always required to detect very low concentrations so the use of the classification to show change since 1990 is hampered for rivers characterised by low concentrations of orthophosphate (grades 1 and 2). Similarly, phosphate was not measured routinely in all rivers before 1994.

Like phosphate, background nitrate concentrations differ between rivers due to natural geographical factors. Inputs from human activities, especially farming and sewage works, have increased nitrate concentrations in rivers. A scheme for grading river nitrate concentrations which will relate to legal standards in the Surface Water Abstraction Directive (75/440/EEC) and ecological effects is being developed. The results for 1995 are shown in concentration bands (as annual averages) selected to illustrate the range in values across the country.

A5.4 The Aesthetic General Quality Assessment

Rivers can also be judged to a large extent by their visual appearance. This is an important factor affecting how a river will be used. Rivers in high grades for chemistry or biology may be perceived as being of poor quality if they are littered, visibly polluted or have an unusual smell.

The aesthetic quality of a river is determined by a mix of perceptions including the clarity of the water, odour, stagnation, colour and the presence of oil, litter or foam. The Agency scheme makes assessments by surveying the river and its bank. A standard method has been devised. Sites are assessed on both banks, or one, depending on public access. The unit of survey is a stretch of the bank 50 metres long and five metres wide. The number of items of litter are counted, a visual inspection is made of the cover by oil, foam, fungus and ochre, and the colour and odour of the water is noted. Each type of measurement (litter, odour and colour) is graded from 1 to 4 and each is given a weighted score for each class according to its acceptability based on the findings of a public perception study. Sewage litter is weighted as the most unacceptable. The site is then graded from 1 to 4, described as Aesthetically Good Quality, Fair Quality, Poor Quality and Bad Quality respectively.

Table A5.6 gives the scoring system for categories
within the aesthetic GQA.

Table A5.6
*GQA for aesthetic
quality*

Litter (number of items)

Type of litter	Class 1	Class 2	Class 3	Class 4
Gross	none	2	6	>6
General	5	39	74	>74
Sewage	none	5	19	>19
Faeces	none	3	12	>12

Oil, scum, foam, sewage fungus, ochre (percentage cover)

Class 1	Class 2	Class 3	Class 4
0	5	25	>25

Colour

Intensity	Blue / Green	Red / Orange	Brown / Yellow / Straw
Colourless	Class 1	Class 1	Class 1
Very pale	Class 1	Class 2	Class 1
Pale	Class 3	Class 3	Class 2
Dark	Class 4	Class 4	Class 3

Odour

Definitions:	
Group I	Tolerated or less indicative of water quality. Musty, Earthy, Woody.
Group II	Indicators of poor quality. Farmy, Disinfectant, Gas, Chlorine.
Group III	Indicators of very poor quality. Sewage, Polish or Cleaning Fluids, Ammonia, Oily Smells, Bad Eggs (Sulphide).

Classification:			
Intensity of odour	Group I	Group II	Group III
None	Class 1	Class 1	Class 1
Faint	Class 1	Class 2	Class 3
Obvious	Class 2	Class 3	Class 4
Strong	Class 3	Class 4	Class 4

Table A5.7 shows how classes within the aesthetic GQA are combined into an overall score.

Parameter	Allocation of points for each class			
	class 1	class 2	class 3	class 4
Sewage Litter	0	4	8	13
Odour	0	4	8	12
Oil	0	2	4	8
Foam	0	2	4	8
Colour	0	2	4	8
Sewage Fungus	0	2	4	8
Faeces	0	2	4	6
Scum	0	1	3	5
Gross Litter	0	0	1	3
General Litter	0	0	1	3
Ochre	0	0	0	1

The points allocated for each parameter are summed to give the Total Score. The Grade is then assigned as:

Parameter	Allocation of points for each class	Total Score
Grade 1	Good	1, 2 or 3
Grade 2	Fair	4, 5,6 or 7
Grade 3	Poor	8, 9, 10 or 11
Grade 4	Bad	more than 11

A5.5 Results of the chemical, biological and pilot nutrient GQA

Table A5.8
*Chemical results for
1990*

Region	Length of River in Each Chemical Grade (km) in 1988-90						
	A	B	C	D	E	F	Total
Anglian	36.0	758.8	1691.3	1189.3	785.2	102.1	4562.7
Midlands	449.9	1514.0	1610.2	992.7	1002.8	130.7	5700.3
North East	852.3	1619.7	554.1	447.0	606.0	170.3	4249.4
North West	718.6	618.2	556.1	442.8	648.0	208.7	3192.4
Southern	237.8	713.1	668.9	292.0	238.3	32.8	2182.9
South West	1644.7	2670.8	1239.9	737.1	358.0	68.0	6718.5
Thames	315.9	981.2	1050.3	577.6	560.6	46.2	3531.8
Welsh	1782.5	1412.9	426.6	228.7	133.3	39.2	4023.2
England & Wales	6037.7	10288.7	7797.4	4907.2	4332.2	798.0	34161.2

Region	Percentage length of River in Each Chemical Grade in 1988-90					
	A	B	C	D	E	F
Anglian	0.8	16.6	37.1	26.1	17.2	2.2
Midlands	7.9	26.6	28.2	17.4	17.6	2.3
North East	20.1	38.1	13.0	10.5	14.3	4.0
North West	22.5	19.4	17.4	13.9	20.3	6.5
Southern	10.9	32.7	30.6	13.4	10.9	1.5
South West	24.5	39.8	18.5	11.0	5.3	1.0
Thames	8.9	27.8	29.7	16.4	15.9	1.3
Welsh	44.3	35.1	10.6	5.7	3.3	1.0
England & Wales	17.7	30.1	22.8	14.4	12.7	2.3

Table A5.9
Chemical results for 1995

Region	Length of River in Each Chemical Grade (km) in 1993-5						
	A	B	C	D	E	F	Total
Anglian	269.8	1619.0	1473.7	840.9	582.4	28.0	4813.8
Midlands	764.8	2175.9	2126.7	912.7	542.6	66.1	6588.8
North East	2008.0	1687.3	855.3	594.7	731.1	81.9	5958.3
North West	1156.8	1952.4	1036.3	694.4	773.5	131.9	5745.3
Southern	275.8	968.5	589.0	213.8	152.0	20.0	2219.1
South West	2312.4	2251.8	1058.1	218.3	193.9	27.2	6061.7
Thames	538.2	1338.8	1178.3	517.6	211.0	13.2	3797.1
Welsh	3468.2	1142.1	240.2	106.7	79.6	6.1	5042.9
England & Wales	10794.0	13135.8	8557.6	4099.1	3266.1	374.4	40226.9

Region	Percentage length of River in Each Chemical Grade in 1993-5					
	A	B	C	D	E	F
Anglian	5.6	33.6	30.6	17.5	12.1	0.6
Midlands	11.6	33.0	32.3	13.9	8.2	1.0
North East	33.7	28.3	14.4	10.0	12.3	1.4
North West	20.1	34.0	18.0	12.1	13.5	2.3
Southern	12.4	43.6	26.5	9.6	6.8	0.9
South West	38.1	37.1	17.5	3.6	3.2	0.4
Thames	14.2	35.3	31.0	13.6	5.6	0.3
Welsh	68.8	22.6	4.8	2.1	1.6	0.1
England & Wales	26.8	32.7	21.3	10.2	8.1	0.9

Region	Length of River in Each Chemical Grade (km) in 1994-6						
	A	B	C	D	E	F	Total
Anglian	284.1	1518.8	1480.6	908.1	587.3	26.5	4805.6
Midlands	843.6	2211.7	2074.8	865.0	665.9	58.2	6719.2
North East	1831.0	1873.8	1086.8	686.9	792.6	136.5	6407.6
North West	1162.4	1853.4	1196.4	622.9	753.2	155.5	5745.3
Southern	315.7	892.6	575.9	220.9	199.7	14.3	2219.1
South West	2452.1	2190.7	938.4	266.7	201.6	18.4	6067.9
Thames	499.0	1359.5	1022.2	581.2	325.2	9.0	3796.1
Welsh	3679.7	933.9	263.7	79.0	82.4	4.2	5042.9
England & Wales	11067.6	12839.6	8638.8	4230.7	3604.4	422.6	40803.7

Region	Percentage length of River in Each Chemical Grade in 1994-6					
	A	B	C	D	E	F
Anglian	5.9	31.6	30.8	18.9	12.2	0.6
Midlands	12.6	32.9	30.9	12.9	9.9	0.9
North East	28.6	29.2	17.0	10.7	12.4	2.1
North West	20.2	32.3	20.8	10.8	13.0	2.7
Southern	14.2	40.2	26.0	10.0	9.0	0.6
South West	40.4	36.1	15.5	4.4	3.3	0.3
Thames	13.1	35.8	26.9	15.3	8.6	0.2
Welsh	73.0	18.5	5.2	1.6	1.6	0.1
England & Wales	27.1	31.5	21.2	10.4	8.8	1.0

Table A5.10
Chemical results for 1996

Table A5.11
*Comparison of
1990 and 1995:
chemistry*

Comparison of 1990 Chemistry on 1995 Chemistry (km)

		1988/90						
		A	B	C	D	E	F	Total
	A	4492.5	3425.3	453.6	59.6	60.8	4.4	8496.2
	B	1160.1	5154.8	3240.7	1072.4	353.2	33.7	11014.9
1993/95	C	156.1	1192.6	3063.0	1864.1	963.4	88.0	7327.2
	D	19.3	104.5	717.1	1235.2	1218.3	137.1	3431.5
	E	0.0	25.3	141.0	566.0	1578.8	356.1	2667.2
	F	0.0	2.5	8.3	5.9	68.1	156.1	240.9
Total		5828.0	9905.0	7623.7	4803.2	4242.6	775.4	33177.9

Length of river upgraded = 13330.7km
Length of river downgraded = 4166.8km
Net improvement = 9163.9km

Comparison of 1990 Chemistry on 1995 Chemistry (percentage length)

		1988/90						
		A	B	C	D	E	F	Total
	A	13.5	10.3	1.4	0.2	0.2	0.0	25.6
	B	3.5	15.5	9.8	3.2	1.1	0.1	33.2
1993/95	C	0.5	3.6	9.2	5.6	2.9	0.3	22.1
	D	0.1	0.3	2.2	3.7	3.7	0.4	10.3
	E	0.0	0.1	0.4	1.7	4.8	1.1	8.0
	F	0.0	0.0	0.0	0.0	0.2	0.5	0.7
Total		17.6	29.9	23.0	14.5	12.8	2.3	100.0

Length of river upgraded = 40.2 per cent
Length of river downgraded = 12.6 per cent
Net improvement = 27.6 per cent

Summary of Net Changes from 1988/90 to 1993/5

(Percentage length changing Grade)

Region	Up	Down	Net Change
Anglian	48.9	11.7	37.2
Midlands	41.5	15.8	25.7
North East	35.0	9.9	25.1
North West	33.0	18.5	14.5
Southern	34.2	16.4	17.8
South West	38.9	10.5	28.4
Thames	43.4	14.2	29.2
Welsh	41.7	6.4	35.3
England & Wales	40.2	12.6	27.6

Table A5.12
Summary of changes from 1990 to 1995: chemistry

Summary of Net Changes from 1988/90 to 1994/6

(Percentage length changing Grade)

Region	Up	Down	Net Change
Anglian	46.5	11.6	34.8
Midlands	43.0	13.7	29.3
North East	30.6	20.8	9.8
North West	31.0	21.2	9.8
Southern	32.4	18.2	14.2
South West	41.0	9.5	31.5
Thames	39.8	14.9	24.9
Welsh	44.3	5.4	38.8
England & Wales	39.6	13.7	25.8

Table A5.13
Summary of changes from 1990 to 1996: chemistry

Table A5.14
Biological results for 1990

Region	Length of River in Each Biological Grade (km) in 1990						
	a	b	c	d	e	f	Total
Anglian	465.3	1420.2	1522.6	482.7	208.8	70.1	4169.7
Midlands	327.8	806.0	1213.6	770.5	469.8	223.6	3811.3
North East	1335.9	1174.4	519.8	409.3	379.4	313.5	4132.3
North West	426.2	1071.4	692.6	333.6	617.5	880.4	4021.7
Southern	397.5	452.6	396.9	128.3	34.0	10.0	1419.3
South West	2142.8	2113.0	826.2	222.9	153.3	88.3	5546.5
Thames	716.9	996.5	689.3	346.5	236.3	107.2	3092.7
Welsh	1395.2	1441.9	613.7	242.8	97.9	15.5	3807.0
England & Wales	7207.6	9476.0	6474.7	2936.6	2197.0	1708.6	30000.5

Region	Percentage length of River in Each Biological Grade in 1990					
	a	b	c	d	e	f
Anglian	11.2	34.1	36.5	11.6	5.0	1.7
Midlands	8.6	21.1	31.8	20.2	12.3	5.9
North East	32.3	28.4	12.6	9.9	9.2	7.6
North West	10.6	26.6	17.2	8.3	15.4	21.9
Southern	28.0	31.9	28.0	9.0	2.4	0.7
South West	38.6	38.1	14.9	4.0	2.8	1.6
Thames	23.2	32.2	22.3	11.2	7.6	3.5
Welsh	36.6	37.9	16.1	6.4	2.6	0.4
England & Wales	24.0	31.6	21.6	9.8	7.3	5.7

Region	Length of River in Each Biological Grade (km) in 1995						
	a	b	c	d	e	f	Total
Anglian	1053.9	2023.3	1166.8	347.6	123.0	16.8	4731.4
Midlands	965.9	1683.7	1788.9	918.5	357.8	122.3	5837.1
North East	2264.4	1201.6	734.0	515.4	479.5	267.6	5462.5
North West	961.1	1534.4	902.9	497.4	808.0	262.1	4965.9
Southern	976.9	718.8	298.3	163.0	29.0	4.6	2190.6
South West	3325.5	1897.0	533.6	103.4	54.5	21.0	5935.0
Thames	1132.2	1116.3	792.9	345.6	157.7	24.3	3569.0
Welsh	2316.7	1682.2	676.0	151.3	32.7	4.9	4863.8
England & Wales	12996.6	11857.3	6893.4	3042.2	2042.2	723.6	37555.2

Region	Percentage length of River in Each Biological Grade in 1995					
	a	b	c	d	e	f
Anglian	22.3	42.8	24.7	7.3	2.6	0.4
Midlands	16.5	28.8	30.6	15.7	6.1	2.1
North East	41.5	22.0	13.4	9.4	8.8	4.9
North West	19.4	30.9	18.2	10.0	16.3	5.3
Southern	44.6	32.8	13.6	7.4	1.3	0.2
South West	56.0	32.0	9.0	1.7	.9	0.4
Thames	31.7	31.3	22.2	9.7	4.4	0.7
Welsh	47.6	34.6	13.9	3.1	0.7	0.1
England & Wales	34.6	31.6	18.4	8.1	5.4	1.9

Table A5.16
Comparison of 1990 and 1995: biology

Comparison of 1990 Biology on 1995 Biology (km)

		1990						
		a	b	c	d	e	f	Total
	a	6599.6	4255.3	899.3	58.9	56.5	10.7	11880.3
	b	2097.3	4308.4	2616.0	347.9	66.8	24.3	9460.7
1995	c	253.0	720.2	2126.0	1424.8	429.5	46.3	4999.8
	d	11.2	60.5	416.6	784.3	688.6	163.5	2124.7
	e	0.0	7.1	28.6	138.7	627.1	422.6	1224.1
	f	0.0	0.0	0.0	25.4	92.5	196.2	314.1
Total		8961.1	9351.5	6086.5	2780.0	1961.0	863.6	30003.7

Length of river upgraded = 11511.0km
Length of river downgraded = 3851.1km
Net improvement = 7659.9km

Comparison of 1990 Biology on 1995 Biology (percentage length)

		1990						
		a	b	c	d	e	f	
	a	22.0	14.2	3.0	0.2	0.2	0.0	39.6
	b	7.0	14.4	8.7	1.2	0.2	0.1	31.5
1995	c	0.8	2.4	7.1	4.7	1.4	0.2	16.7
	d	0.0	0.2	1.4	2.6	2.3	0.5	7.1
	e	0.0	0.0	0.1	0.5	2.1	1.4	4.1
	f	0.0	0.0	0.0	0.1	0.3	0.7	1.0
Total		29.9	31.2	20.3	9.3	6.5	2.9	100.0

Length of river upgraded =38.4 per cent
Length of river downgraded =12.8 per cent
Net improvement =25.5 per cent

Summary of net changes from 1990 to 1995

(Percentage length changing Grade)

Region	Up	Down	Net Change
Anglian	49.3	9.9	39.4
Midlands	36.0	14.3	21.7
North East	36.1	10.7	25.4
North West	46.0	16.3	29.6
Southern	34.7	5.9	28.8
South West	33.7	12.5	21.2
Thames	36.9	15.2	21.8
Welsh	32.6	14.4	18.2
England and Wales	38.4	12.8	25.5

Table A5.18
*Comparison of
1995 chemical
grade with 1995
biological grade*

Comparison of Chemical GQA on Biological GQA (km) for England & Wales in 1995

		Chemistry						
		A	B	C	D	E	F	
	a	5788.9	4874.1	1556.1	319.3	162.3	8.3	12709.0
	b	3552.1	4603.4	2540.6	713.6	334.5	7.0	11751.2
Biology	c	893.5	2192.3	2116.0	834.7	722.1	42.9	6801.5
	d	130.7	656.5	860.9	768.8	493.9	50.9	2961.7
	e	56.4	329.0	454.1	498.4	590.9	67.5	1996.3
	f	6.7	20.2	96.6	123.0	332.3	112.8	691.6
Total		10428.3	12675.5	7624.3	3257.8	2636.0	289.4	36911.3

Biology better than Chemistry = 12727.8km
Chemistry better than Biology = 10202.7km
Difference = 2525.1km

Comparison of Chemical GQA on Biological GQA (percentage length) for England & Wales in 1995

		Chemistry						
		A	B	C	D	E	F	
	a	15.7	13.2	4.2	0.9	0.4	0.0	34.4
	b	9.6	12.5	6.9	1.9	0.9	0.0	31.8
Biology	c	2.4	5.9	5.7	2.3	2.0	0.1	18.4
	d	0.4	1.8	2.3	2.1	1.3	0.1	8.0
	e	0.2	0.9	1.2	1.4	1.6	0.2	5.4
	f	0.0	0.1	0.3	0.3	0.9	0.3	1.9
Total		28.3	34.3	20.7	8.8	7.1	0.8	100.0

Biology better than Chemistry = 34.5 per cent
Chemistry better than Biology = 27.6 per cent
Difference = 6.9 per cent

Region	Length of River in Each Chemical Grade (km) in 1988-90						
	1	2	3	4	5	6	Total
Anglian	0.0	189.1	268.5	381.1	1794.9	1766.0	4399.6
Midlands	11.5	102.3	64.0	162.5	471.1	682.4	1493.8
North West	841.5	712.0	419.1	349.0	643.9	386.8	3352.3
South West	750.8	1602.0	868.3	1234.0	1840.1	406.5	6701.7
Southern	3.5	260.8	313.5	359.6	647.2	521.3	2105.9
Thames	55.0	246.1	161.5	225.1	700.8	1433.9	2822.4
Welsh	182.9	960.2	262.1	310.2	346.6	65.1	2127.1
England & Wales	1845.2	4072.5	2357.0	3021.5	6444.6	5262.0	23002.8

Region	Percentage length of River in Each Chemical Grade in 1988-90					
	1	2	3	4	5	6
Anglian	0.0	4.3	6.1	8.7	40.8	40.1
Midlands	8	6.8	4.3	10.9	31.5	45.7
North West	25.1	21.2	12.5	10.4	19.2	11.5
South West	11.2	23.9	13.0	18.4	27.5	6.1
Southern	0.2	12.4	14.9	17.1	30.7	24.8
Thames	1.9	8.7	5.7	8.0	24.8	50.8
Welsh	8.6	45.1	12.3	14.6	16.3	3.1
England & Wales	8.0	17.7	10.2	13.1	28.0	22.9

Table A5.20
Phosphate results for 1995

Region	Length of River in Each Chemical Grade (km) in 1993-5						
	1	2	3	4	5	6	Total
Anglian	11.3	658.4	344.1	703.1	2348.9	742.4	4808.2
Midlands	0.0	497.1	302.5	432.8	991.6	946.7	3170.7
North East	733.8	1073.4	435.3	609.8	989.0	325.5	4166.8
North West	1099.4	1697.9	779.8	594.2	1084.2	416.0	5671.5
South West	716.2	1838.9	804.7	996.7	1539.1	115.0	6010.6
Southern	0.0	454.8	416.4	411.7	662.4	258.4	2203.7
Thames	0.0	392.2	256.7	510.7	1658.3	978.2	3796.1
Welsh	2577.1	1275.7	492.5	376.8	259.9	54.1	5036.1
England & Wales	5137.8	7888.4	3832.0	4635.8	9533.4	3836.3	34863.7

Region	Percentage length of River in Each Chemical Grade in 1993-5					
	1	2	3	4	5	6
Anglian	0.2	13.7	7.2	14.6	48.9	15.4
Midlands	0.0	15.7	9.5	13.6	31.3	29.9
North East	17.6	25.8	10.4	14.6	23.7	7.8
North West	19.4	29.9	13.7	10.5	19.1	7.3
South West	11.9	30.6	13.4	16.6	25.6	1.9
Southern	0.0	20.6	18.9	18.7	30.1	11.7
Thames	0.0	10.3	6.8	13.5	43.7	25.8
Welsh	51.2	25.3	9.8	7.5	5.2	1.1
England & Wales	14.7	22.6	11.0	13.3	27.3	11.0

Comparison of 1988/90 Grade on 1993/5 Grade (km)

		1988/90						
		1	2	3	4	5	6	Total
	1	1103.6	800.8	74.6	35.8	7.5	6.2	2028.5
	2	525.8	2419.4	1061.6	481.7	162.0	27.0	4677.5
1993/95	3	57.9	340.5	823.5	893.9	355.8	37.0	2508.6
	4	38.6	72.5	224.5	1272.9	1389.9	53.9	3052.3
	5	3.0	42.6	41.6	151.5	4209.7	2540.0	6988.4
	6	0.0	1.2	8.1	3.9	76.4	2522.5	2612.1
Total		1728.9	3677.0	2233.9	2839.7	6201.3	5186.6	21867.4

Length of river upgraded = 7927.7km
Length of river downgraded = 1588.1km
Net improvement = 6339.6km

Comparison of 1988/90 Grade on 1993/5 Grade (percentage length)

		1988/90						
		1	2	3	4	5	6	
	1	5.0	3.7	0.3	0.2	0.0	0.0	9.3
	2	2.4	11.1	4.9	2.2	.7	0.1	21.4
1993/95	3	0.3	1.6	3.8	4.1	1.6	0.2	11.5
	4	0.2	0.3	1.0	5.8	6.4	0.2	14.0
	5	0.0	0.2	0.2	0.7	19.3	11.6	32.0
	6	0.0	0.0	0.0	0.0	0.3	11.5	11.9
Total		7.9	16.8	10.2	13.0	28.4	23.7	100.0

Length of river upgraded = 36.3 per cent
Length of river downgraded = 7.3 per cent
Net improvement = 29.0 per cent

APPENDIX 6

Sources of Groundwater Contamination

Entec UK Ltd was commissioned by the NRA to undertake a detailed study of sources of groundwater pollution from May 1995 to May 1996, using information readily available, largely from the NRA itself. The survey of groundwater sources linked contamination to different land uses. The land use categories used in the NRA survey were as follows:

Chemicals (pharmaceuticals, wood treatment plants, paint works)

Petrochemicals (oil refineries, fuel storage depots)

Metals (iron & steel works, smelters, electroplating/anodising/galvanising works)

Energy (gasworks, power stations)

Transport (garages, maintenance shops, railway depots/sidings)

Waste Disposal (landfill sites)

Water Supply & Sewage Treatment (septic tanks, sewage-treatment plants)

Agriculture (leaking silage clamps, pesticide preparation)

Residential (fuel oil spills, leaking fuel oil tanks)

Retail (retail parks, fuel oil spills)

Military (Ministry of Defence sites e.g. military airbases)

Petrol Service Stations (spillages, leaking underground storage tanks)

Light Industrial (light industrial warehouses, premises)

Pits and Quarries (sand & gravel extraction, quarrying)

Mines and Spoil Heaps (abandoned mines and associated spoil heaps)

Miscellaneous (docks, wharfs, quays, sites not falling into any other category).

A subjective assessment of the point source severity was applied in an attempt to prioritise sites on a scale of national importance and thus provide an indication of the magnitude of groundwater pollution in England and Wales. The severity codes and number of point sources in each category are given in Table A6.1.

Table A6.1
Severity of groundwater contamination

Severity code	Description	Number of point sources
1. High Significance	Gross contamination of major aquifer	96
2. Medium-High Significance	Moderate contamination of major aquifer	203
3. Medium Significance	-	339
4. Medium-Low Significance	-	387
5. Low Significance	Slight contamination of minor aquifer	180

APPENDIX 7

Landscape Evaluation Matrix

The National Rivers Authority developed methods for assessing landscapes. Evaluation matrices have been devised for both the river landscape and the river channel types but they include broadly similar criteria which, in our view, are factors which make a particularly important contribution to the quality of the riverside or channel. They are divided into three main groups: factors affecting the visual qualities of the landscape; those affecting the environmental quality of the riverside and channel; and those affecting activities along the river and appreciation of the river landscape. They include:

aesthetic appeal: whether the river or channel landscape is judged to be generally attractive or unattractive;

condition: whether the landscape and its components are generally in a good, well-managed or poor, neglected condition;

visual harmony: whether the character of the landscape is generally harmonious or discordant, both in itself and as part of a wider scene;

appropriateness of character: whether the landscape 'fits in' well with its surroundings or is it out of character with its immediate context;

environmental quality: whether the landscape provides a hospitable or hostile environment, for example, whether it is exposed or sheltered, hard or soft in character, tranquil or noisy, light or dark;

accessibility: whether there is a good access provision to and along the river or whether the riverside is inaccessible;

connectivity: whether riverside access is well-used or poorly used.

Each division of the riverside and river channel has been assessed subjectively against these criteria, allocating a plus (+) where a landscape type scores particularly positively, a minus (−) where it scores particularly poorly and a '●' in all other cases. An appropriate value class is then attributed as follows:

1. mostly positive attributes (generally looks attractive, a pleasant place to be, well-used, well managed, land-use contributes positively to character, etc.);

2. a mix of positive and negative attributes (with the balance not tending towards either direction);

3. mostly negative attributes (has an unsightly appearance or degraded condition, is out of context with its surroundings, has a hostile or poor environmental quality, restricted access and isolated from its hinterland etc.).

The allocation of intervention strategies helps to indicate where positive action is required to maintain or enhance the river landscape. It does not however, indicate what form the intervention should take, by whom and whether the action is feasible within the short or longer term. The categories of intervention follow the standard nomenclature:

C   Conservation (low intervention)
emphasis on conservation of existing character and appropriate management or enhancement of particular features which contribute to this character.

R   Restoration (moderate intervention)
emphasis on restoring a positive, strong and coherent character to areas where the existing landscape is being degraded. This does not necessarily imply restoration to a former character but strengthening of a new identity. This level of intervention may be achieved through a range of mechanisms, including development or management activities.

E   Enhancement (high intervention)
emphasis on creating new landscape character in those areas which are highly degraded or derelict and have almost totally lost their former identity.

References

ADAMOWICZ W.L., GARROD G.D. AND WILLIS K.G., 1995.
Estimating the passive use benefits of Britain's inland waterways.
Research report. Centre for Rural Economy, University of Newcastle upon Tyne.

BEEBEE T.J.C., 1977.
Environmental change as a cause of Natterjack Toad (Bufo calamita) declines in Britain.
Biol Conserv (II), 87-102.

BEEBEE T.J.C., FLOWER R.J., STEVENSON A.C., PATRICK S.T., APPLEBY P.G., FLETCHER C., MARSH C., NATKANSKI J., RIPPEY B., AND BATTARBEE R.W., 1990.
Decline of the Natterjack Toad Bufo calamita in Britain: Palaeoecological, Documentary and Experimental Evidence for Breeding Site Acidification.
Biological Conservation 53 (1990) 1-20

BOLLEN J., DOWNING R., MAAS R., VAN ALST R. AND MOLDAN B., 1994.
Framework for the Selection of Policy Actions on the Basis of Europe's Environment – The Dobris Assessment.
Draft Discussion Paper. National Institute of Public Health and Environmental Protection, Bilthoven and Centre for Environmental Scholarship, Charles University, Prague.

BRADSHAW A., 1996.
Otter postmortem examinations – a summary report.
Report to the Environment Agency.

BUISSON R.S.P., AND BRADLEY P., 1994.
Human pressures on natural wetlands: sustainable use or sustained abuse?
In Wetland management, Ed. Falconer, RA and Goodwin, P. Institute of Civil Engineers, p35-46

CENTRE FOR ECOLOGY AND HYDROLOGY, 1996.
An Overview of UK Water Resources prepared for the UK Round Table on Sustainable Development. 16pp.

CHEMICAL INDUSTRIES ASSOCIATION, 1996.
The UK indicators of performance 1990-1995. Chemical Industries Association, London.

CHILTON P.J. AND MILNE C.J., 1994.
Groundwater Quality Assessment: A National Strategy for the NRA.
British Geological Survey Report WD/94/40C.

CLARKE G.P., KASHTI A., MCDONALD A. AND WILLIAMSON P., 1997.
Estimating Small Area Demand for Water: A New Methodology.
J. CIWEM, 11(3) p186-192

COOKE A.S., 1972.
Indications of recent changes in status in the British Isles of the frog (Rana temporaria) and the toad (Bufo bufo).
J Zool, London 167, p161-178

CRATHORNE B., FIELDING M., OAKES D.D.B., HEGARTY B.F., HART J., BUCKLAND J., MATHIAS H. AND ARNOLD J.C., 1995.
A study of the economics of restriction on the use of pesticides.
WRC/Gould Rural Environment report to DoE, WRc report no. DoE 355/P. Medmenham.

CRITICAL LOADS ADVISORY GROUP, FRESHWATERS SUB-GROUP, 1995.
Critical Loads of Acid Deposition for United Kingdom Freshwaters.
Prepared at the request of the Department of the Environment, September 1995. ISBN 1-870393-25-2

DEPARTMENT OF THE ENVIRONMENT, 1993.
Countryside Survey 1990.
Main Report. Prepared by the Institute of Terrestrial Ecology and the Institute of Freshwater Ecology. 174pp. HMSO

DEPARTMENT OF THE ENVIRONMENT, 1994.
Biodiversity, The UK Action Plan.
HMSO, London. 188pp. ISBN 0-10-124282-4

DEPARTMENT OF THE ENVIRONMENT, 1995a.
Biodiversity: The UK Steering Group Report 1995,
HMSO, London. ISBN 0-11-753218-5

DEPARTMENT OF THE ENVIRONMENT, 1995b.
Projections of Households in England to 2016,
HMSO. ISBN 0-11-753055-7

DEPARTMENT OF THE ENVIRONMENT, 1995c.
Review of the composition of leachates from domestic wastes in landfill sites.
Report by Aspinwall & Company Ltd. to DoE Waste Technical Division, Report no. CWM/072/95, DoE, London.

DEPARTMENT OF THE ENVIRONMENT 1995d.
Landfill design, construction and operational practice.
Waste Management Paper 26B. HMSO, London.

DEPARTMENT OF THE ENVIRONMENT AND WELSH OFFICE, 1996.
Water Resources and Supply: Agenda for Action.
The Stationery Office.

DEPARTMENT OF THE ENVIRONMENT, 1996a.
Review of the potential effects of climate change in the United Kingdom.
Second report of the United Kingdom Climate Change Impacts review Group. HMSO. ISBN 0-11-753290-8

DEPARTMENT OF THE ENVIRONMENT, 1996b.
Environmental Protection Expenditure by Industry.
HMSO 76pp. ISBN 0-11-753300-9

DEPARTMENT OF THE ENVIRONMENT, 1996c.
Household Growth: Where Shall We Live? Cm 3471,
HMSO 72pp. ISBN 0-10-134712-X

DEPARTMENT OF THE ENVIRONMENT, 1996d.
United Kingdom Climate Change Impacts Review Group 1996.
Review of the potential effects of climate change in
the United Kingdom. Second Report, prepared at the
request of the DoE. HMSO, London. ISBN 0-11-
753290-8

DEPARTMENT OF THE ENVIRONMENT, 1996e.
Digest of Environmental Statistics no. 18.
London. ISBN 0-11-753297-5

DEPARTMENT OF THE ENVIRONMENT, TRANSPORT
AND THE REGIONS, 1997.
Digest of Environmental Statistics, no. 19.
The Stationery Office, London. 284pp. ISBN 0-11-
753399-8

DEPARTMENT OF TRANSPORT, 1996.
Transport, The Way Forward. The Government's Response to the
Transport Debate.
HMSO 138pp. ISBN 0-10-132342-5

ECOTEC RESEARCH AND CONSULTING LIMITED,
1993.
Evaluating a cost benefit analysis of reduced acid deposition.
A contingent valuation study of aquatic ecosystems.
Working paper five, report to the Department of the
Environment. Birmingham.

ENGLISH NATURE, 1997.
Wildlife and Fresh Water, an Agenda for Sustainable Management.
56pp. ISBN 1-85716-260-9

ENGLISH NATURE, 1997b.
Personal Communication.

ENVIRONMENT ACT, 1995.
Chapter 25.
HMSO, London. 394pp. ISBN 0-10-542595-8

ENVIRONMENT AGENCY, 1996a.
The Environment of England and Wales: A Snapshot.
Environment Agency, Bristol. 124pp.

ENVIRONMENT AGENCY, 1996b.
Groundwater pollution: evaluation of the extent and character of
groundwater pollution from point sources in England and Wales.
14pp.
Environment Agency, Solihull.

ENVIRONMENT AGENCY, 1996c.
Radioactive Substances Report for 1995, Bristol.

ENVIRONMENT AGENCY, 1997a.
Viewpoints on the Environment. Developing a National
Environmental Monitoring and Assessment Framework. 48pp.
Environment Agency, Bristol.

ENVIRONMENT AGENCY, 1997b.
Saving Water: Taking Action. The responses to the consultation report
on water conservation and demand management. 56pp.
Environment Agency, Bristol.

ENVIRONMENT AGENCY, 1997c.
Distribution of Macroinvertebrates in English and Welsh Rivers based
on the 1995 Survey.
School of Computing, Staffordshire University. R&D
Technical Report E12.

ENVIRONMENT AGENCY, 1997d.
Series of Groundwater Vulnerability Maps available in
hardcopy or on CD-ROM from the Stationery Office.

ENVIRONMENT AGENCY, 1997e.
An Environmental Strategy for the Millennium and Beyond. 28pp.
Environment Agency. Bristol.

ENVIRONMENT AGENCY, 1997f.
The Identification and Assessment of Oestrogenic Substances in
Sewage-Treatment Works Effluents.
The Stationery Office, London. 56pp. ISBN 0-11-
310124-4.

ENVIRONMENT AGENCY, 1997g.
Policy and Practice for the Protection of Floodplains. 21pp.
Environment Agency, Bristol.

ENVIRONMENT AGENCY, 1998a.
The River Habitat Survey. Report in preparation.

ENVIRONMENT AGENCY, 1998b.
Endocrine-Disrupting Substances in the Environment: What should
be done?
Environmental Issue 1. 16pp. Environment Agency,
Bristol.

EUROPEAN ENVIRONMENT AGENCY, 1994.
European Rivers and Lakes: Assessment of their Environmental State.
Ed. P. Kristensen and H. Ole Hansen, EEA
Environmental Mongraphs 1. 122pp. ISBN 87-
901980-1-8

EUROPEAN ENVIRONMENT AGENCY AND UNITED
NATIONS ENVIRONMENT PROGRAMME, 1997.
Water Stress in Europe — can the challenge be met?
Copenhagen 16pp. ISBN 92-916702-5-1

FMA, 1997.
The Fertilizer Review.
Fertilizer Manufacturers Association, Peterborough.
10pp.

FORESTRY COMMISSION AND ENVIRONMENT AGENCY, 1997.
Phytophthora disease of Alder.
Leaflet available from Environment Agency, Bristol. 6pp.

FOSTER S.S.D. AND GREY D.R.C., 1997.
Groundwater Resources.
Balancing Perspectives on Key Issues Affecting Supply and Demand. J CIWEM, II (3), 193-199.

FOUNDATION FOR WATER RESEARCH, 1994.
Urban Pollution Management Manual: A planning guide for the management of urban waste water discharges during wet weather.
FR/CL 0002, Foundation for Water Research (FWR), Marlow 324pp. ISBN 0-9521712-1-X

FOUNDATION FOR WATER RESEARCH, 1996.
Assessing the benefits of surface water quality improvements.
Manual. FWR, Marlow. 167pp.

GEORGE D.G., HEWITT D.P., LUND J.W.G. AND SMYLY W.J.P., 1990
The Relative Effects of Enrichment and Climate Change on the Long-Term Dynamics of Daphnia in Esthwaite Water, Cumbria.
Freshwater Biology, 23, p55-70.

GEORGE D.G. AND TAYLOR A.H., 1995.
UK lake plankton and the Gulf Stream.
Nature 375, p 139.

GIBBS J.N. AND LONSDALE D., 1996.
Phytophthora disease of Alder: the situation in 1995.
Forestry Commission Research Information, Note 277. 4pp.

GREY D.R.C., KINNIBURGH D.G., BARKER J.A. AND BLOOMFIELD J.P., 1995.
Groundwater in the UK. A Strategic Study. Issues and Research Needs.
Groundwater Forum Port FR/GFI 70pp. Publ. Foundation for Water Research. ISBN 0-9521712-2-8

HARRIES J.E., JOBLING S., MATTHIESSEN P., SHEAHAN D.A. AND SUMPTER J.P., 1995.
Effects of trace organics on fish — phase 2.
Report to the DoE, Foundation for Water Research, Marlow, Report no. FR/D 0022.

HEATHWAITE A.L., 1995
The Impact of Disturbance on Mire Hydrology.
In Hydrology and Hydrochemistry of British Wetlands. Ed Hughes and Heathwaite. Wiley

HERRINGTON P., 1996.
Climate Change and the Demand for Water.
Department of the Environment. HMSO, London. ISBN 0-11-753138-3

HIRSCH R.M. AND SLACK J.R., 1984.
A nonparametric trend test for seasonal data with serial dependence.
Water Resources Research, 20(6). p.727-732.

HMIP, 1995.
HMIP Monitoring Programme, Radioactive Substances Report for 1994.

HOLDEN P. AND SHARROCK J.T.R., 1994.
The RSPB Book of British Birds, Third Edition.
Macmillan London Ltd. ISBN 0-333-60722-8.

HOUSE OF COMMONS ENVIRONMENT COMMITTEE, 1995.
The Environmental Impact of Leisure Activities.
Fourth Report, Vol 1. HMSO.

HOUSE OF COMMONS ENVIRONMENT COMMITTEE, 1996.
First report, Water Conservation and Supply,
The Stationery Office, London. ISBN 0-10-201397-7

HUGHES J.S. AND O'RIORDAN M.C., 1993.
Radiation exposure of the UK population — 1993 review.
Chilton, NRPB-R263. HMSO, London.

HUNT I.D., 1996.
High and Dry.
The Impacts of Over-abstraction of Water on Wildlife. Ed. F. MacGuire. 40pp. Publ. Butterfly Conservation, Friends of the Earth, RSPB, WWF, Plantlife, The Wildlife Trust (The Biodiversity Challenge Group).

INSTITUTE OF FRESHWATER ECOLOGY, 1995.
Annual Report, 1994-95

INSTITUTE OF HYDROLOGY, 1996.
Report No. 130. Flood risk map for England and Wales.

JOINT NATURE CONSERVATION COMMITTEE/INSTITUTE OF TERRESTRIAL ECOLOGY, 1995.
Atlas of amphibians and reptiles in Britain.
ISBN 0-11-701824-4

KINNIBURGH J.H., TINSLEY M.R. AND BENNETT J., 1997.
Orthophosphate Concentrations in the River Thames.
J. CIWEM, 11(3), 178-185.

LITTLEWOOD I.G., WATTS C.D., GREEN S., MARSH T.J. AND LEEKS G.J.L., 1997.
Aggregated river mass loads for Harmonised Monitoring Scheme catchments grouped by PARCOM coastal zones around Great Britain.
A Report to the Department of the Environment (EPG 1/8/26) by the Institute of Hydrology.

LLOYD J.W. AND TELLAM J.H., 1995.
Groundwater-fed wetlands in the UK.
In Hydrology and Hydrochemistry of British Wetlands. Ed Hughes and Heathwaite. Wiley

MAFF, 1989.
Report of the Working Party on Pesticide Residues, 1985-1988.
Food Surveillance Paper no.25. HMSO, London.

MAFF, 1995.
Radiation in Food and the Environment, Annual Report 1995.

MAFF, 1996.
Radioactivity in Food and the Environment, 1995.
ISSN 1365-6414. Publ. MAFF

MAFF, 1997.
Radioactivity in Food and the Environment, 1996.
ISSN 1365-6414. Publ. MAFF

MARCHANT J. AND BALMER D., 1994.
Waterways Bird Survey 1992-1993 population changes.
British Trust for Ornithology News 191, 8-10.

MARSH T.J., 1996.
The 1995 UK Drought – A Signal of Climatic Instability?
Proceedings of the Institute of Civil Engineers, Water,
Maritime and Energy 118:189-195.

MASON C.F. AND MACDONALD S.M., 1993a.
Impact of organochlorine pesticide residues and PCBs on otters (Lutra lutra) in eastern England.
The Science of the Total Environment 138, p.147-160.

MASON C.F. AND MACDONALD S.M., 1993b.
PCBs and organochlorine pesticide residues in otter (Lutra lutra) spraints from Welsh catchments and their significance to otter conversation strategies.
Aquatic Conservation: Marine and Freshwater
Ecosystems 3, p.43-51.

MASON C.F. AND MACDONALD S.M., 1994.
PCBs and organochlorine pesticide residues in otters (Lutra lutra) and in otter spraints from South West England and their likely impact on populations.
The Science of the Total Environment 114, p.305-312.

MAYBECK M. AND HELMER R., 1989.
The quality of rivers: from pristine stage to global pollution.
Palaeogeography, Palaeoclimatology, Palaeoecology
75, 283-309.

MINISTRY OF HOUSING AND LOCAL
GOVERNMENT, AND WELSH OFFICE, 1970.
Taken for Granted.
Report of the Working Party on Sewage Disposal,
HMSO. 66pp.

MORRIS D.G. AND FLAVIN R.W., 1996.
Flood Risk Map for England and Wales.
Report No130, Institute of Hydrology. ISBN 0
948540 75 3.

MOSS B., JOHNES P. AND PHILLIPS G., 1996.
The monitoring of ecological quality and the classification of standing waters in temperate regions: a review and proposal based on a worked scheme for British waters.
Biological Review, 71, 301-339

MOUNTFORD J.O., 1994.
Floristic Change in English Grazing Marshes: the impact of 150 years of drainage and land-use change.
Institute of Terrestrial Ecology. Watsonia 20, 3-24

NEWSTEAD S. AND WAKERLEY M., 1994.
Supplies in England and Wales, Monitoring Radioactivity in Water.
Proceedings of a workshop on harmonisation of East-West Radioactive Pollutant Measurement,
Standardization of Techniques, Considerations of
Socio-Economic Factors.

NOP SOCIAL AND POLITICAL, 1997.
Environment Expenditure.
A report prepared for the Environment Agency.
December. Jn 46510. 7pp.

NRA, 1990.
Discharge Consent and Compliance: A Blueprint for the Future.
Water Quality Series No.1, NRA Bristol.

NRA, 1992a.
Policy and Practice for the Protection of Groundwater.
NRA. 52pp.

NRA, 1992b.
Economic value of changes to the water environment.
Report by CNS Scientific and Engineering Services,
NRA R&D Note 37. Bristol.

NRA, 1993.
Faunal richness of headwater streams.
Stage 2, Catchment Studies. Main report. R&D Note
221. Bristol

NRA, 1994a.
The Quality of Rivers and Canals in England and Wales (1990-1992).
NRA Water Quality Series No.19, HMSO, London.
ISBN 0-11-886519-6

NRA, 1994b.
River Darent low flow alleviation.
NRA Southern Region, Worthing.

NRA, 1994c.
Contaminated land and the water environment.
Water Quality Series no 15, HMSO. 60pp. ISBN 0-11-886521-8.

NRA, 1995a.
Saving Water.
The NRAs approach to Water Conservation and
Demand Management: A Consultation Report. 70pp.

NRA, 1995b.
Contaminants Entering the sea.
NRA Water Quality Series no.24, HMSO, London.
94pp. ISBN 0-11-886514-5

NRA, 1995c.
Pesticides in the Aquatic Environment.
NRA Water Quality Series no26, HMSO, London.
92pp. ISBN 0-11-310101-5

NRA, 1995d.
Impact of Recreation on Wildlife.
R&D Note 408. Project no. 498. 90pp.

NRA, 1995e.
Total impact assessment of pollutants in river basins – pesticide impact modelling.
R&D Note 404. Bristol

NRA, 1995f.
Annual Report and Accounts 1994/95.
129pp. ISBN 1-873160-29-9.

NRA, 1996a.
River Habitats in England and Wales, A National Overview.
River Habitat Survey Report No.1.

NRA 1996b.
A Strategy for the Management of Salmon in England and Wales.
36pp.

NRA, 1996c.
The Impact of Land Use on Salmonids. A study of the River Torridge Catchment.
R&D Report 30 in conjunction with MAFF. HMSO.
ISBN 0-11-3101104. 48pp.

OECD, 1982.
Organisation for Economic Cooperation and Development.
Eutrophication of water, monitoring, assessment and control.
OECD, Paris. ISBN 92-64-12298-2

OECD, 1994.
Organisation for Economic Cooperation and Development,
Environmental Performance Reviews: United Kingdom 1994.
OECD, Paris. ISBN 92-641-4260-6

OFFICE FOR NATIONAL STATISTICS, 1997.
Social Trends 27.
ISBN 0-11-620838-4

OFWAT, 1993.
Customer preferences and willingness to pay for selected water and sewerage services.
A summary report to the Office of Water Services by the Flood Hazard Research Centre, Middlesex University.

OFWAT, 1994.
Future Charges for Water and Sewerage Services, The Outcome of the Periodic Review.
58pp. ISBN 1-87423-411-6

OFWAT, 1995.
1994-95 report on the financial performance and capital investment of the water companies in England and Wales.
OFWAT, Birmingham. 56pp. ISBN 1-87423-418-3

OFWAT, 1996a.
Leakage of water in England and Wales.
25pp. ISBN 1-874234-22-1

OFWAT, 1996b.
1995/96 Report on the Cost of water delivered and sewage collected.
29pp. ISBN 1-87423-425-6

OFWAT, 1996c.
Report on Recent Patterns of Demand for Water in England and Wales.
16pp.

ONSTAD C.A. AND BLAKE J., 1980.
Thames Basin Nitrate and Agricultural Relations.
Proc. Symposium on Watershed Management '80.
ASCE/Boire, ID/July 21-23, 1980. p.961-973.

ORMEROD S.J., O'HALLORAN D., GRIBBIN S.D. AND TYLER S.J., 1991.
The ecology of dippers (Cinclus cinclus) in relation to stream acidity in upland Wales: breeding performance, calcium physiology and nestling growth.
Journal of Applied Ecology 28, 416-433.

PATRICK S., MONTEITH D.T. AND JENKINS A., (EDITORS) 1995.
UK Acid Waters Monitoring Network: The first five years.
Published for the DoE and DoE (Northern Ireland) by ENSIS Publishing. 320pp.

PALUTIKOF J.P., SUBAK S. AND AGNEW M.D., 1997.
Economic Impacts of the Hot Summer and Unusually Warm Year of 1995.
Prepared for the Department of the Environment. Pub. University of East Anglia, Norwich. 178pp.
ISBN 0-902170-05-8.

PERRINS C., 1997.
Swans on the Thames, Personal Communication.

PRESTON AND CROFT, 1997.
Aquatic Plants of Britain and Ireland.
Institute of Terrestrial Ecology. 365pp.
ISBN 0-946589-55-0

PURDOM C.E., HARDIMAN P.A., BYE V.J., ENO N.C., TYLER C.R. AND SUMPTER J.P., 1994.
Oestrogenic effects of effluents from sewage-treatment works.
Chemistry and Ecology 8, 275-285.

RACKHAM O., 1986.
The History of the Countryside.
Dent, London

RATCLIFFE D.A., 1984.
Post-medieval and recent changes in British vegetation: the culmination of human influence.
New Phytologist 98: 73-100.

ROYAL COMMISSION ON ENVIRONMENTAL POLLUTION, 1992.
Sixteenth Report on Freshwater Quality.
HMSO: London 291pp. ISBN 0-10-119662-8

ROYAL COMMISSION ON ENVIRONMENTAL POLLUTION, 1994.
Transport and the Environment.
Eighteenth Report, Cmd 2674, HMSO, London. ISBN 0-10-126742-8

ROYAL COMMISSION ON ENVIRONMENTAL POLLUTION, 1996.
Nineteenth Report, Sustainable use of soil. Cm 3165, HMSO, London. ISBN 0-10-131652-6

RSPB, 1996.
A Review of Habitat Land Cover and Land-Use Survey and Monitoring in the UK.
RSPB

SCOTTISH ENVIRONMENTAL PROTECTION AGENCY AND ENVIRONMENT AGENCY, 1997.
A Guide to Sustainable Urban Drainage. 25pp.
ISBN 1-901322-01-7.

SIMPSON V.R., 1997.
The health status of otters (Lutra lutra) in south west England.
Report to the Environment Agency.

SOCIAL AND COMMUNITY PLANNING RESEARCH, 1997.
UK Day Visits Survey: A summary of the 1996 survey findings.
SCPR

SPORTS COUNCIL, 1991.
A digest of sports statistics for the UK.
ISBN 1-872158-25-0

STANNERS AND BOURDEAU, 1995 (EDITORS).
Europe's Environment. The Dobris Assessment.
European Environment Agency Task Force, Copenhagen, 676pp. ISBN 92-8265-409-5

STEVENS P.A., ORMEROD S.J. AND REYNOLDS B., 1997.
Final report on the Acid Waters Survey for Wales.
Volume I. Institute of Terrestrial Ecology (NERC) report to the Environment Agency, Welsh Office, Countryside Council for Wales and Forestry Authority. Bangor.

STRACHAN R. AND JEFFERIES D.J. 1993
The water vole Arvicola terrestris in Britain 1989-1990: its distribution and changing status.
The Vincent Wildlife Trust, London.
ISBN 0-946081-23-9

TECHNICAL COMMITTEE ON DETERGENTS AND THE ENVIRONMENT, 1993.
Second report, Appendix G, Sodium tripolyphosphate as a detergent builder — and its contribution to phosphate in the environment.
HMSO.

UK CRITICAL LOADS ADVISORY GROUP, 1995.
Critical Loads of Acid Deposition for United Kingdom Freshwaters. Sub-group report on fresh waters.
Prepared at the request of the DoE, London.

UK REVIEW GROUP ON IMPACTS OF ATMOSPHERIC NITROGEN, 1994.
Impacts of Nitrogen Deposition on Terrestrial Ecosystems.
Prepared at the request of the DoE, London. ISBN 1-87039-322-8

UK ROUND TABLE ON SUSTAINABLE DEVELOPMENT, 1997a.
Freshwater. 46pp.

UK ROUND TABLE ON SUSTAINABLE DEVELOPMENT, 1997b.
Housing and Urban Capacity. 76pp.

THE VINCENT WILDLIFE TRUST, 1996.
Otter Survey of England 1991-1994.
The Vincent Wildlife Trust, London.
ISBN 0-946081-31-X

WALLEY W.J. AND MARTIN R.W., 1997.
Distribution of macroinvertebrates in English and Welsh rivers based on the 1995 survey.
Environment Agency R&D Technical Report E12.

WATER SERVICES ASSOCIATION, 1996.
Waterfacts 1996.
WSA 75pp. ISBN 0-947886-39-7

WEATHERLEY N.S., DAVIES G.L. AND ELLERY S., 1997.
Polychlorinated biphenyls and organochlorine pesticides in eels (Anguilla anguilla L.) from Welsh rivers.
Environmental Pollution, 95, 127-134.

WHITE P., LABADZ J.C. AND BUTCHER D.P., 1996.
The Management of Sediment in Reservoired Catchments.
Journal Chartered Institute of Water and Environmental Management, 10, 183-189.

WIERINGA K., 1995 (EDITOR).
Environment in the European Union. Report for the review of the Fifth Environmental Action Programme.
European Environment Agency, Copenhagen. ISBN 92-8275-263-1

WORLD HEALTH ORGANISATION, 1993.
Guidelines for Drinking Water Quality.
Volume 1. Recommendations. Second edition.

WMO/UNEP, 1996.
Climate Change 1995, The Science of Climate Change.
Summary for Policy makers and Technical Summary
of the Working Group I Report. Intergovernmental
Panel on Climate Change. 56pp.

WRIGHT J.F., BLACKBURN J.H., GUNN R.J.M., FURSE
M.T., ARMITAGE P.D., WINDER J.M. AND SYMES K.L.,
1996.
*Macroinvertebrate frequency data for the RIVPACS III sites in Great
Britain and their use in conservation evaluation.*
Aquatic Conservation: Marine and Freshwater
Ecosystems, vol 6, p141-167.

Glossary of Terms

Acidification, acid deposition, acid rain | *Acidification is the process by which acid rain, correctly termed acid deposition, increases the acidity of soils and fresh waters, damaging the life they support. Cloudwater, rain and snow are made more acidic than normal by emissions of sulphur and nitrogen compounds from the combustion of fossil fuels.*

Algae | *Simple microscopic (sometimes larger) plants.*

Algal bloom | *Rapid growth of algae (see above) which when excessive can cause problems to water users and other life.*

Alkaline | *Water of pH greater than 7. Lowland waters or those on chalk or limestone are typically alkaline. The opposite of acidic.*

Alpha activity | *A measure of emissions of ionising nuclear particles by radioactive substances.*

Ammonia | *A substance found in water often as the result of pollution by sewage or livestock effluent. Ammonia affects fish and abstractions for potable water supply.*

Amphibians | *Amphibians are soft skinned vertebrates such as frogs, toads and newts. They can live on land or in water. They breed in water and their eggs undergo external fertilization with a larval (tadpole) stage before becoming adults.*

Aquifer | *Underground water source — water bearing rock.*

Average Score Per Taxon (ASPT) | *Measurement used in the biological assessment of rivers. The total BMWP score divided by the number of invertebrate taxa (see below).*

Baseflow | *The rate of river flow under normal dry conditions with a high proportion of groundwater and a low proportion of surface runoff.*

Benthic | *Associated with the bed of a waterbody.*

Best Available Techniques Not Entailing Excessive Cost (BATNEEC) | *The level of pollution control required for sites regulated under the Environmental Protection Act 1990. Includes the technology and management of the site to prevent the release of prescribed substances, or to reduce the release to a minimum and to render harmless any other substances that might cause harm if released.*

Best practicable environmental option (BPEO) | *The BPEO procedure establishes, for a given set of objectives, the integrated pollution control option that provides the most benefit or least damage to the environment as a whole, at acceptable cost, in the long as well as the short term.*

Beta activity | *A measure of emissions of ionising nuclear particles by radioactive substances.*

Bioaccumulation | *The build up of toxic substances in living organisms at concentrations often many times those of the surrounding environment.*

Biochemical oxygen demand (BOD)	The quantity of dissolved oxygen in water (mg/l) consumed under test conditions during a given period (five days) through the microbiological oxidation of biodegradable organic matter present in waste waters. One of the standard tests used to characterise effluent quality. Allylthiourea is added to suppress oxygen consumption by nitrification.
Biodegradation	The process by which materials are transformed (degraded or decomposed) by the actions of living organisms, e.g. bacteria, fungi, moulds or insects. Biodegradation involves both physical and chemical breakdown.
Biodiversity	The number of different plant and animal species, including variants within each species, in an ecosystem. The variety of life.
Biological Monitoring Working Party (BMWP)	The BMWP established an index of biological quality based on the presence or absence of river invertebrate taxa with differing sensitivity to pollution. This is the BMWP Score for a site.
Biota	All living organisms, plant and animal.
Blue-green algae	A group of algae (see above) including some species that release toxic chemicals.
Borehole	A hole for the abstraction of groundwater, usually by pumping.
Buffer zone	Land next to a watercourse managed to protect the water from the physical or polluting effects of human land-use e.g. farming.
Catchment	Area drained by a river or river system. Also area drained by a sewage system.
Chlorophyll	A plant pigment, of which chlorophyll 'a' is a common measure. Used as a measure of abundance of planktonic algae.
Coarse fish	Freshwater fish of the family Cyprinidae (e.g. roach, carp and pike) and eels.
Coliform bacteria	A group of bacteria found in the intestine and faeces of most animals. Coliforms can sometimes be found in untreated water. The treatment process removes them and disinfection prevents their reappearance in the distribution system. In water receiving discharges, faecal coliform bacteria are used to indicate the presence of sewage.
Combined sewer overflow (CSO)	Most sewers receive sewage and rainfall runoff from roads and other surfaces. After heavy rainfall, the flows may exceed the capacity of the sewers or the sewage treatment works. CSOs allow the dilute and excess flow to discharge to a receiving water.
Confined aquifer	A confined aquifer is bounded above and below by impermeable rocks. It has no potential for contact with the atmosphere. An unconfined aquifer is not bounded above and consequently its upper surface may come into contact with, or be influenced by, the atmosphere.
Consent	A statutory document issued by the Agency which defines the legal limits and conditions on the discharge of an effluent to a watercourse.
Controlled water	Controlled waters include all rivers, canals, streams, brooks, drainage ditches, lakes, reservoirs, estuaries, coastal waters and groundwater to which British pollution control legislation applies. Small ponds and reservoirs which do not themselves feed other rivers or watercourses are not included within the definition of "controlled waters" unless the Secretary of State defines them as such – which he has done in the case of water supply reservoirs in the Controlled Waters (Lakes and Ponds) Order 1989.

Critical load	*In relation to acidification (see above), an estimate of the amount of acid deposition below which significant harmful effects on sensitive parts of the environment do not occur.*
Cryptosporidium	*A waterborne parasitic micro-organism, believed to originate from livestock. Cryptosporidia have been identified as responsible for a small number of acute diarrhoea cases (cryptosporidiosis).*
Cyprinid	*Freshwater fish of the family Cyprinidae, e.g. roach, carp, pike.*
Dangerous Substances	*Substances defined by the European Commission as in need of special control because they are toxic, accumulate in plants or animals and are persistent (Dangerous Substances Directive, 76/464/EEC).*
Diatom	*A type of microscopic plant.*
Diffuse source	*A source of pollution which is not an identifiable point discharge but includes field or urban runoff, atmospheric emissions or numerous poorly defined discharges.*
Directive	*Legislation issued by the European Community which requires a member state to implement its requirements, for example to achieve specified environmental standards.*
Direct Toxicity Assessment (DTA)	*A method for testing the quality of effluent or water using the response of standard test organisms which will show the overall toxicity of a mixture of chemicals.*
Dissolved oxygen (DO)	*Oxygen dissolved in a liquid, the solubility depending on temperature, partial pressure and salinity, expressed in milligrams per litre. Tables giving values for the solubility of oxygen in water have been published in standard methods.*
Drought	*A prolonged period of dry weather, said to exist if, for at least 15 days, on each day rainfall has been less than 0.25mm.*
E-coli (Escherichia coli)	*A bacterium taken as an indicator of faecal contamination.*
Ecosystem	*All life and non-living matter within a defined space, such as a river or a lake, and their interactions.*
Effective rainfall	*The amount of rainfall reaching surface and groundwater after losses to the air by evapotranspiration.*
Effluent	*Water discharged from a site which may be contaminated, for example with sewage or waste substances from industrial processes.*
Endocrine disruption	*Any disruption of the normal functioning of the endocrine (hormonal) system by either artificial or naturally occurring chemicals, thereby affecting those physiological processes which are under hormonal control.*
Environmental Quality Index (EQI)	*A measure of biological quality based on river invertebrates. The ratio of the number of taxa or average score per taxon found in samples to those predicted by the RIVPACS model.*
Environmental Quality Objective (EQO)	*The description of water quality required to maintain an identified use of a body of water.*

Environmental Quality Standard (EQS)	The concentration for example, of a substance in the environment which should not be exceeded in order to protect natural or human uses.
Eutrophication	The enrichment of water by nutrients, especially compounds of nitrogen and/or phosphorus, causing an accelerated growth of algae and higher forms of plant life to produce disturbance to the balance of organisms present in the water and to the quality of the water concerned.
Evapotranspiration	The loss of water to the air from the ground surface and plants by evaporation and through the leaves of plants (transpiration).
General Quality Assessment (GQA)	The Environment Agency's classification scheme for water quality. Assesses quality through a set of 'windows', including chemical and biological, placing each reach into one of six classes for each window.
Groundwater	Water occurring in permeable underground rocks, e.g. chalk and sandstone.
Groundwater Protection Policy (GPP)	The Environment Agency's policy for the protection of groundwater, based on groundwater vulnerability, the definition of source protection zones and the control of activities including abstraction, discharges and waste disposal.
Hardness	Characteristic of waters containing dissolved calcium and magnesium salts.
Harmonised Monitoring Scheme (HMS)	The DETR programme for monitoring river quality, based on chemical sampling at the tidal limit of rivers or the downstream end of major tributaries.
Heavy metals	A general term for those metals which are toxic when present in elevated concentrations. These include elements such as zinc, copper, lead, nickel and mercury, all of which are commonly used by industry.
Integrated Pollution Control (IPC)	Applied by the Agency under the Environmental Protection Act 1990 to control the most complex and polluting industrial processes. It integrates the control of emissions to air, land and water to seek the best overall option.
Intersex	An intersex individual (or hermaphrodite) is an organism in an ambiguous sexual state, where they cannot function as either male or female. For example, an intersex condition may arise as a result of endocrine disruption during early development.
Invertebrates	Animals without backbones. They include, for example, insects, crustaceans, worms and molluscs living on the river bed.
Leach, leachate	The movement of substances through soils and rocks to surface and groundwaters is known as leaching and the solution they are carried in is the leachate.
Load	The quantity or mass of any substance transported in an effluent per unit time (the product of concentration of pollutant and effluent flow).
Local Environment Agency Plan (LEAP)	The process by which the Agency plans to meet all the environmental issues in a catchment. A consultation plan is published followed by an action plan which is reviewed at five year intervals.
Low flow river	A river identified by the Agency as having excessively low flows and requiring action to improve the situation.

Macroinvertebrate	An invertebrate animal of sufficient size to be retained in a net with a specified mesh size, usually about one millimetre.
Macrophyte	Macrophytes (literally 'big plants') are any plants large enough to be seen with the naked eye and include aquatic reeds, pond weeds and seaweeds.
Mean	An average value. In precise terms the arithmetic mean.
Mean Trophic Index (MTI)	A measure based on plants to describe the nutrient status of rivers in relation to the risk of nutrient enrichment or eutrophication.
Median	The middle (50 percentile) of a set of numbers arranged in numerical order.
Mesotrophic	Oligotrophic water bodies are characterised by low concentrations of nutrients and low plant production. Eutrophic water bodies have high concentrations of nutrients and high plant production. Mesotrophic waters are less well defined and are generally thought to be in a state of transition between these two extreme conditions.
Net catches	The number of fish caught by licensed fishermen using nets
Nitrate Sensitive Area (NSA)	Area designated by the Ministry of Agriculture, Fisheries and Food, with advice from the Environment Agency, where agricultural activities are controlled to reduce nitrate contamination of groundwaters.
Nitrate Vulnerable Zone (NVZ)	Area designated under the EC Nitrate Directive (91/676/EEC) where changes to agricultural practice will be required to protect waters vulnerable to nitrate pollution.
North Sea Conference	Forum in which states surrounding the North Sea established agreements to cut the discharge of certain pollutants to the sea via rivers.
Nutrient	A substance such as nitrogen or phosphorus which provides nourishment to organisms.
Ochre	A reddish-brown deposit of oxidised iron, typical of minewater pollution.
Oestrogen(ic)	Oestrogen is the name for a class of hormones produced in ovaries which are important in regulating the reproductive system of female animals. Oestrogen is carried by the blood to other parts of the body where different responses are triggered eg. in the uterus of humans oestrogen triggers the growth of the tissue lining the womb in anticipation of a possible pregnancy. 'Oestrogenic' is the adjective used to describe any chemical compound which mimics oestrogen.
Organic pollution	Substances which consume dissolved oxygen in rivers as they are degraded by bacteria, including sewage, farm and food wastes.
Organochlorines	Organochlorine insecticides are formed by the chlorination of hydrocarbons. They include DDT, aldrin, dieldrin, endrin, chlordane, lindane and hexachlorobenzene. They were used most extensively from the mid 1940s to the 1960s. Their low volatility, chemical stability, fat solubility and environmental persistence led to their bioaccumulation in food chains. These compounds have the ability to disrupt the endocrine (hormonal) or enzyme systems of many animals. Some organochlorine pesticides can cause gross birth defects, especially in birds.

Organophosphates	The organophosphorus insecticides are a large group of potent pesticides, which account for about 40 per cent of total registered pesticides in the world. They act by attacking the nervous systems of animals. Organophosphates are highly toxic to humans and other mammals but are less persistent than organochlorines.
Oslo and Paris Commissions (OSPARCOM)	Conventions under which member states have adopted conventions for the prevention of marine pollution.
Percentile	A statistic which describes how data are distributed among all the possible values they could take. For example, a pollutant concentration which has a 95 percentile of 20 mg/l will have 95 per cent of all concentrations below 20 mg/l. Similarly, if the 10 percentile is 5 mg/l then only 10 per cent of concentrations will fall below 5 mg/l. Consequently, 50 per cent of concentrations will be above (and below) the 50 percentile, or median value. To test river quality against a 95 percentile standard requires an estimate to be made of the 95 percentile quality, from measured concentrations, which will then be compared against the standard.
Pesticide	A chemical used to control biological pests, includes insecticides, herbicides and fungicides.
pH	A measure of acidity based on a logarithmic scale of concentrations of hydrogen ions. Neutral is pH 7, acidic is below pH 7, alkaline is above pH 7; pH 6 is ten times as acidic as pH 7, and pH 5 is 100 times as acidic as pH 7.
Phyto-oestrogen	Phyto-oestrogen is the name for natural compounds produced by plants which are oestrogenic.
Phytoplankton	Plankton is the collective name for drifting microscopic organisms at any depth in the sea or fresh water. The phytoplankton is the plant part of the plankton.
Planktonic	Microscopic plants or animals that float or swim freely in the water.
Point source	A source of pollution which is a discrete identifiable discharge, such as a sewage outfall or industrial discharge.
Polychlorinated biphenyls (PCBs)	The commercial production of the group of chemicals called PCBs began in 1930. They have been widely used in electrical equipment and as fire resistant liquids. PCBs are extremely persistent in the environment and bioaccumulative. They have been detected since the early 1970s in most materials and locations, including remote polar regions. PCBs accumulate in the fatty tissues of animals and have caused toxic effects. The skin and liver are most affected but the intestines, the immune system and the nervous system are also targets. Some PCBs may be carcinogenic.
Polycyclic aromatic hydrocarbons (PAHs)	Semi-volatile organic compounds are produced when a material containing hydrogen and carbon is burned incompletely, such as in domestic fires, during refuse burning or in car engines, and some occur naturally. PAHs are amongst the most significant of these organic compounds because many of them are known to be carcinogenic.
Potential evaporation (PE)	This is the amount of water which could theoretically be evaporated or transpired by plants from the land surface.

Precipitation	The means by which water is deposited on the earth's surface from the atmosphere. Usually water vapour in air condenses to form raindrops or snowflakes which fall to earth from clouds. Occasionally water vapour also condenses directly onto the earth's surface as dew.
Primary treatment	The physical treatment of sewage effluent, usually settlement, to remove gross solids and reduce suspended solids by about 50 per cent and BOD by about 20 per cent.
Pyrethroids	Synthetic pyrethroid insecticides are currently the most widely used pesticides. They are very potent insecticides with low toxicity to mammals. They act by attacking the nervous system of animals.
Riparian	Refers to the land alongside watercourses.
River gauging stations	A building, structure or instrument for measuring the velocity, flow or volume of water passing a point in a river. It can be simple as in a pole or weir calibrated in terms of river depth, or complicated like acoustic or magnetic sensors with computerised telemetry to a base station.
River Habitat Survey (RHS)	The Environment Agency's scheme for monitoring the physical form and vegetation of river banks and in the river channel.
River Invertebrate Prediction and Classification System (RIVPACS)	A computer based system used to predict the invertebrate life in a river under natural conditions. Used to calculate the Environmental Quality Index.
Rod catches	The number of fish caught by rod licence holders over a specified time-period.
Salmon Action Plan	Local plan for the management of salmon, prepared by the Environment Agency.
Salmonid	Fish of the family Salmonidae, notably salmon, brown trout and sea trout.
Secondary treatment	Biological treatment and secondary settlement of sewage effluent, normally following primary treatment, capable of producing a substantial reduction in BOD and suspended solids.
Sensitive Area (Eutrophic)	Area designated under the Urban Waste Water Treatment Directive (91/271/EEC) as affected by or at risk from the adverse effects of nutrient enrichment.
Septic tank	A type of sedimentation tank in which the sludge is retained sufficiently long enough for the organic content to undergo anaerobic digestion. When sludge is eventually removed to a sewage treatment works, some is left in the tank to act as a 'seed' to initiate further digestion. Used for receiving the sewage from houses and other premises which are too isolated for connection to a foul sewer.
Sewage Treatment Works (STW)	A term for the structures, plant and equipment used for collecting and treating sewage, normally with some sludge drying.
Site of Special Scientific Interest (SSSI)	Site designated by English Nature or the Countryside Council for Wales under the Wildlife and Countryside Act 1981 for its importance to nature conservation.
Special Area for Conservation (SAC)	Sites notified under the Habitats Directive (92/43/EEC) for their conservation value.

213

Special Protection Area (SPA)	Site designated under the Conservation of Wild Birds Directive (79/409/EEC).
Storm sewer overflow	See combined sewer overflow (above). Storm sewers may contain only runoff or also sewage, as in a combined sewer overflow.
Surface water	All streams, rivers and lakes at the ground surface.
Suspended sediment/solids	Particles suspended in water, measured as milligrams per litre by evaporation or filtering.
Sustainable development	Development that meets the needs of the present without jeopardising the ability of future generations to meet their own needs.
Taxa, Taxon	Taxa is the plural of taxon, which is the species, family or other group to which an organism belongs.
Tertiary treatment	Any treatment following secondary treatment which produces a high sewage effluent quality by means of, for instance, grass plots, microstrainers or nutrient removal.
Thermocline	A thermocline is a region of large vertical temperature gradients. Typically, a deep lake will form a thermocline due to solar heating of its surface waters in spring and summer. The deeper water, below the thermocline, may be several degrees cooler than the surface water.
Toxicity Based Consent	A consent (see above) which contains as a criterion the degree of toxicity of the discharge to a standard test organism.
Trade effluent	A discharge to water from a commercial or industrial site.
Turbidity	The opacity of a liquid to light (its cloudiness) due to particles in suspension. May be used as a measure of suspended solids.
UK Biodiversity Action Plan	Produced on behalf of the government by the UK Biodiversity Steering Group in response to the United Nations Conference on Environment and Development 1992 (the Rio "Earth Summit").
Urbanisation	Land cover by housing, industrial development, roads or similar structures.
Vascular plants	Vascular plants are those which have vessels for transporting fluids around the plant.
Vitellogenin	Vitellogenin is an egg-yolk protein usually produced only by female animals in the liver in response to oestrogen released from the ovaries. Vitellogenin is passed from the liver to the ovaries in the blood where it is incorporated into eggs. Males do not produce eggs but their livers will produce vitellogenin if they are exposed to elevated levels of oestrogen. So, vitellogenin levels in males are good indicators of exposure to oestrogen or oestrogenic compounds.
Water Level Management Plan	A statement covering the management of water levels which balances the needs of agriculture, flood defence and conservation.
Water table	The level below which soils and rocks are saturated. Where the water table meets the ground surface springs, streams, rivers and lakes occur.

Printed in the United Kingdom for The Stationery Office.
J0048496, C10, 5/98, 5673.